MORE MEMORIES OF
CASTLE CARY AND ANSFORD

Clearing the snow around the Horse Pond, 25th. April 1908. The Horse Pond is a residual element of a moated manorial complex, itself a successor to the castle of which only earthworks and foundations remain. In the background is the parish church, another link to Cary's early history.

MORE MEMORIES OF CASTLE CARY AND ANSFORD

The Living History Group
Castle Cary
2012

Cover Illustrations

Front:

An aerial view of the town taken in the 1990s looking south. All Saints' Church and the Old Vicarage are near the top while in the centre is Manor Farm before this was redeveloped for housing as Castle Rise. At the bottom are the earthworks, the only visible remains of the Norman castle.

Castle Cary Museum.

Back:

An amusing Castle Cary postcard from c.1905 produced by Birn Bros. of London as one of a set of six cards on similar themes, two of which featured two girls. The 'milestone' design, series 2452, was overprinted for use in many towns.

A.V.Pearse collection.

'On the road' – a steam traction engine hauls Pither's removal van and team in the early years of the twentieth century.

A.V.Pearse collection.

First published 2012

© Copyright the Living History Group and the individual contributors

Artwork & Design by Wincanton Print Company Limited

Printed by Wincanton Print Company Limited
01963 33643 www.wincanton-print.com

ISBN 978 1 902247 05 2 (Standard edition)
         978 1 902247 06 9 (Limited Edition)

*In memory of Julien Nicholls,
1936-2010
A longtime Castle Cary resident
and one of the founders of the
Living History Group*

Contents

	Page No.
Preface	9
Introduction	11
John Cannon	13
Bygone Days *by Cornelius Martin*	23
Joseph Chapman *by Colin Taylor*	43
Harvesting at Manor Farm *by John Mackie*	47
The Story of a Wedding Dress *by Stanley Hodge*	49
Memories of Butwell House *by Alan Bliss*	53
A Strand in Britain's Story, T S Donne & Sons Ltd.	59
David Stickland	81
The British Timber Trade *by Norman Hetherington*	87
An Old Somersetshire Industry, John Boyd & Co	91
The Horsehair Industry of Somerset *by Norman Wymer*	97
Memories of Miss Longshaw	103
The Delaware Veterinary Group	107
Robert John Norris 1900-1983	115
Life as a Wartime Evacuee at Ansford *by Keith Crane*	119
Childhood Memories of Ansford *by Gordon Groves*	121
Yvonne Francis	129
Raymond Boyer	135
Farming Around Castle Cary *by Raymond Boyer*	149
Veronica Stickland	163
Stella Clothier	167
Memories of Castle Cary by a wartime evacuee *by Jack Yockney*	171
National Service Years *by Julien Nicholls*	175
Clarks at Castle Cary *by Julien Nicholls*	181
A Cary Childhood *by Graham Wheelan*	185
The History of Dimmer Tip *by Raymond Boyer*	189
Mill Lane Dairy *by Eileen Pattle*	193

Memories of Lower Cockhill Farm House *by Olive Boyer*	195
The Old House at Lower Cockhill Farm *by Pek Peppin*	199
A Tale of Two Houses *by Chris Hicks*	205
Some Early Memories *by Valerie Nicholls*	209
Childhood Memories of Castle Cary *by Richard Burrows*	219
Roger Otton	227
House Fire in Winter *by Tony Price*	231
Janet Hutchfield	235
Memories *by Jean Barnes*	239
Hazel Merrifield	243
88 Not Out! *by Kenneth Clothier*	249
Thoughts on Cary *by Maurice Adams*	263
Castle Cary and Ansford Street Names *by Will Vaughan*	271
Index	311

Preface

The Castle Cary and Ansford Living History Group was formed in 1995, since which time in addition to the staging of exhibitions and other events, it has published three books on the town and contributed to another, and amassed a considerable archive of photographs and ephemera relating to the area. *Memories of Castle Cary and Ansford* was published in 1998, and the Group is now pleased to present a second collection.

Members of the Group involved in the compilation and production of this book are as follows:

RAY and OLIVE BOYER were married in 1955 and were founder members of the Living History Group. After a lifetime in agriculture they retired to live in Lower Ansford. Ray has lived his whole life in the parish of Castle Cary, and was one of the first pupils at the new school at Ansford in 1940; he also served on the Parish Council for thirty five years. Olive came from the village of Lovington and before marriage worked for her father on the farm. They have two sons, David and Philip.

ANN BRITTAIN has lived in Castle Cary her entire life. She was educated at Castle Cary Primary School and Ansford Secondary Modern School and worked at Centaur Services for thirty-three years. She has a great interest in Castle Cary and its history.

ADRIAN COOK was born at High Wycombe in 1961 and brought up in Beaconsfield for the next eighteen years. He then spent four years in Plymouth doing an Engineering degree, followed by various jobs in project engineering. He settled in Bristol, working at Strachan & Henshaw until 2006, when he moved to Castle Cary and a post at Augusta Westland, the helicopter manufacturer at Yeovil. He was a keen member of Avon Wildlife Trust and a member of the committee; and has a keen interest in his genealogical roots. Between working and sport he has time to fit in some metal detecting which he has been doing for seventeen years.

LYNN EMSLIE moved to Alford, near Castle Cary, with her husband in 1993. Originally from Lytham St Anne's in Lancashire, Lynn has a life-long interest in history and archaeology and has been an active member of several local history groups.

CHRIS HICKS was born and worked in Oxford until he moved, with his wife Karen, to Castle Cary in 2009. A bookbinder for nearly fifty years he has also been at various times an antiquarian bookseller, private press printer and publisher. In this last role he edited and published two books on the history of Summertown in Oxford where he was brought up. He also spent twenty years as a primary school governor. Researching the history of his new house brought him into contact with the Living History Group and he soon began to be involved in their activities.

JANET HUTCHFIELD née Lush was born in 1930 at Blackworthy, Castle Cary. She was six months old when her father took over the butcher's shop in the High Street, and has lived in Castle Cary her whole life. She was educated at Castle Cary Primary School and Ansford Secondary Modern School. Leaving school at 14 she joined the family business. Always keen on sport in her youth Janet played netball, hockey, tennis and cricket and later in life took up bowls.

RUTH LODGE was born at Ditcheat in 1932 and spent her childhood at Wyke Champflower, attending schools at Lamyatt and Bruton. She moved to Castle Cary in 1944, and attended Ansford Secondary Modern School. On leaving school she trained as a cheesemaker, but after her marriage in 1953 became a cook, spending many years at the George Hotel, and more recently, prior to her retirement, at South Cary House.

BRIAN LUSH has lived in Castle Cary his entire life, and is the third generation of his family to do so. He has seven siblings, his father is one of six, and grandfather Reginald was one of twenty. The Lush connection with Castle Cary began when his great-grandfather Eli started a butchery business in Castle Cary in 1888, which transferred to the present High Street shop in 1894. From these premises the family have been serving the community for 124 years, the oldest family run business in Castle Cary. Brian has lived in Clanville for six years, and has now retired from the family business, moving on to pastures new. He is especially interested in local and family history, and joined the Living History Group in 2000. He is also a member of the Museum committee.

VALERIE NICHOLLS has lived in Castle Cary all her life and was educated at Miss Grosvenor's Southend Girls' School, Castle Cary Junior School, and Ansford Secondary Modern School. Together with her late husband Julien, she has been a member of the Living History Group since its formation in 1995. She is proud of the Group's achievements and continues to play an active part in recording past and recent history of Castle Cary and Ansford for future generations.

ANNETTE PEARCE came to live in Castle Cary with her husband and six year old son in 1972. It proved to be the best thing they had ever done, as within a month she obtained a position at Haynes Publishers, and later, for a number of years up to her retirement, she worked at Cooper and Tanner, Estate Agents, in the town. She finds Cary such a lovely place to live - and the people are great too!

ADRIAN PEARSE was born in 1958 and currently farms at East Pennard. Through his mother, the late Sarah Barrett of Ansford, he descends from generations of Cary residents, including members of the town's Scottish influx. Chairman of the Living History Group since 2006, he takes a keen interest in editing the Group's publications. He is also Chairman of East Pennard Parish Council, and of the trustees of East Pennard United Charities; and Vice-Chairman of Mendip Postcard Club; as well as a committee member of other local bodies; and regularly gives talks in the area on local history topics.

JOHN PITMAN was born in South Street, Castle Cary, in 1934 and attended Castle Cary Infants and Junior School, and Ansford Secondary Modern School. He moved with his parents to Venus Cottage in 1939, leaving school in 1949 and serving as an apprentice carpenter and joiner in Bath. Returning to Castle Cary, he found employment with local builders. He married in 1957, and became self-employed in 1960. John played soccer and cricket for Castle Cary and was a member of the Robins skittles team for fifty years. He served on Castle Cary Parish Council for eight years, and his interests include sport and local history.

DAVID REID has resided in the Castle Cary area for over thirty years with an interest in Natural History and the historic use and development of the landscape.

Introduction

Welcome to *More Memories of Castle Cary and Ansford*; the second collection of reminiscences and allied material to be produced by the Living History Group.

The range and type of material presented here may at first glance appear a disparate assemblage, stretching as it does from the early eighteenth century to comparatively recent times, and recording personal experiences as well as aspects of the structural and social environment of the town. What is clearly revealed, however, to those that seek them, are the connections through time and space, of many of the contributions in terms of the nature of the town they describe, its folklore, and its inhabitants.

During the period covered in this collection, Castle Cary grew from little more than an overgrown village, indeed a veritable backwater, to the bustling small town we have today, while Ansford remained a very small and entirely rustic community in the shadow of its larger neighbour, until very recent decades; aspects of this process of evolution are revealed by the selection here presented. Cary's fairs and markets were a long established function of the town, connecting it to a wider hinterland, and to them were added small scale industrial development utilizing local resources, especially in the field of textiles and associated products, from the late eighteenth century onwards. Building on these modest beginnings, the mid-nineteenth century influx of Scottish entrepreneurial skills and acumen was to have a major impact on the subsequent industrial and business development of the town, as well as its social and cultural context, the effects of which remain to this day. Castle Cary had also been an important stop on coaching routes, and the coming of the railways in 1856 ensured the continuance of wider connections and the concomitant prosperity which again continues into present times.

Over these centuries, the physical appearance of the town changed out of all recognition, though the basic mediaeval plan of the core areas remains intact to a surprising degree. Later fronts to buildings certainly conceal much from earlier periods, and there are still fragments from earlier buildings to be seen, as well as some astonishing survivals, as at Cockhill; while other aspects of the town's more distant history are preserved in the local nomenclature. Throughout the passing decades trades have changed, and tradesmen come and gone, but the range of businesses and their associated shopfronts, as well as modes of operating, has been rich and varied, and reveals a great deal about contemporary customs and lifestyles. Some may deplore recent changes, but when viewed with a longer perspective, they simply fit with the pattern of development over time.

The two World Wars had a direct impact on Castle Cary and the local area, with compulsory military service taking her sons to distant parts of the globe, many never to return. For those that did, there were new experiences and realities, and the wider effects of the conflicts affected others in terms of wartime service in the Women's Land Army, National Service, and with the direct effect on local industries, of rationing, and of the bombing of the railway station. Children were also evacuated to the locality, and the newly built Ansford School hosted a contingent from Southampton – strangely reinforcing a link with Cary's strong association with the sinking of RMS Titanic in 1912.

Rural activities also faced a dramatic and unparalleled process of change – from a period where all depended on the labour of man and horse to one of state-of-the-art technology. The majority of smallholdings, and indeed many more substantial farms have gone, and with them their workforce and associated rural crafts, to leave a handful of enterprises operating on a significant scale. The process of adaptation has been for many a difficult and uncertain one, but remorseless none the less.

Castle Cary has always faced change, and over time has adapted very well to new circumstances. Certainly, the memories recorded here are full of nostalgia, and often trivial and patchy in nature, and give but a partial glimpse of their subject, but "what cannot be totally known, ought not to be totally neglected; for the knowledge of a part is better than the ignorance of the whole". They also reveal many of the hidden strengths of the town and its people.

Adrian V. Pearse, Editor

John Cannon

John Cannon

John Cannon was born in 1684 to a prosperous farming family in West Lydford and during his lifetime compiled a comprehensive memoir, an edited version of which has recently (2010) been published as *The Chronicles of John Cannon, Excise Officer and Writing Master* ed. John Money, in two volumes by the Oxford University Press. The original manuscript is the property of the Somerset Archaeological and Natural History Society, and may be consulted at the Somerset Records Centre.

Cannon's account, remarkable as it is in extent and complexity, is also almost unique for the period from this social level. Castle Cary was one of Lydford's neighbouring market towns and is frequently mentioned: the following extracts provide detail of the town's physical and social aspects at a time when other sources are almost entirely lacking.

"To illustrate these memoirs and before I shall proceed in the annals of my life I beg an opportunity to give ye topographical discription of ye place of my nativity as also of Castle Cary and other adjacent places it being my design to give some brief hints of all such towns & places where I had any employment or concern and in the introduction of these memoirs I at first promised."

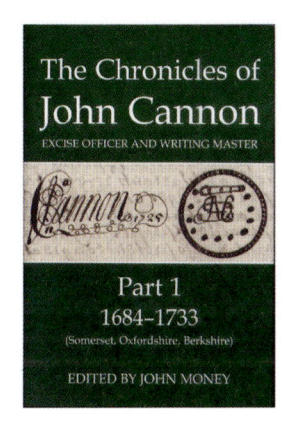

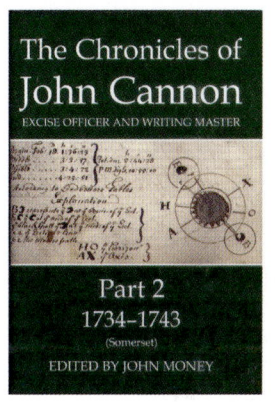

The OUP / British Academy edition of John Cannon's Chronicles, edited by John Money and published in 2010.

Grange Farm, John Cannon's birthplace at Fair Place, West Lydford, from a postcard c.1905.
A.V.Pearse collection.

Cannon's topography of Castle Cary is largely based - indeed in part copied from - the *Magna Britannia* published in c.1727, but has supplementary material relating to the parish church and a series of mills powered by the River Cary, which were the fore-runners of the town's industrial development at the end of the century.

"... CASTLE CARY the manor & estate of the family of St Maur of whom Nicholas St Maur who had been summoned to parliament among the barons from 25 Ed III to ye 34 of ye same King. His heir was Nicholas St Maur his eldest son then 9 years of (age) who dying before he came of full age his brother Richard succeeded him 10 Rich II in his honour & estate and died possessed of this manor. His heir was a daughter & named Alice who was in ye minority after his death but being come to full age married Sir William le Zouche and carried this manor wth divers other estates in this & other Counties into his family, by whom he had Sir William le Zouche who bore ye title of Lord Zouche and S Maur who died 8 Ed. IV seized of this manor of Castle Cary & ye hamlets thereunto belonging being Handspen Honywick and Almsford leaving them to John his son who being attainted in parliament 1 Hen. VII for taking part wth Richard III his estate was seized into ye Kings hands but his son John being restored in blood recovered this manor being of his grandmother's inheritance. It is at present a small market town ye market on Teusday weekly but like other paultry markets beginning at 10 of ye clock and ending at noon. Here are 4 or 5 good fairs yearly for sheep

'Cannon country' – a section from Robert Morden's Somerset map of 1695 shows West Lydford in relation to Castle Cary, and other local towns and villages.
A.V.Pearse collection.

& cattle viz May 1st, (Septem)ber 18, ye Teusday before palm Sunday & Whit Teusday & a weekly market for a month before ye feast of ye nativity of our Saviour. It is scituated in a very fine healthy air, has a neat Church with a small spire & in it 5 fine tuneable bells & near ye manor house late Mr. Lucy's. In the pond arises a brook wch in a short space drives 4 or 5 mills one of which cost a great sum in ye building & contrivance said to grind 100 bushells of wheat in a day, ye builders one Morley & Company from Bristol being at such a charge that they faild soon after it was erected. This Brook being called Cary runs to Babcary, Cary fitzpain, Little Cary, Lites Cary and north by Somerton where is a bridge over it called Carybridge. This Manor now is vested in Tho. Player Esq. & Madam Etrick. Near this town is a medicine well called Carywell but it is in ye Lordship of Alford formerly of good repute."

Cannon's initial training for excise employment included a very frank account of an incident involving his supervisor at Castle Cary in 1706:- "John Altrop was born at Kettering in Northamptonshire, of very honest parents, had some small share of English literature, bred an engineer. Whether his friends had ability to set him up is not certain; however, I found him at Castle Cary as an officer of excise. He was a very facetious person if humour'd, otherwise rough and ill-tempered, given to brawling and fighting, a lover of songs, musick and dancing, very unchast and inconstant to his wife, a true devotee to the school of Venus, of which I saw one remarkable instance. For coming into a cellar at the Katharin Wheel at one John Gibbs's, it being one of the houses in my instruction book, I caught my master in the very act of criminal conversation with Miss Lucy, youngest daughter of ( ) Lucy, Esquire, a lunatick, then under the care of Bernard Compton, a doctor, & who had lately stolen the said Miss. Lucy & married her though a great disparity in their ages, his is above 50 and she not 14. She & my master had been quondam friends before. This act so barefaced surprised me, and starting back withdrew and rounded Gibbs, who being their confident and procurer, & might have forewarned me. His wife would often question me about her husband's doings but would be answered negatively. Her sisters was truly apprehensive of his lasciviousness, his delight being in obscene & filthy songs with which he would often times make merry and then I should reprove him, but he would caution me to keep all his secrets from his wife or any of her family."

The 'Katherine Wheel' mentioned here was later to become the 'Angel Inn' bordering The Pitching on the west side of the Market Place, where in the following year, 1707, Cannon relates an incident where he was almost press-ganged for military service.

"May 1st. This day now being a fair at Castle Cary being an annual fair & noted for a fine show of milking pails carried abt in procession by the young men and maids with musick & other mirth in a very solemn manner which brings a great company of spectators & other loitering people. And it happened that my father sent me with some goods to sell; & my old companions, they also went thither for to have a peal or two when I was at leisure after my business was done to attend them. So it happened that I sold the goods & was waiting or loitering abt the fair for my dealers to take my money & deliver the goods. I standing in a certain place with my hands behind me looking on some who were gaming as is usual in all fairs for some who having no calling or other business to attend, a certain serjeant with a drum coming by at that instant, & seeing me in a careless posture, slapped a guinea in my hand which I felt & turning about asked him what he meant by being so kind as to give me money. He replyed it was himself that did it & I had taken the Queen's money, that I were enlisted & must now go

The George Hotel – one of the few buildings in Castle Cary surviving from Cannon's time, possesses a date stone for 1673, though the Market Place elevation was re-fronted in the eighteenth century, and parts of the structure around the inn yard behind re-built after a fire in the nineteenth century.
A.V.Pearse collection.

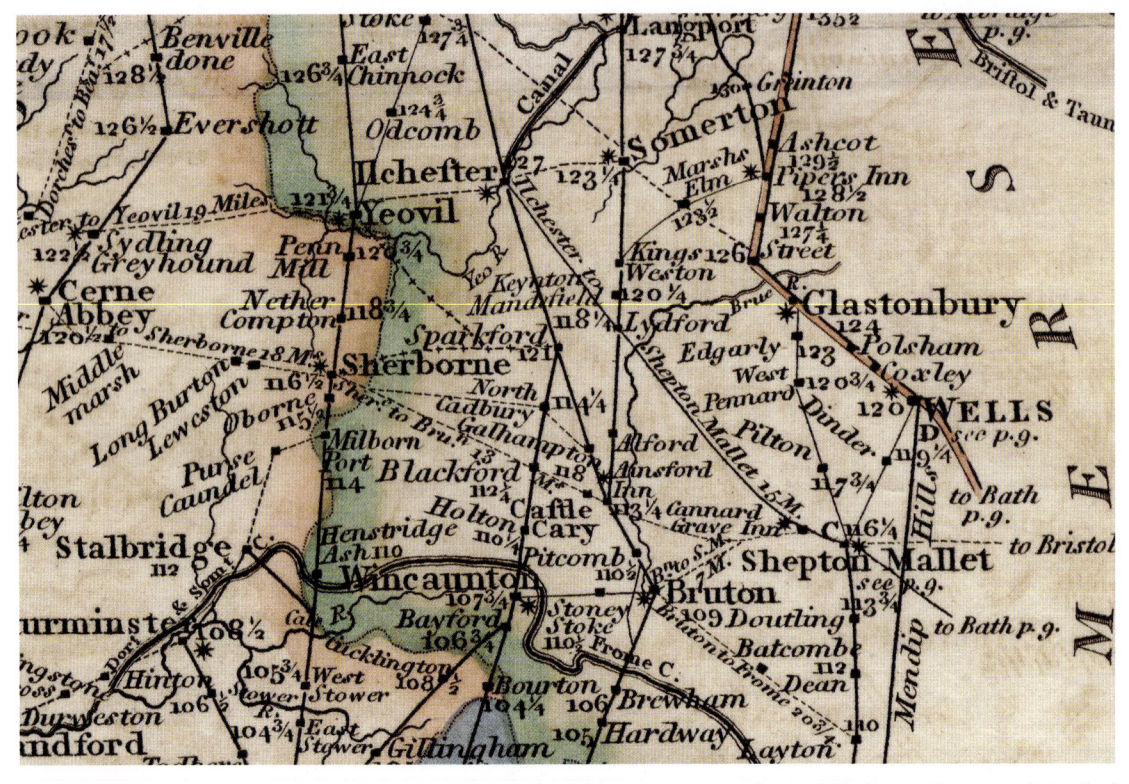

Castle Cary was a noted stopping point on several coaching routes, served especially by the George and Ansford Inns. The extract from Laurie and Whittle's map of 1806 illustrates the coaching routes, primarily running in an east-west direction.
A.V.Pearse collection.

with them. I answered not so hastily & withal I threw the piece on the ground, upon which arose a great scuffle & fray for I had many sided with me and fell foul on the serjeant & soundly thrashed him. Others cut the drumhead but they alleadged what they had done to be justifiable. On the other hand, I told them that for the warrant of their act, I would appeal & immediately go & they should by foul or fair meanes go with me into the George Inn before Mr. Justice Hunt and other gentlemen which I knew was there present & if their act was warrantable I would submit. If not, they must expect to abide by what the justices would order so in we went & the case being laid before them, the serjeant was severely reprimanded for meddling with those who had any business for their parents or masters & then ordered the serjeant to depart the town & that he would make him know that the civil power in many cases was superior to the militaryalthough in time of war. However, I kept with my Companions in a body who was my lifeguard being merry on this exploit though the serjeant threatened to take me yet wherever he could light on me, but he was deceaved of his expectation & hopes. And what became the guinea was uncertain. And as for the serjeant, I saw him in Oxfordshire at Watlington some years after recruiting again where calling him into the Cross Keys Inn, we were merry together & relating former passages, I told him that I then served Her Majesty though in another way."

Later in his life Cannon was undertaking accountancy work at Maperton, near Wincanton, and gives a fascinating contemporary account of the murder committed in 1730 at the spot on the Castle Cary - Wincanton road ever since immortalized as 'Jack White's Gibbet' and oft-recounted in local folklore.

"During my transacting in these parts, a horrid & barbarous murder was committed by one William White of Wincanton, weaver, on one Anthony Sutton, a shoemaker of Shaftsbury. The latter being employed by Mr. Still of Shaston (Shaftesbury) to carry a letter & a message to his brother-in-law, Mr. Howe of Somerton, & calling at the house of one John Gilbert at The Sun in Wincanton (I being then in the same house), enquired the way to Somerton. White being there also was very busy above others to direct him & offered him his company as far as Castle Cary, on which Sutton seemed to be exceedingly glad & therefore they joyned company & drank plentifully & in paying the reckoning White perceived a piece in Sutton's hand which he took to be gold, whereas it was no more than a counter of yellow mettal. The devil then entred into his heart, & casting the fear of God behind his back he coveted to be possessor of the said piece - however, in some time, they set out on the intended journey together as far as Holbrook House, the seat of Nath (aniel) Farwell Esq., (where) they broke out of the road into the enclosure to avoid the dirt (&) the said White took up a hedge stake being a dry black thorn & pretended to make it his walking staff. And so going on about a mile they met two women with whom White began to be rude striving to kiss them & endeavouring to thrust his hand into the bosom of one of them, which dealing she opposed, on which he struck her with the said hedge stake on the arm, and Sutton more civil than White reproved him for his rude behaviour towards the women. He presently began a quarrel with Sutton & leaving the women they went on quarrelling a field or two on the way where both of them laid down to sleep; & Sutton awaking first awakening (ed) also his pretended guide, & getting up they again went on quarrelling about the women till coming to a place near a village called Bratton, White took an occasion to knock down Sutton with the hedge stake who resisted awhile but that blow being followed by more proved fatal to poor Sutton, & White being enraged with malice never left him till he killed him on the spot, after which he forced the said stake into the mouth of the deceased, tore out the cheeks on both sides from ear to ear very barbarous, & then dragged the body a small distance & left it. But thinking it not safe, came again & went & came again till at last he hauled the body to a certain ditch a little north of Bratton Church, & set it upright as on a chair in the said ditch which ran over his legs & thighs with water, it being a current stream. About four days after the body was discovered by two labouring men of Shepton Montacute who came athwart the grounds to Bratton & fortuned to come over the hedge at the very place where the poor murthered man was placed as aforesaid, who alarmed the neighbourhood as also Wincanton, & abundance of people shock't to see it, among which this White & one Molly went also, & according to a tradition several touched the deceased and White also, on which it bled, as reported, by which (they) suspected him guilty as also the former circumstances & the women people began to talk it for certain. However another thing happened which confirmed in some an entire belief of his being the murtherer, was as the said Molly & he was returning from Bratton, two hounds came about them fawning & leaping up against White, & as Molly said they often changed their colour & shape, appearing very dismal sometimes & off at a distance & then near following them to Wincanton & then disappeared. Next day the coroner sat on the body & White was taken up on suspicion, & the jury adjourned to the house of one widow Jewel in Wincanton being the Rainbow, where the coroner examined White, & I being in the company looked on White & charged him directly accessory & guilty of the murther on which he vowed he would be avenged on me for my hard though just censure. At last he was committed by the coroner to Ilchester Gaol, where by a stratagem contrived by some fellow prisoners, he confessed the fact, & at Taunton Assizes next following was hanged up *In Terrorem* near Bratton on the road where he perpetuated the said fact."

Late in December 1742 John Cannon writes to Rev. Samuel Woodforde regarding employment as schoolmaster at Castle Cary, but just over a week later his memoir ends and he vanishes from the historical record, presumed dead. Samuel Woodforde's son James is shortly to greatly augment the story of Castle Cary and locality in the mid eighteenth century, and many of Cannon's descendants would eventually reside in the town, notably those deriving from his two daughters, by which route the current editor, Cannon's five and six - great grandson, descends.

John Cannon's cipher.

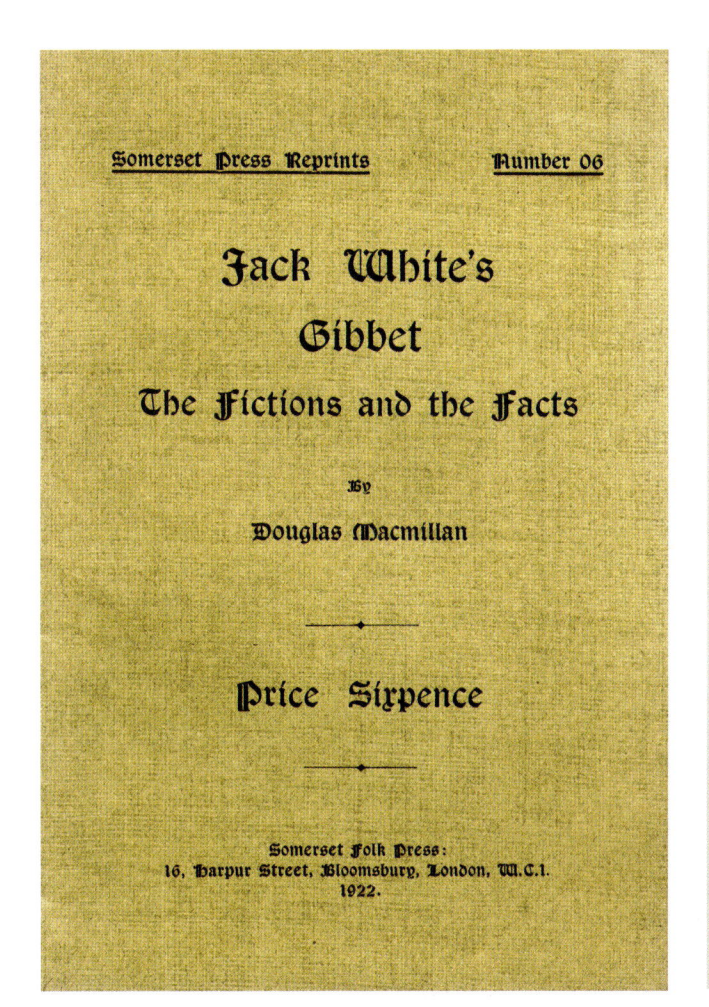

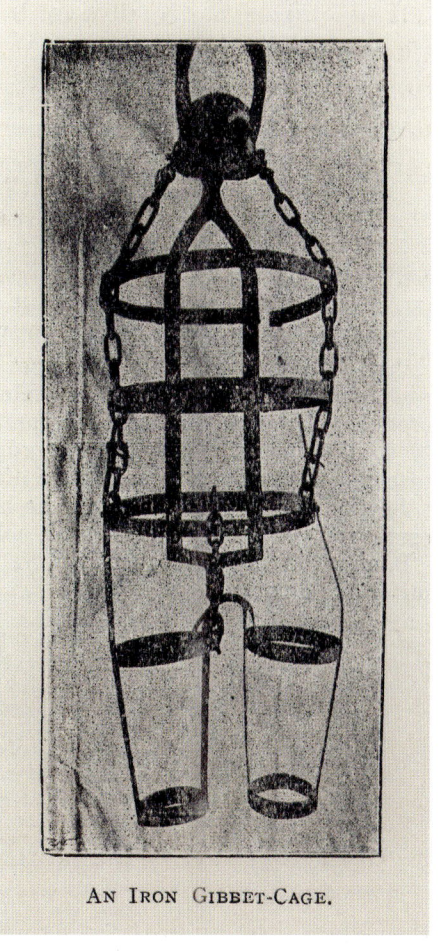

The story of 'Jack White' became a staple of Castle Cary folklore, and was greatly embellished and corrupted as the years progressed. Douglas Macmillan produced a booklet recounting the tale in 1922, including a photograph of an iron cage of the type used to suspend the murderer's corpse.
A.V.Pearse collection.

SQUIRE WOODFORDE'S STORY.

Some considerable time after the execution of Jack White, 'Squire Woodforde, of Castle Cary, had occasion to pass the gibbet late one night after dining at Wincanton. He had declared that he was not afraid of the corpse, and would speak to it as he passed. Accordingly on reaching the spot he remarked: "Well, Jack, how be you?" To his horror he heard the corpse reply: "Jack's cold,—turble cold!" The 'Squire did not subsequently walk that way after late dinners.

Parts of the gibbet survived well into the nineteenth century, ensuring remembrance of the tale.

Near the south-eastern extremity of the beautiful and fertile county of Somerset, stands the small, but ancient market-town of Castle-Cary, deriving its name from a castle, which was for some centuries the property and the residence of the noble family of Carey or Cary, earls of Monmouth, and lords of the manor on which the town stands. It is difficult to discover the precise period at which it was relinquished by its noble occupants; but this much is certain, that it was a place of no small importance in the wars of the Roses, and that, during the troubled reign of the first Charles, it was garrisoned for that monarch by a party of Sir Bevil Granvilles's cavaliers; in consequence of which, it was completely dismantled by Colonel Weldon, the parliamentary commander, who passed through the town on his way to Taunton; and thus, after being the scene of many a splendid pageant, in which the "gentil knights and fayre ladye" of the olden time displayed their prowess and their beauty, it has undergone the fate of all sublumary things, and its mouldering and ruined walls are now used as a granary for the principal inn in the town. The spacious court, erewhile the theatre on which the steel-clad heroes of a former age exhibited their skill and courage, in the pompous and spirit-stirring tilt and tournament, and gained from applauding beauty the reward of successful valour, has now degenerated into an inn-yard, and the castle-moat administers to the comfort of the equestrian lieges in the shape of a horse-pond. Leaving to the curious in antiquarian research, who delight in dragging from their time-worn sepulchers the musty relics of antiquity, and who wade, with laborious and unwearied zeal, through the obscure records of bygone centuries, to demonstrate the etymology of a name, the task of deciphering the rude, and almost obliterated inscription which adorns the massy portal of the ancient edifice, I shall, sans farther introduction, proceed to state, that the town of Castle-Cary, like most country towns of a similar size, consists of one long street, which extends nearly a mile in an irregular line from north-east to south-west; and, from a narrow entrance at either end, descends by a very gradual declivity to the centre, where it expands into and area of considerable size, from whence a branch diverging takes a circuit of a few hundred yards, and again merges in the main street. The street at its greatest width, is denominated the market-place, in the centre of which stood formerly a stone cross, of elaborate and costly workmanship. Among the modern structures which surrounded it, and with which it had no sympathy, if we may so speak, the ancient column reared its venerable head, and seemed as much out of place as the gigantic John of Gaunt, in his mailed habiliments, would appear in an assembly of the starched and perfumed military dandies of the present day. A few years since, however, this vestige of popery – a monument at once of the genius and the superstition of our ancestors – was removed to facilitate the approach and departure of the increasing number of stage-coaches to and from the principal inn. This structure, which stands directly opposite to the site of the cross, was then, and is still, known by the name of "The George;" and the warlike saint himself, in close combat with his formidable enemy the dragon, rudely carved in stone, formerly adorned the key-stone of the spacious gateway which led to the interior of the inn. But, alas! for human vanity, however potent the doughty St George might have been in defending himself from the assaults of the poisonous monster, all his prowess was found insufficient to resist the silent and insidious attacks of time. The pride of a modern occupier aspired to decorate the building with a new front. Dragon, and steed, and hero, were taken down a few years ago, in a dilapidated state; and like the cross, its contemporary, administered to the comfort of passengers by repairing the rutted street in front of the inn; but, in order that the fame of the champion might not be involved in the same ruin with his effigy, the seal of the landlord and the pencil of a country artist have perpetuated the memory of the famous triumph of the saint over his scaly adversary, by rearing in the market-place, on the summit of a lofty pole, a painted resemblance of the stone figures which formerly announced to the weary traveler the welcome vicinity of "The George" – the modern sign being rendered still more attractive by the gaudy colours in which the florid fancy of the rural Rubens has exhibited it; to which might be added another advantage it has over its predecessor, in the gift it possesses of luring the benighted and way-worn passenger by the monotonous creaking of its rusty iron hinges, but which, for the hungry and tired pedestrian, has more charms than the sweetest note ever extracted from the "light guitar" by the skilful fingers of the Venetian serenaders, when seeking to gain the applause of his lovely mistress.

A somewhat fanciful and greatly embroidered account of Jack White's Gibbet was produced by George C. Dyke and published in Vol. IV of The Republic of Letters – A selection in Poetry and Prose from the Works of the Most Eminent Writers, with many Original Pieces by A. Whitelaw in 1833, and subsequently in other periodicals. The description of Castle Cary Market Place in the late eighteenth century is of interest, though of questionable reliability.

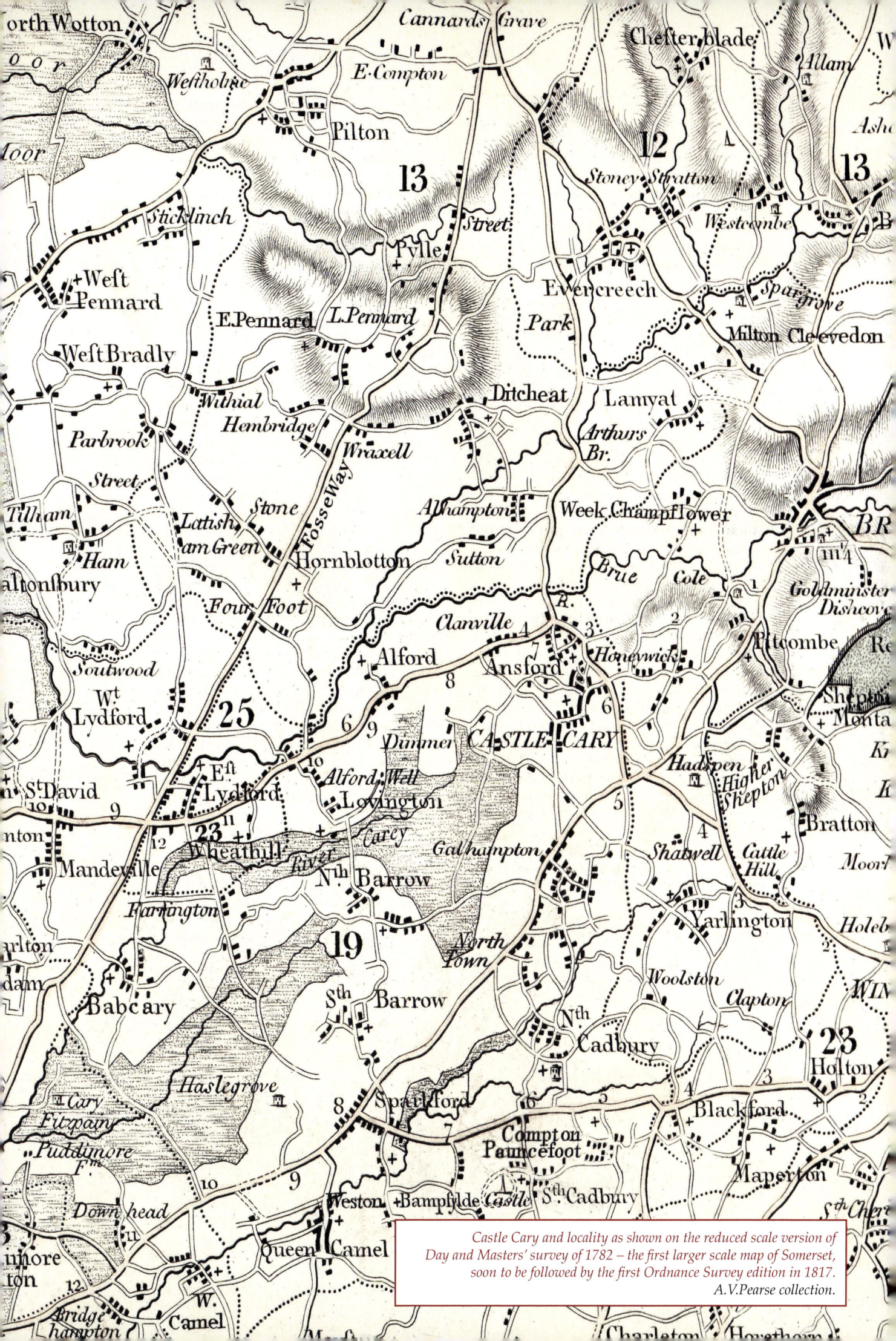

Castle Cary and locality as shown on the reduced scale version of Day and Masters' survey of 1782 – the first larger scale map of Somerset, soon to be followed by the first Ordnance Survey edition in 1817. A.V.Pearse collection.

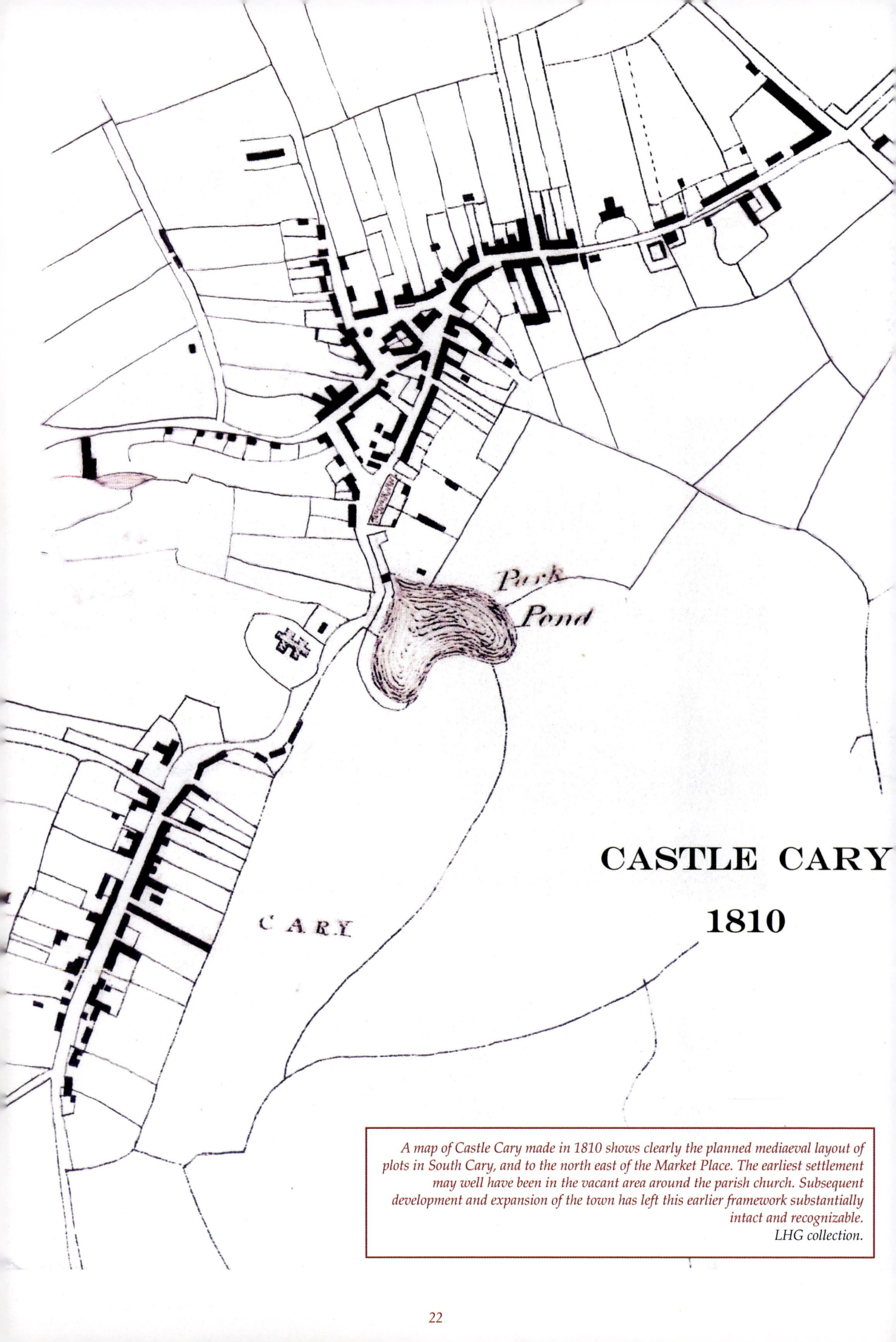

CASTLE CARY 1810

A map of Castle Cary made in 1810 shows clearly the planned mediaeval layout of plots in South Cary, and to the north east of the Market Place. The earliest settlement may well have been in the vacant area around the parish church. Subsequent development and expansion of the town has left this earlier framework substantially intact and recognizable.
LHG collection.

Bygone Days

Bygone Days by Cornelius Martin

My first acquaintance with Castle Cary was about the year 1860 when I was taken by my father to "Cary Market," at that time one of the most important cattle markets in that part of mid-Somerset. The market was held in the streets near and branching out from the Town Hall; the cattle were kept in place by the drovers who had brought them in from the districts around extending over a radius of 8 to 10 miles. The bulls were tethered to strong posts in Ansford Lane - nicknamed Bull Street. The pigs and some sheep were in pens at Bailey Hill under the charge of "Benny" Bowles. This is how I found the market in 1875 when coming to reside here; it continued to function for some years after, then the introduction by some of the leading auctioneers of the repository system - at Sparkford on the south and Shepton Mallet on the north and Evercreech Junction between - soon brought about its decline.

Cornelius Martin was born at Baltonsborough and moved to Castle Cary in 1875, founding a business that bears his name to this day.

Gas at the above date was 8/4 per 1000 feet but was soon reduced to 7/6 and in a few years had sunk to 3/4 - a record price for such a small town. The reason for this was occasioned by the fact that the principal shareholder had extended a factory and he found that cheap gas was more to his advantage than dividends and thus a benefit was conferred on the whole community.

"Thou sayest not wisely that the former days were better than these" - so said Ecclesiastes, the preacher. A general truth, but it has its exceptions. I think it will be admitted that the middle of the last century was a church going age and this habit had not faded out in 1875 when I settled in Cary. Three places of worship - all fairly well attended - met the requirements of the town. Canon Meade at the Parish Church with its curates Revs. Thompkins and Alford; Rev. W. Cotton at "Zion", and J.F. Masters at the Wesleyan

An attractive Cornelius Martin billhead from c.1900.
A.V.Pearse collection.

Church. A flourishing Temperance cause was represented by the Concord lodge of Good Templars. There was a vigorous Band of Hope and prosperous Sunday Schools in connection with each place of worship - so that I think we can say the religious morale of the town was well sustained. Such is my reflection at a "look-back".

Now what was the commercial and industrial state at the time (1875)? The two leading industries were as now T.S. Donne & Sons Rope and Twine Works, at that time at Torbay and Florida, employing men, women and boys; and John Boyd's Horsehair Works at High Street. A good deal of the latter was carried on in various cottages where looms had been erected and where could be heard their throb from "early morn till dewy eve". This however was soon altered by the extension of factory buildings and the erection of improved machinery in the High Street. James White had also made a start in Bailey Hill as a Horsehair Manufacturer. The Cheese Factor Store in South Cary, established by James Mackie, was also one of the most important commercial enterprises of the town.

A stoneware flagon produced for C. Martin's shops in South Street and the Market Place.
H.&A.Gifford collection.

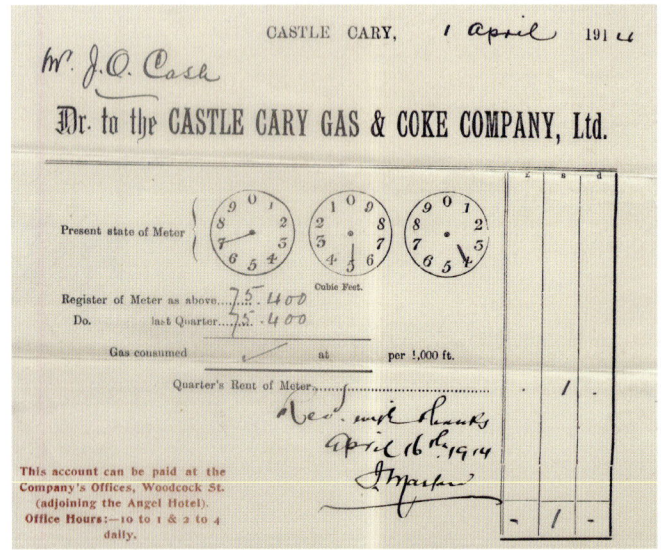

Castle Cary Gas and Coke Company billhead.
A.V.Pearse collection.

T. S. Donne and Sons – one of the town's principal industries.
A.V.Pearse collection.

TELEGRAMS:—
"JAMES WHITE,
CASTLE CARY."

Castle Cary, Somerset, Sept 5th 1896

Treasurer Constitutional Club c Cary

Bot of James White & Son,
Horsehair Merchants,

FEATHERS, FLOCKS, TICKS. WEBS, HESSENS, TWINES &c. &c.

MANUFACTURERS OF HAIR SEATINGS, CURLED HAIR, CIDER CLOTHS, BRUSH MAKER'S DRAFTS &c. &c.
TERMS   CONVEYANCE
EMPTIES NOT ALLOWED FOR UNTIL ACTUALLY RECEIVED IN GOOD CONDITION.

James White had extensive premises on Bailey Hill.
LHG collection.

Folio P-169

Castle Cary, *September* 1880
SOMERSET,

M Messrs. of the late Mr James Tabbott

Bought of **H. BUNCOMBE,**

Furnishing, Agricultural, and General Ironmonger.

Terms _____ INTEREST CHARGED ON OVERDUE ACCOUNTS.

Henry Buncombe's ironmongery store facing the Market Place was well sited to capture the agricultural trade.
A.V. Pearse collection.

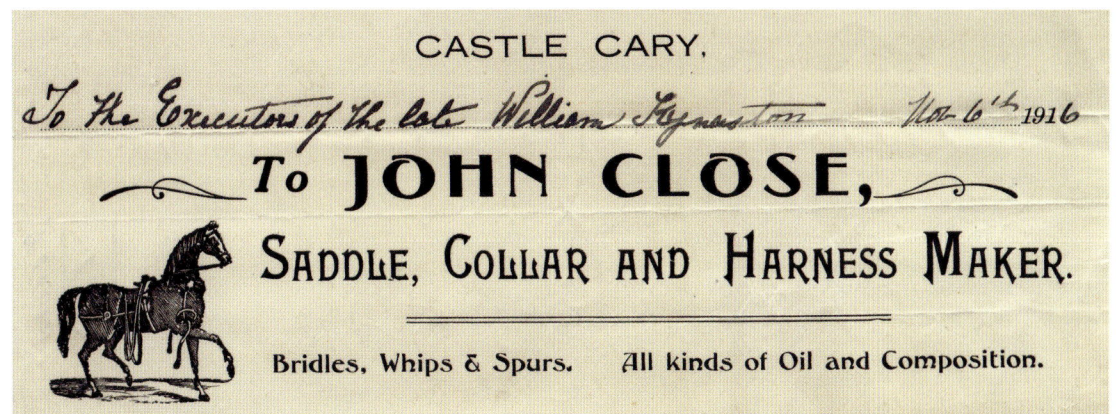

CASTLE CARY.

To the Executors of the late William Keynston   Nov 6th 1916

To JOHN CLOSE,

SADDLE, COLLAR AND HARNESS MAKER.

Bridles, Whips & Spurs.   All kinds of Oil and Composition.

The Close family provided harness and saddlery requirements in the Market Place.
A.V. Pearse collection.

[ESTABLISHED 1827.]

CASTLE CARY, *Christmas* 1883

C. Russ Esq

Bought of **F. S. MOORE,**

DISPENSING AND FAMILY CHEMIST,
PRINTER, BOOKSELLER, AND STATIONER.

THE DAILY PAPERS REGULARLY SUPPLIED.
A LARGE ASSORTMENT OF PAPER HANGINGS IN STOCK
And Patterns by the principal Manufacturers.

Francis Samuel Moore had a printing business in Fore Street.
A.V. Pearse collection.

The principle trades of Castle Cary when I arrived in 1875 were in the hands of the following; ironmongery, Buncombe & Son; drapery, Messrs. Clarke, Green and Whitelock; grocery, Tom Coles, Market Place - Obadiah Bird, opposite Horse Pond - C. Butt, Fore Street - and "Patty Bowles", Woodcock Street; butchers, Toogood, Market Place - Powell, Fore Street; also Bartlett, a weekly visitor from Galhampton. H. Close & Son, saddlers and harness-makers, were conspicuous in the Market Place (it was the horse age); carriage-builder, Mr. Bellringer, who did an extensive business with the gentry and farmers of the neighbourhood; chemists, F. S. Moore, who shared the printing business of the town with Thomas Daniell of the Market Place. A high-class tailoring business was conducted by Lemon & Sons at the corner of Ansford Lane and Upper High Street; Joseph Churchouse also carried on an old-established tailoring trade in Fore Street; George Baker was a furniture dealer in the Market Place, his business being taken over shortly after by Charles Pither and greatly extended by him. Painters and plumbers were provided by J. Penny & Sons, South Cary - also Day Bros., South Cary; and Mr. Bartholomew was a hairdresser. The public were well supplied with the staff of life by Messrs. Ellis of Fore Street, Biggin, Market Place; and Eason, miller and baker of Torbay. Mr. Samuel Snook was the hardware merchant and marine store dealer, while William Ridout, High Street, was a bootmaker, and Enos Wines a general store dealer on Bailey Hill.

The premises of Joseph Green, in Fore Street.
A.V.Pearse collection.

A brass harness plate.
A.V.Pearse collection.

Buttons possibly from flannel underwear, made by Messrs. Churchouse and Lemon.
A.V.Pearse collection.

ESTABLISHED 1850.

BAILEY HILL, CASTLE CARY, *April* 18*96*

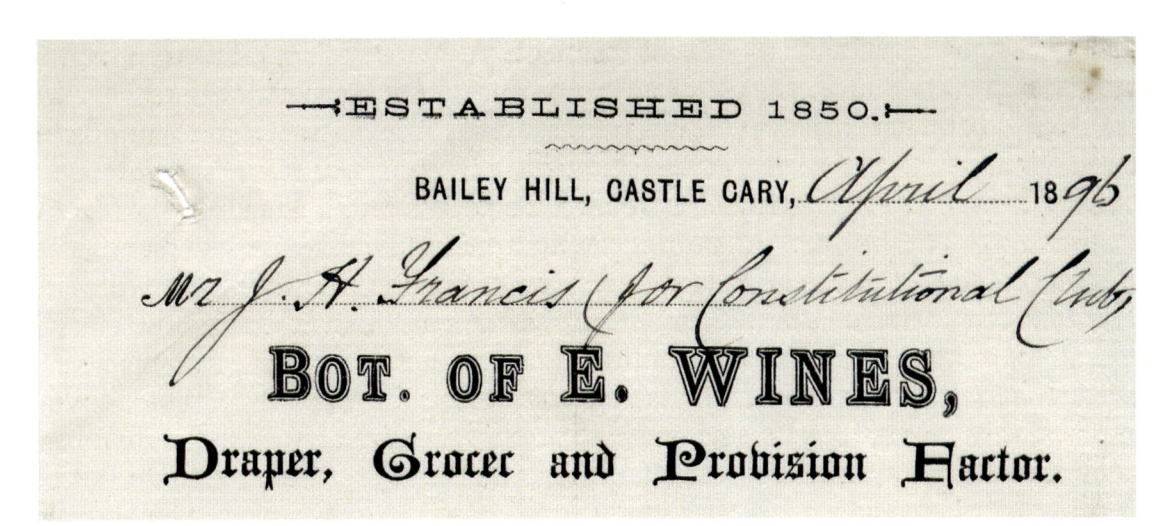

Mr *J. H. Francis (for Constitutional Club)*

BOT. OF E. WINES,
Draper, Grocer and Provision Factor.

Enos Wines was a draper and grocer on Bailey Hill.
LHG collection.

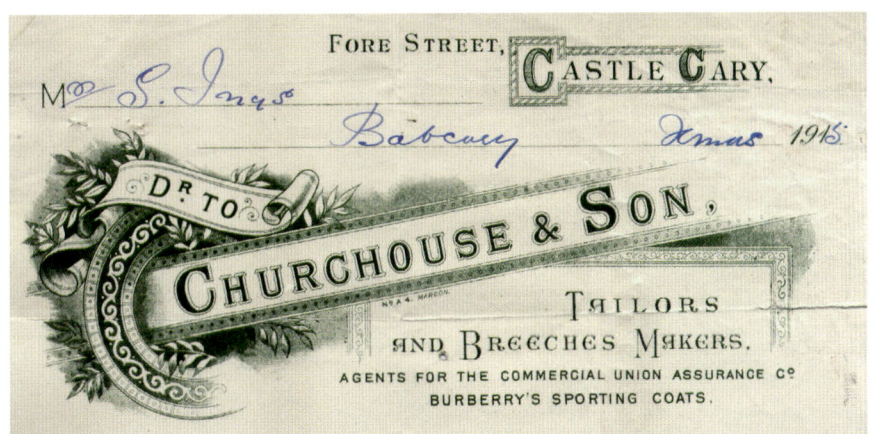

CASTLE CARY, 18
SOMERSET.

Mr *T Pawlett 12 Clifton Park Rd Clifton Bristol*

BOUGHT OF N. LEMON & SONS,
Tailors, Habit and Breeches Makers.
HOSIERS, HATTERS & SHIRTMAKERS.

5 PER CENT INTEREST CHARGED AFTER 12 MONTHS.
SUN FIRE OFFICE AND CLERICAL, MEDICAL & GENERAL LIFE OFFICES.

FORE STREET, CASTLE CARY,

Mr *S Ings*
Babcary Xmas 1915

DR TO **CHURCHOUSE & SON,**
TAILORS AND BREECHES MAKERS.
AGENTS FOR THE COMMERCIAL UNION ASSURANCE Co
BURBERRY'S SPORTING COATS.

Nathaniel Lemon and Son, and Joseph Churchouse and Son, tailors and outfitters.

STEAM FLOUR MILLS,

Castle Cary, 189*7*

The Late Mr H Gartele

Bought of **R. EASON,**
MILLER, CORN FACTOR, ETC.

1895

Robert Eason was a corn dealer and water miller at Torbay.
A.V. Pearse collection.

George Baker's furniture and removals business was taken over and expanded by Charles Pither and Son, with extensive workshops in 'Pithers' Yard'.

A postcard was issued illustrating work in the various departments, the larger view is of the cabinet workshop. LHG and A.V.Pearse collections.

GEORGE HOTEL, CASTLE CARY.

Sept 10 1903

Mr H. W. Harrold — Mr Hamlin's Sale

Dr. to C. & E. M. HARROLD,

GENUINE WINES AND SPIRITS.

The Harrold family were long established landlords of the George Hotel.
A.V.Pearse collection.

The hotel and public-house licences were held by the following; "George Hotel," Mrs. Harrold and family; "Britannia," Mr. Andrews; "Angel," Mr. Taylor, who also conducted a Posting business; "Waggon & Horses," John Hamblin; "Heart & Compass," Thomas White; "Railway Hotel," Mr. Pearce; "Mitre," Mr. Brake; the "Alma," T. Baker; "Savage Cat," Mr. Coleman, Smallway; "Fox & Hounds," Mr. Newport.

It will be noticed that only three names still persist in the town today, and only one in the same business, viz. that of Churchouse, and that is still a flourishing concern and on the same spot as in the last two generations. Mr. Horner was a baker who occupied the premises now in use by Mr. Asher as baker and confectioner. I should say they are the only ones in the town that can claim such a long succession - Horner, Biggin, Barber, Asher - quite 200 years in the same trade.

Mention should be made of the little colony of Scottish drapers settled principally in South Cary who did a good business in the surrounding district - the Hunters, the Hodges, and the Lees - all employing young men as travellers with their "packs" from Monday till Friday.

Private residents were: George Gray, Manor House; Captain Phelps, High Street; Mr. Tidcombe, Church Villa; two retired doctors, Mr. Lemon, sen. and Tom Gifford in South Cary.

The building industry was represented by E. O. Francis & Sons and Silas Hoskins & Sons. There was also a quaint old man named "Sammy" Ward who was quite a character, of very strong theological opinions on the Calvinistic side, with whom I had some discussion.

The legal profession was represented by the Russ Bros. at "The Pines," High Street with Arthur Harrold as chief clerk; and by George Woodforde (father of the late Randolph Woodforde) at Ansford Cottage.

Dr. Carey Coombs had succeeded Dr. Taylor and established himself as the leading medical practitioner in the district; his fine presence and known high distinction in the profession and his high moral and religious character made him a conspicuous personality. Richard Corner was the manager of Stuckey's Bank and very popular with the trading community. The handsome gold paten and chalice (after Nettlecome pattern) and wafer-box, still in constant use in the Parish Church, bear the inscription - Offered by Richard Corner, 1902.

The Post Office in those early days was part of the Buncombe premises (now occupied by Martins Stores) and conducted by the Misses Buncombe.

Naturally the heads and families of the two manufacturers were the most influential - personalities in the town. I well remember 65 and more years ago watching Salisbury Donne morning after morning on one of his high stepping horses on his way from South Court to the Mill at Torbay - also his eldest son, Stephen, was frequently to be seen on his high mettled steed in full hunting kit on his way to the "meet" of the Blackmore Vale Foxhounds. A handsome man and possessing a very kindly disposition, who, unfortunately, was struck down in the very prime of life; leaving a widow and young family to mourn their loss. That they had the greatest sympathy of the inhabitants was manifested by the large and representative gathering at the funeral. John Donne, his younger brother, who afterwards built Florida House, took a prominent place in the town, received H. M. 'commission of peace,' and for some years attended the magistrates' meeting at the Wincanton Petty Sessions. The further history of the Donne family is well known to all.

John Boyd, who turned his business into a Limited Company in 1882, carried on as J. Boyd & Co., Ltd. Previous to this, in Queen Victoria's Jubilee year (1887) he had built a block of cottages in Ansford Road, calling them "Jubilee Cottages," which he endowed by passing over shares in Boyd & Co. Old and disabled employees of the firm were placed in them as life-tenants, free of rent, with a weekly allowance that the shares produced.

The Francis family manufactured bricks and tiles and operated as building contractors. A.V.Pearse collection.

Copies are still extant of a photograph of from 40 - 50 of the leading businessmen taken in front of the Market Hall in the Jubilee year 1887, of whom (in 1944) I am the only survivor.

Two or three more personalities are suggested in addition to those already noted. The name of William Macmillan stands out vividly. Coming to the town in 1860s as an assistant to Mr. Boyd, he had a progressive spirit and soon gathered about himself some of the more intelligent members of the community and formed what was known as the Y.M.S. (Young Men's Society) which held regular meetings in a room at the Town Hall where public matters of the day were discussed and debated. Among the members I recall John Knight, chief clerk at Messrs. Donne's, who had a keen mind and some debating power, and it was not unusual for him and Mr. Macmillan to find themselves in an interesting combat over some controversial subject - politics or otherwise. There were also J. H. Francis, Joseph Green, Sergeant Elliott (Rifle Corps instructor). Rev. E. Cotton, and others. This Society became popular, for many years providing occasional public entertainment - and once a year a free tea for all old inhabitants.

William Macmillan, as is well known, played a very important part in the town life for many years, was appointed a Justice of the Peace for Somerset, and afterwards elected a member of the County Council.

Dr. Carey Coombs.
LHG and A.V.Pearse collections.

The gardens belonging to the Jubilee Cottages on the east side of Ansford Lane (now occupied by Hanover Court) from a postcard of c.1905.
LHG collection.

Another prominent figure comes to my mind is Silas Hoskins, a mason by trade, who told me that he worked at the building of the Town Hall, also of the Railway Station - at that time called the Ansford Station. A man of fine physique and of sound judgement, he was a kind of local repository of the past history of the town.

Elias Barber, nurseryman and seedsman, is also worthy of mention. Born and bred in Castle Cary, he could give very interesting reminiscences; an outstanding figure in the Wesleyan community as a local preacher and office-bearer. His daughters also were active workers in that church.

In these reminiscences I have purposely not included personalities of to-day. The names of Drewett, Pither, and others could not be omitted in writing of the public life of the town. But Charles Pither, who is no longer with us, certainly has every claim. Coming to Castle Cary in 1877, he deserves to be remembered for his business capacity and mental endowments as well as for the benefit of his personal influence upon his fellow-men.

It is on record that in the year 1800 there was in Castle Cary an up-to-date (for that period) good middle-class boarding and day school conducted by a Mr. Paull where sons of the well-to-do farmers and tradesmen of the neighbourhood received their education. About the year 1858 the present writer was a pupil of a daughter of Mr. Paull who had started a school for boys at Baltonsborough; she was a very gifted lady and a real disciplinarian. Her father's school here was carried on, or revived, with the arrival in the 1860s of the Rev. James Grosvenor, a retired Congregational Minister; a man of a retiring disposition but of considerable gifts of speech and manner; he lived to an advanced age. His wife also had an 'academy' for girls, which still survives at Scotland House, South Cary.

Rev. James Grosvenor is seated to right, holding a boater, in this school group taken at Scotland House c. 1908.
A.V.Pearse collection.

Elias Barber, nurseryman, billhead.
A.V.Pearse collection.

James Mackie, a Scotsman from Ayrshire, built a cheese store in South Street.
A.V.Pearse collection.

    The brief reference to James Mackie must be amplified. Over six feet tall, with a slight stoop and a long stride, he was a very arresting figure. He was the first chairman of the Parish Council, a 'canny Scot' and so a keen business man, yet of a generous disposition, as many who had sought his help in time of need could testify. As a young man in the local Rifle Corps he represented his battalion at the annual competitions at Wimbledon (now transferred to Bisley). As a judge of cheeses he was in great demand at the Southern Counties' shows. When he died in 1909 he left a greatly extended business to be carried on by his sons and grandsons.

    Castle Cary, when I first knew it in 1875, was much the same as it is today. Cumnock Terrace and Florida House were built soon after; much later came the allotments in South Cary, and other houses in various parts have increased the accommodation.

    Features of the town include the Parish Church of All Saints - built in the Perpendicular style in 1855 with embattled western tower and pinnacles and lofty octagonal spire adjoined the spacious vicarage with its umbrageous surroundings; Lodge Hill - rising to a height of 400 ft., with its graceful terrain; and the Park pond, once (before its contraction) a beauty spot, and the Horsepond - with its continuous flow from the never-failing hill reservoir; where there has since been added the granite Cross mounted on three tiers of steps to the memory of the 46 men of the parish who fell in the last war. Mention must be made of the "George Hotel" - with its ancient front, that had seen several generations of traders pass through its doors, and deals and bargains ratified by many a foaming glass. The "George," where the unfortunate traveller of Gibbet fame 200 years ago ate his last meal and met his fate, as legend tells, at the hand of his unknown brother, Jack White, at the Bratton crossroads. The "George," that for some years ran the 'yaller bus' to and from the G.W.R. station, bringing many 'carpetbaggers' to offer their wares to Cary tradesmen, and, in its cosy bar, when the day's duties were done, to relate to its wondering frequenters tales of their travels in distant parts of the land. At the old Hostelry at its back Jim the ostler combined the craft of a basket-maker with his regular duties. The old "George" - there it still stands, but, alas! the stable is without horses and the yard minus its 'yaller bus,' but there is parking space for cars of all descriptions. Who knows what changes in this ancient institution are in store when the new world towards which we are all looking is come?

The next old building of note in High Street is the 'Villa' (as it used to be called), the house where John Wesley was entertained; we find this note in his Journal - in 1790 - "Since my last visit (he visited our town five times) God has taken to Himself Mrs. Clarke who with a fine presence and good understanding combined a very uncommon degree of deep religion." Some years later the followers of the Wesleys worshipped in a humble edifice in what was known as 'Horner's Yard' at the back of what is now Pither's emporium and workshop. In 1839 the present Wesleyan (now Methodist) chapel was erected upon a ridge in the lower slopes of Lodge Hill, with the help of friends in Shepton Mallet; when its centenary was observed five years ago many interesting facts connected with its history were related.

Zion Chapel in South Cary, of much older history than the 'Wesleyan,' is content to retain the retired spot facing the Park where devoted and sometimes persecuted pastors of the flock have preached the Gospel to several generations of worshippers. Long may it continue its witness to the saving truths it proclaims.

The parish church is portrayed on this rare glass paperweight dating from about 1870.
A.V.Pearse collection.

Benjamin Ferrey's design for the rebuilt and enlarged parish church, showing a smaller south porch than the structure actually acquired, as the porch from the original church, with chamber above, was retained. Engraved by W. Dickes.
A.V. Pearse collection.

A silver 'sweetheart' brooch depicting Castle Cary church, hallmarked in Birmingham in 1892.

The coming to Castle Cary in 1845 of Prebendary R. J. Meade was a notable event in its history since for a hundred years previously no resident clergyman had ministered in the Church. The building of the spacious Vicarage was made possible by his generosity and enterprise. He took a very active part in the annual meetings of the Somerset Archaeological Society which was started four years after his arrival. At a Bruton gathering he gave a paper on the history of Castle Cary, and another later on its Church; both can be seen to-day in the 1857 issue of the Society's records. In 1863 Mr. Meade was made a Canon of Wells Cathedral, the town thus being honoured by that ecclesiastical distinction for seventeen years until his death in 1880. He was keenly interested in the Church Day School and on one of his visits to it he questioned the elder boys on the Catechism. Asking a rather promising lad "What is your name?" he received the somewhat gruff reply "Mannel" - which the master interpreted to the Vicar as "Emmanuel." But when to the next question "Who gave you this name?" the puzzled boy at length answered "I'm d - d if I know," - well, no doubt the Vicar saw that greater attention was given to this subject in the future. "Mr. Meade's Club" was composed of a good number of the working and artisan class of a more temperate and steady character than the members of another club which the new Vicar found on his arrival. I can well remember the handsome equipage drawn by two upstanding dappled bay carriage horses by which the Canon and his household were periodically conveyed to Wells when official duties required his attendance at the Cathedral. Some of my readers will recall an erection on Lodge Hill which, owing to its shape, was commonly called 'Canon Meade's Extinguisher' and could be seen from Wells (the Canon in one of his addresses to the Somerset Archaeological Society referred to the Hill as "that eminence overhanging the town.")

There are members of the working class of those times who deserve a place among the notabilities. One such was Edward Noble - a 'drawer' at Boyd's. He was a good specimen of the intelligent artisan, a man with an interest in public matters - political and religious. As an amateur caterer for teas, dinners, etc., he distinguished himself. I think he also acted as a 'go-between' of employer and employed, having the confidence of master and man. In industrial affairs such men have saved many a disastrous 'strike' to the benefit of the community.

A fine Georgian residence 'The Villa', now known as Beechfield House, rebuilt after a fire, is set back and screened from the High Street by a high wall and trees.

Castle Cary vicarage, built by Canon Meade in 1846, and very much a gentleman's residence. A.V.Pearse collection.

A view from the 1890s of the Wesleyan Methodist Chapel built in 1839. The wooden hut was utilized by Professor Gyngell as a photographic studio. LHG collection.

Friendly societies were a common means by which artisans and members of the working class made provision for welfare benefits, and were associated with ceremonial club days and festivities. Members carried poles, decorated with ribbons, and surmounted with brass emblems particular to their organization. Shown here are nineteenth century pole heads for the Ansford and Ditcheat society, left; and Castle Cary society, right. A.V.Pearse collection.

Another such representative character was Richard Gibbs, of the Park Cottages, a shoemaker, but with several side-lines - viz, that of bombaily, bill-poster, emergency postman, town-crier - one of the most active men of his age and class I have ever known. As town-crier he would leave his cobbler's stool and waxed thread, take his 'Bill of Authority' and proclaim from north to south of the town some coming event after crying 'Oh yes Oh yes' in a ringing tone, all for the price of one shilling and accomplished in the shortest possible time. In his early 'bombaily' days his duties had their possible risks. One cold damp winter's night he was in possession of the household effects of a certain creditor when the enraged householder returned and seizing Dick by the scruff of his neck hurled him through the doorway into the midden outside, and there he was left for the night until the authorities could come and assert his rights to possesssion.

I fancy I hear someone say "What about Georgie Woodrow?" Well, space must just be found for him among these fragments of the long ago. He was a weaver who came here from Kidderminster in the 'sixties,' first working a loom in his cottage and afterwards employed in Boyd's Factory as a foreman over women-workers. If he appeared dictatorial, it was only due to a high sense of what his duties demanded of him. Yet George allowed himself to relax on Saturday afternoons during the football season. A most energetic backer-up of the home-team at matches, he was always ready with his lemons at half-time to refresh his favourites. He was a fanatical teetotaller and would give no quarter to those who differed from him on this point. Of small stature, but possessing a vigorous frame, and a man of strong convictions, no worthier appointment was ever made to the Jubilee Cottages, in one of which he ended his days.

Cornelius Martin took over J. Sessions' ironmongery business in the Market Place, as advertised on an issue of the Castle Cary Thunderer.
LHG collection.

[Editor's note. Cornelius Martin originated from a long established Baltonsborough family, coming to Cary in 1875 and establishing a grocery business in South Cary. He expanded his business, purchasing premises in the Market Place by 1889, and soon after the adjoining ironmongery business of J. B. Sessions, to create the 'Central Stores,' later to become 'Cornelius Martin & Sons': the South Cary shop remaining a grocery branch and warehouse. His sons, Cornelius Charles and Richard William took over the running of the grocery and ironmongery businesses respectively, while Cornelius senior moved to Gillingham in 1904 as managing director of the Hudson and Martin private limited company, until his retirement in 1935 at the age of 84. His reminiscences of Cary were published in a series of articles in the Cary Parish Magazine in 1944, and under several subsequent ownerships Martin's Stores continues to thrive.]

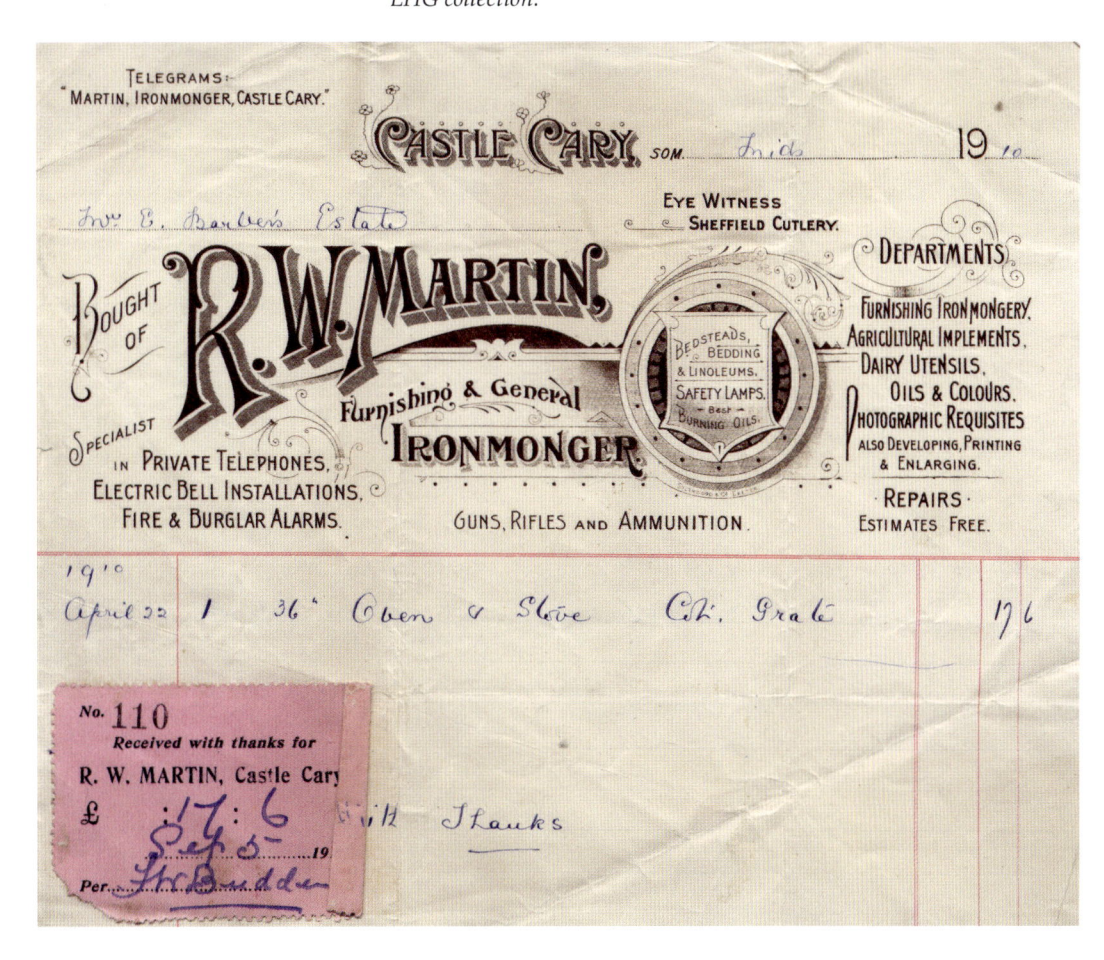

CASTLE CARY,
Somerset, *Feby* 1912

M*r* Stickman

Dr. to R. W. Martin,

Ironmonger and Engineer.

DEPARTMENTS
Furnishing
Ironmongery
Agricultural
Implements
Dairy
Utensils
Oils & Colors

R. W. MARTIN, CASTLE CARY. SOM.

TELEGRAMS
MARTIN,
IRONMONGER
CASTLE CARY

DEPARTMENTS
Photographic
Requisites.
Domestic
Electricity.
Specialist
in Telephones.

TELEGRAMS:
"MARTIN, ELECTRICIAN, CASTLE CARY."

INSTALLATIONS for	INSTALLATIONS of
Lighting by Air-Gas, Electricity, or Acetylene.	Telephones, Fire & Burglar Alarms, Electric Bells.

661

RICHARD W. MARTIN,
ENGINEER,
Authorised as Plumber by the Castle Cary Water Co., Ltd.

CASTLE CARY,
SOMERSET,

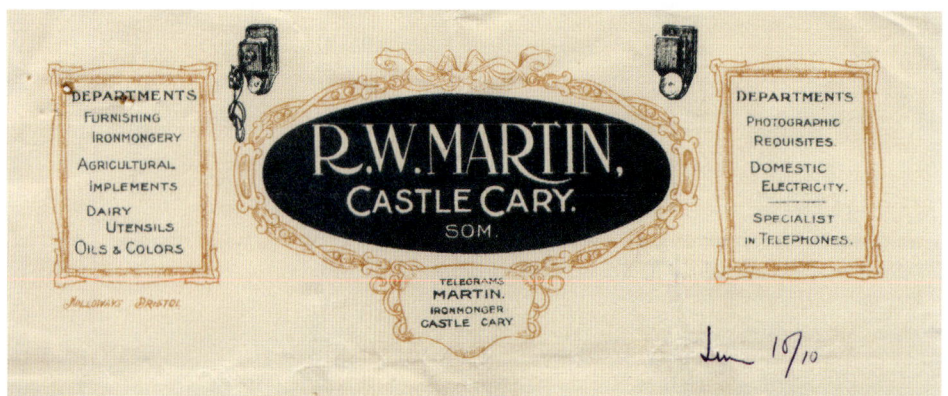

Cornelius Martin's son Richard William took over the ironmongery side of the business in the former Sessions' premises and soon expanded into the photographic and electrical areas of retailing. He died as a result of injuries received in a motorcycle accident at Arthur's Bridge, near Ditcheat, in 1916.
A.V.Pearse collection.

Cornelius C. Martin

Branch Shop & Warehouses,
SOUTH STREET.

Telegraphic Address
MARTIN, GROCER, CASTLE CARY.

Central Stores,
Market Place,
CASTLE CARY,
SOMERSET.

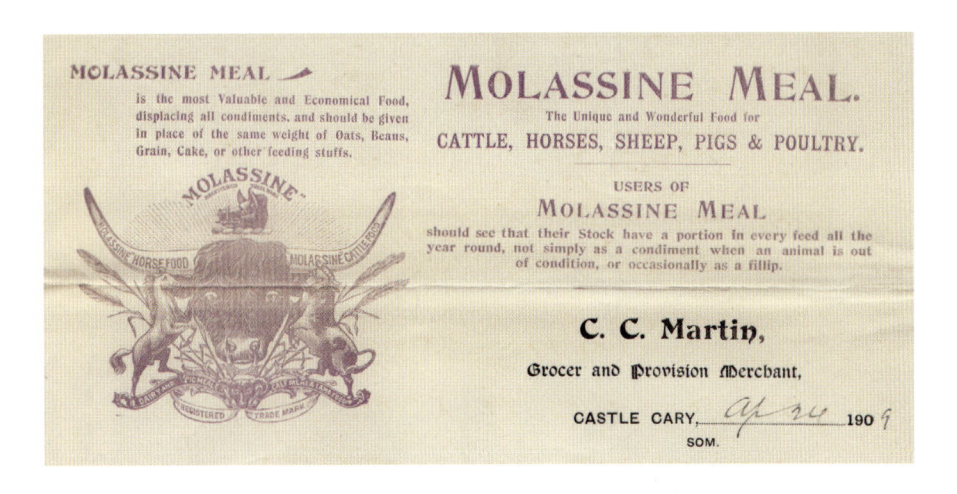

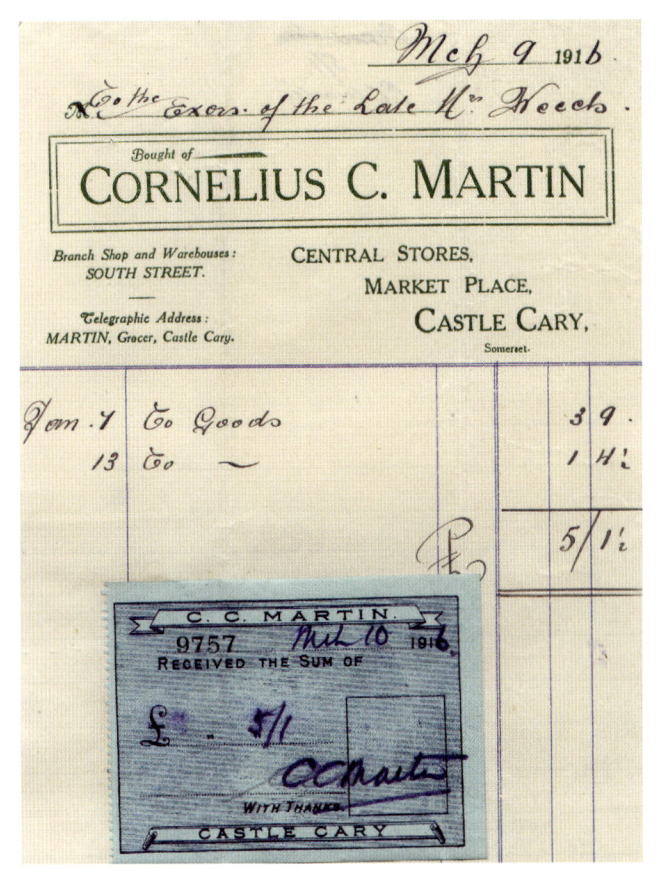

Cornelius Charles Martin operated the grocery department, including the branch shop in South Street.
A.V.Pearse collection.

Willoughby Wyatt joined Cornelius Charles Martin as a partner in 1918, eventually taking over the concern. Under successive owners the business continues to thrive.
A.V.Pearse collection

Martins Stores occupies a prime location in the Market Place and continues to supply groceries to the locality, though the interior has undergone radical alterations since Cornelius Martin's time.
LHG collection.

The painted brick frontage of Martins Stores conceals an older building incorporating much re-used material, including this Norman arch, complete except for the label stops, used as a window head in the west elevation and rarely noticed by passers-by, and perhaps deriving from the castle ruins.
A.V.Pearse collection.

Joseph Chapman

Joseph Chapman by Colin Taylor

Joseph Chapman was my great-grandfather - his daughter, Nora, married my grandfather Godfrey Taylor, the former stationmaster of both Bruton and Whitham. His eldest son was Kenneth Taylor, my father, who as a child frequently went to Boyd's factory with his aunt, Gladys Joyce, former licensee of the Half Moon, and devoted member of Ansford Church.

Chapman came to prominence in Ansford and Cary when he re-designed the original hair-picker mechanism, still in use today on Henderson's power looms in Boyd's factory, such that it had three chances of successfully selecting a single hair in the same time span that it took the original version to select just one hair, with obvious commercial potential.

He was born in Ilford, Essex, in 1848, the son of a bookseller also called Joseph Chapman, and worked initially at the North London Locomotive Company in Bow, Middlesex, where he met Henderson in 1866. They worked together for the next two years, until Chapman left the company in 1868 as a journeyman engineer, after which Henderson quit in early 1869. Chapman had met his future wife, Annie Jemima Lowe, of Woodeford Green, Essex, daughter of Thomas Lowe, a builder, but her parents withheld their consent, and in a vain bid to forget her, Chapman left his employer in 1868 and travelled to Argentina where he worked on their railways and later joined a ship's company as its engineer. On one occasion while sailing between Buenos Aires and Montivideo a fire broke out threatening the lives of all on board. Chapman seized control of the ship and rammed it onto a sand bar where the passengers escaped to safety.

Joseph Chapman, born in Ilford in 1848. He came to Ansford in the early 1870s to work for John Boyd. C.Taylor collection.

Joseph Chapman's wife Annie Jemima, from Woodeford Green, Essex. C.Taylor collection.

Annie Jemima Chapman in the porch of Woodford Cottage, near the junction of Tucker's Lane and Ansford Hill.
C.Taylor collection.

The Chapman family outside Woodforde cottage in 1887.
Left to right, back row: Annie Jemima; Gertrude; Joseph; front row; Ethel; Gladys; Frank; Nora; Lily.
C.Taylor collection.

In the middle of 1871 Chapman arrived in England and returned to Ilford, where he found Annie Lowe still single and unattached, but marriage was still not on the agenda. When he heard that Henderson was in Cary, Chapman set out to find him, and thus started a journey that linked his name with Boyd's textile company for the next 40 years. Soon after he married Annie, and his father came to Ansford to live with the newly married couple in 1875 at Woodforde Cottage, and remained for some years before returning to London, where he died aged 87 at Manor Park, Essex in 1901.

Attached to Joseph Chapman's home at Woodforde Cottage was a fully equipped engineering workshop and forge, where he refined Boyd's horsehair power looms and increased their range of geometric patterns. He is best remembered for his invention of the 'picker' mechanism, which had a major impact on the local horsehair industry, but which he never had patented, and was largely responsible for constructing John Boyd's prototype loom. Boyd rewarded Chapman with a box of drawing instruments, stamped 'Reward - Department of Science and Art' - now in my possession; and offered him accommodation in one of his prestigious terraced houses of Cumnock Terrace, reserved for his senior staff and family members. Family tradition recounts that he also built a velocipede, or penny-farthing bicycle, and other machines including aspirations to construct a 'flying machine'. He and his family integrated into the Cary community, and identified with the Congregational Church, where Boyd was the 'registrar' for many years. He was elected to be a parish councillor from 1895 until 1919, during which time he oversaw the 'stoning of the dirty part of Solomon's Lane', and the construction of the footpath from the railway station to Ansford Hill. In 1906, along with F. C. Wride, he was apointed an 'Overseer' of Ansford to assess the needs of the local poor.

Chapman remained as Boyd's engineer, attending to the machines he had invented, until he was 70 years of age. After the death of his wife in 1914 he lived with his youngest daughter, Lily Lowe, first and then with his daughter Nora Taylor at 6 Wyke Cottages at Wyke Champflower, until his death in 1933 aged 86. He was buried in Ansford churchyard, beside his wife, and just a few yards away from his daughter Constance Marion Winifred. His looms, now moved to the Torbay factory, have never been improved upon, and now serve a growing range of products for a worldwide market.

Joseph Chapman in later life, on Creech Hill. He died in 1933, and is buried at Ansford.
C.Taylor collection.

Harvesting at Manor Farm

Harvesting in the 1880s at Manor Farm – the reminiscences of John Mackie in 1943

What happy times those harvest days recall! In June or July, when we sat at lunch in some pook of fragrant hay, or beneath the half-made rick, eating our lunch of bread and cheese, and listening to the stories of old and hard days, when bread was a shilling a loaf, and barley bannock was almost the only fare of the farm labourer. Dear old John Nash, one of Nature's truest gentlemen, the aristocrat of our farm, entranced my brother William and me with his account of hardships in his boyhood days. How we both loved that man!

John Mackie was of Scottish descent, and an enthusiast of Somerset dialect, producing several books of poetry and plays, as well as being a frequent contributor to the Somerset Year Books in the 1920s and '30s.
photo. Somerset Year Book 1929.

Manor Farm, situated above Park Pond and on part of the castle site, was the successor to a manorial complex previously occupying this area, which has been occupied since Roman times. The present farmhouse was built in the nineteenth century, replacing a building from the Tudor period.
A.V.Pearse collection.

Then in the cornfields, how hard we worked, but how greatly we loved it. I would that I could go over it all once more. Up in the morning at four o'clock to milk a dozen cows before breakfast. Then out harvesting. We had no reaper and binder in those days of the eighties, nor yet a self-deliverer. Our reaping machine was like an ordinary field grass mower, but it had two seats. My father drove the team, and our fine farm bailiff, John Lumbard, sat with a straight rake and put the sheaves down as the machine progressed, lowering the scrave by a foot gadget, and placing the sheaves, unbound in the wake of the cutter. We had to gather and tie the sheaves and throw them back before the machine could get round again, and it was sometimes tough work, especially when milking time came, and we had to part with some of our workers. Then, too, when we grew wheat after a crop of prize mangolds, the corn was almost as tall as ourselves, and if rain had been heavy the corn was beaten down into a tangle, and we had to straighten it and sometimes make three or four sheaves out of one. Then the thistles!

Thirsty work! – harvesters take a break; from a nineteenth century collotype.
A.V.Pearse collection.

Sheaves of corn were hauled to the rick yard to be built into ricks, sometimes supported on mushroom-shaped stones, called staddle stones, and then thatched, or to a barn, to be threshed at a later time.

We got very tired during the evening, especially as the shortened staff made our work heavier, and we used to go on until sundown. Then to bed, to sleep the sleep, if not of the just, of the tired and happy.

The harvest supper was an event of the year, for then we gathered the farm staff into our dining room, and a great rump of beef and "figged" pudding was the fare. Afterwards there was smoke and song, and the evening was a most convivial entertainment.

I remember, too, the gleaners coming off the land at eventide carrying on their heads the result of their day's work. I had not seen gleaners since those days, until last year I saw a lady coming down from off Salisbury Plain with two great sheaves under her arms. She told me that she gleaned most days of the harvest in order to provide food for her fowls in winter.

The Story of a Wedding Dress

A billhead for Hugh Hodge, who ran a drapery business at Woodville House, and was one of a number of drapers who migrated to Cary from Scotland in the later nineteenth century.
A.V.Pearse collection.

The Story of a Wedding Dress by Stanley Hodge

In the process of researching my family's history I have found that at least two great-great uncles, George and Hugh Hodge, moved from Ayrshire and settled in and around Castle Cary in the second half of the nineteenth century, as part of the influx of Scots to the town, initially, like many of their compatriots, as travelling drapers or 'packmen'. One of them, Hugh, lived in and ran a drapery business from Woodville House, while his wife Susan, a native of Castle Cary and daughter of Richard Cooper, a tailor, was also a dressmaker and milliner at the same address. The Hodges had migrated from Auchinleck and Old Cumnock, neighbouring parishes to Ochiltree, from which Cary's Macmillans had originated.

Every summer my late wife Nan and I visited Somerset from Greenock for several weeks and during these visits I made a point of going to Castle Cary to pursue my research. After leaving a note in the visitors' book at the museum in 2005 I was put in touch with Adrian Pearse, whose great grandmother Elizabeth Amelia Barrett (née Bettey)'s family, by an extraordinary coincidence, turned out

Woodville House, in Woodcock Street, now having a small extension to the western end.

A studio portrait of Elizabeth Amelia Bettey; after her marriage to Wosson Barrett the couple lived in Fore Street.
A.V.Pearse collection.

49

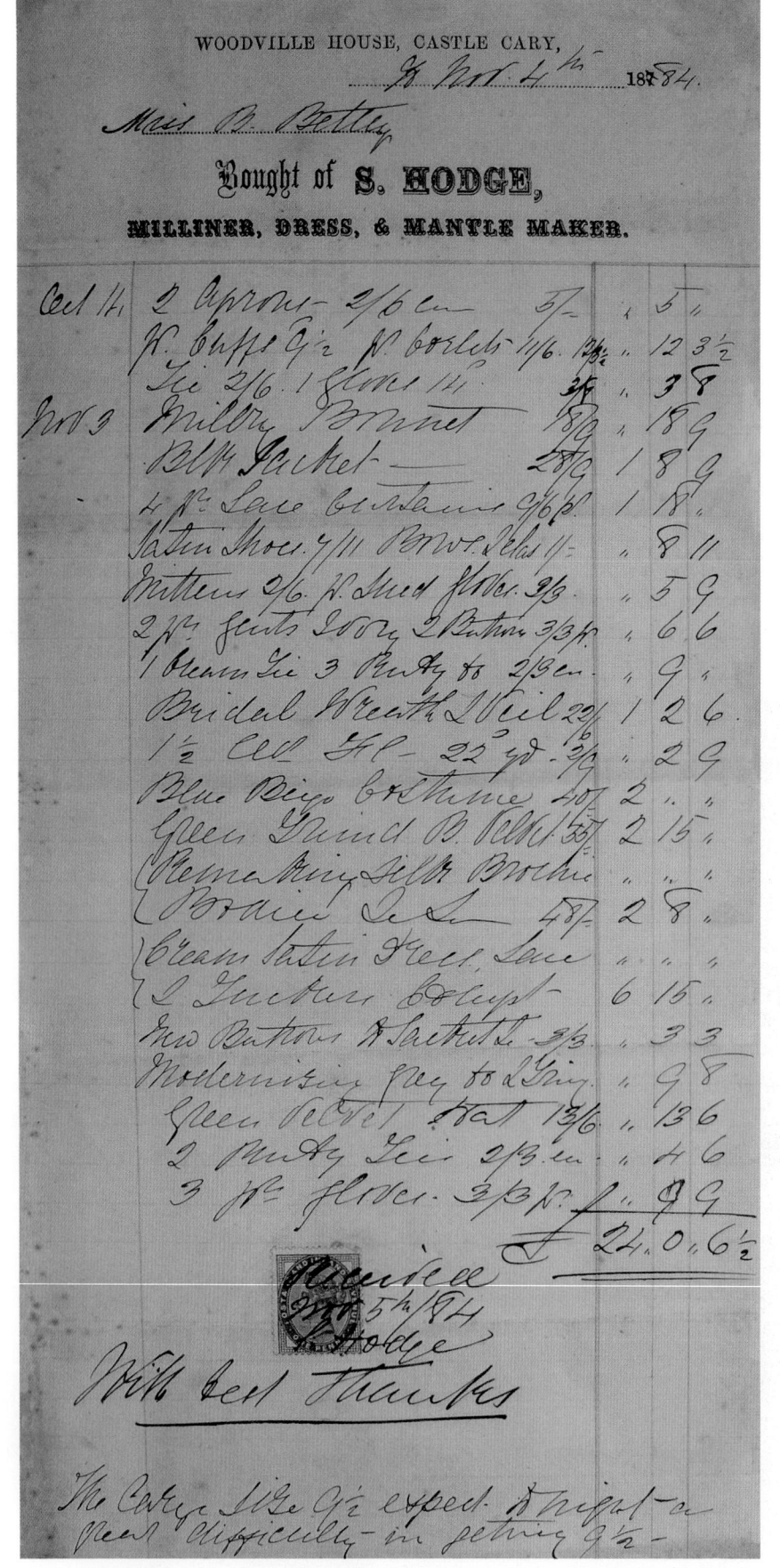

Susan Hodge's invoice for the silk wedding dress at £6-15-00, and additional items at a total of over £24 was a substantial sum in 1884.
A.V.Pearse collection.

to have been friendly with mine in the late 1800s. He was also able to tell me that Susan Hodge had made a wedding dress for her, and supported this with documentation including a photograph of the dress when it was used by his aunt for her wedding during World War II at Ansford, and the original invoice dated 1884.

Evidently another relative had later donated the dress to the costume museum in Totnes, Devon, so in continuation of our holiday we duly visited the Costume Museum on a Thursday afternoon. On explaining the reason for our visit to the lady behind the desk she explained that the current display was on the theme of travelling clothes and unfortunately all the other items had been packed away. As we were talking another lady came into the museum and eventually joined the conversation – this turned out to be Julia Fox, assistant curator in the 1970s and now curator, who attended at the museum only two afternoons per week. When I showed her the 1940s photograph and the invoice she immediately recognized the dress and agreed to let us see it. Nan was quite overwhelmed with the workmanship and sheer beauty of the dress, and surprised that the colour of the silk was pale yellow and not white, but Julia explained that white dresses did not come in to fashion until later. For her part, Julia was delighted to finally have provenance of the dress; it is not every day that someone walks in off the street with such information after 122 years, and how fortunate we were to have chosen one of Julia's afternoons!

Julia Fox shows the dress at Totnes Costume Museum in 2005. S.Hodge collection.

Wartime rationing meant that the dress was used again by Elizabeth Amelia Bettey's grand-daughter, Elizabeth Barrett, for her marriage to Harry Rathbone at Ansford in September 1944.
A.V.Pearse collection.

[Editor's note:- Elizabeth Amelia Bettey was born at Bridge Farm, Alhampton, in 1855, and later lived in the thatched farmhouse at Lower Ansford of which a portion survives and has recently been repaired and given a tiled roof. She was the great – great – great granddaughter of our first contributor, John Cannon, by his daughter Elizabeth, and married her cousin Wosson Barrett in 1884; he being John Cannon's great – great grandson by his daughter Susanna. She died in 1921. Stanley Hodge's grandfather ran one of the main retail businesses in the Greenock area, Mitchell Hodge & Son, house and ship furnishers, founded by his father Mitchell, a brother of George and Hugh at Castle Cary. It closed in the mid 1970s after 150 years.]

Memories of Butwell House

Memories of Butwell House, Ansford by Revd. Alan Bliss

If I could board a time machine and travel back to 1880 1 would learn that my grandmother, Alice Newport, was at school aged 12. I have her poetry exercise book with me; one poem she wrote about was "Oh I'd be a butterfly flitting about from roses to lilies, now in and now out I'd flitter all day in the sun's pleasant ray and with butterfly brothers I'd merrily play"..... Sadly she died in the year I was born; likewise I never met her father Reuben Newport born at Sparkford in 1826. He married later in life as he served in the Royal Marines for 21 years. He was 42 on his discharge in 1866. He first married Amelia Bond at Castle Cary who died in 1872. His second wife was Eliza Moon born in 1835 and died in 1916. They had one daughter Alice Amelia Newport. She and my grandfather Herbert J. Bliss were married by Revd. Colby Price in 1897 at Ansford church.

After leaving the marines Reuben became the Inn Keeper of the Half-Moon in Ansford where in 1880 an auction took place of properties in Ansford, one of which was known as Butwell Cottage, with two cottages adjoining. Reuben obtained the freehold messuage and orchard for £325. Butwell Cottage contained 4 rooms on ground floor, 4 bedrooms, garden, orchard, stable and carthouse. Reuben moved in with his wife and daughter and in 1884 had a wash house built in the court yard by the firm E.O.Francis & Sons, whose letter headed paper states 'Contractors, Builders, Smiths, Wheelwrights, Brick & Tile Manufacturers, Steam Saw Mills and Joinery Works of Castle Cary'.

Correspondence in 1892 mentions the well outside the house. It was to be cleaned out, walls cemented and a pump erected. The tenants and the public had the use of this water so it states, "from time immemorial" so we have the origin of the name 'Butwell'. I remember Mr. & Mrs. Hallett who lived next door always used the water and so did the Bliss's. Butwell House as it came to be known was occupied by Eliza Newport after Reuben died in 1904. From 1916-32 it was let to tenants. In 1932 Herbert John Bliss and his wife Alice moved from Bristol to Ansford. Herbert had retired from G.W.R. but was still active, he became a member of the Parish Council, the Wincanton Rural District Council, a Billeting Officer during the war, not an easy task, but some of the evacuees liked Ansford and stayed on afterwards. He was also a member of the P.C.C. and sidesman at Ansford Church. In 1948 a fire broke out under the stairs, but when some of the walling was removed a baker's oven was found. It was taken out and I remember seeing it before it was taken away for scrap.

I have a limited knowledge of Ansford and Castle Cary, as my parents and I only came to live at Butwell House three or four times a year from 1932 onwards; when at school it became my holiday home. Every year we walked up the station path, though in my early years I was in a pram. I remember Mrs. R. Williams of Hillcroft Farm coming to have a look at me in my pram on the front lawn and saying she wished she had a baby - and sure enough soon afterwards she did. Bobby and Graham were her two sons. As they grew up they worked on the farm and used to deliver the milk in a churn and ladle it out into a jug.

Elaborate hats are a feature in the wedding group photographed in front of Butwell House in 1897, of Alice Newport and Herbert Bliss. Note the elaborate cast iron porch.
A.Bliss collection.

Butwell House, on Ansford Hill, was purchased by Reuben Newport in 1880, and seen here in 1895.
A.Bliss collection.

Contemporary publicity material for the Singer 'Junior', as purchased by Herbert Bliss. It remained garaged after his death, until sold for restoration decades later.
A.Bliss collection.

A field next to the orchard was often grazed and the cows would be milked by hand in there. The farm workers wore long white coats sitting on three legged stools, I often used to watch them milking. In the orchard grew cider apples, plums, pears and apple trees. My uncle Leslie was clever in grafting the trees and in season we could help ourselves to the fruit off the branches. The lower garden was for vegetables; grandfather used to grow everything for the house and my Auntie May made lovely gooseberry pies for Whitsuntide. She also made dandelion wine, and used to take me for walks over the fields pointing out wild plants that you could eat. On Sunday she played the organ in the church and during the week she would have a practice. I often used to pump the organ for this, you had to watch the gauge, and at times she would pull out all the stops. The air would get used up before I had pumped enough in, so there was a terrible sound like the end of a gramophone record that needed winding up, if you know what I mean.

My grandfather had a car, a four seater touring blue Singer AU 9098. It was not my friend as I was always ill in it; the petrol smell was so strong. My Uncle Leslie was the driver and before use it always needed attention. I would have to sit in the driving seat and put my foot on the pedal while my uncle was looking at the engine; "Push harder" he would say and I, perhaps at nine or ten years, could hardly reach the pedal with my foot, I would struggle to do what was required. After my uncle died it was never used until it was sold for restoration.

In the summer time the carnival was full of excitement. My grandfather led the Fancy Dress procession carrying the Union Jack, and what a wonderful time it was. Our family ran the hoopla stall. In the bedroom I slept in at the top of the house was a chest of drawers full of prizes to be won all wrapped up in tissue paper. What a galaxy of treasures! I remember the stall "Bunty Pull the Strings" - we always had a go on that. Uncle Leslie ran the coconut shy and grandfather took the money at the gate.

Now who lived near Butwell House that I can remember? Mr. & Mrs. W. Barrett at the Orchards - they always had the cider apples and you could see the crusher from the lane as you walked by, then Mr. & Mrs. R. Carr at Laylocks, the Clothier Family at Ansford Farm, Mr. & Mrs. Dunford at Orchard Villa, Mr. & Mrs. W.Hallett, Butwell Villa, Mr. & Mrs. Joyce at the Halfmoon Inn, Mr. & Mrs. Lucas at Hill House, Mr. & Mrs. Rathbone at Butwell Cottage, The Church's lived there in the days of the two cottages and I believe George pumped the organ. The Rector was Leslie Taylor who afterwards moved to Wellington, Somerset. I remember also Mr. Basil Bazell was the previous Rector. The Williams of Hillcrest Farm, Alice, Mabel and Helen Woodforde of St. Anselms were all related to the diarist James Woodforde.

There is so much to write about, I recall sitting on the bedroom windowsills and watching the trains go by and the shunting sound never seemed to stop. From the window you could see Ditcheat, and out across the fields to Glastonbury Tor, what a glorious expanse of countryside.

Every holiday we went for walks and I noticed how everyone greeted one another and grandfather would raise his walking stick in acknowledgement. We would walk across the fields to Cary. The Newports were our cousins at the butchers, visit the shops, watch the swans at the Horse Pond end of Fore Street, also walk to Clanville and Ditcheat, often going through the fields. We would return passing the milk factory gaining a lovely smell of milk, hearing the machinery working and the clanging of the milk churns, we would arrive at Butwell

Herbert Bliss leading the fancy dress procession in the Carnival as it passes T. White's ironmongery shop.
A.Bliss collection.

House ready for a meal. The range would have cooked the food, later there was an Aga. Afterwards there was the washing up to do, with those heavy black iron pots. The hot water came from the large black sooty kettle. At night Aunt May would put the warming pan full of red hot coals into my bed to warm it, if it was not the summer season. Grandfather would make hot drinks - cocoa, I would climb the stairs, enclosed they were, and wear my pyjamas - grandfather always wore a night shirt and great- grandfather a night cap with a red tassel - and so to bed - a brass one to climb up into.

The Carnival floats pass through the Market Place in 1931 – the only known stereoview of Castle Cary. It may be seen in 3D using a viewer, or 'freeviewed' with practice.
LHG collection.

A Strand in Britain's Story; T. S. Donne & Sons Ltd.

[Editor's note - the following is extracted from an illustrated souvenir booklet produced by T. S. Donne & Sons in 1947]

The cover of the souvenir booklet showing the Higher Flax Mills from the south-east.

In the closing years of the 18th century important chapters of English history were being written. It was a period which resulted in the birth of the United States of America and the leadership of George Washington; which saw the rise to power of William Pitt, the younger, and two other great figures, Wellington and Nelson, were also making history. We refer, however, to the year 1797 in which on April 21st our own history began. Foremost among the worthy inhabitants of any town should be placed those who introduce new industries and find employment for the people. Such a man was the elder Charles Donne, who was born at Huish Episcopi, Somerset, in the year 1768, and as a young man came to live at Castle Cary. The Donnes originate from an old West of England family, the names of Nicholas Donne and James Donne appearing at Yeovil in a survey in 1545. The will of William, son of John Donne, of Broadwindsor, was administered in 1646, and the Cary branch of the family spring from Hugh Donne who flourished about 1700.

Mr. Charles Donne, looking for a likely place to establish a twine business in the neighbourhood of Yeovil, arriving at Castle Cary, discovered that the people had very little employment. Castle Cary had been famous for its dowlas, tick and knit-hose, but these industries were fast dying out. Here was the golden opportunity that Mr. Donne sought, and in the year 1797 he set up business in cottages at Ansford (the parish adjoining Castle Cary) which served as workshops. A few years later, the business was subsequently removed to a site in Torbay, Castle Cary, Somerset - the name "Torbay" emanating from the fact that the Tor at Glastonbury is almost in a dead line looking across the open country.

Mr. Charles Donne died (at the ripe old age of 87) in 1855. The business was consolidated by his son Thomas Salisbury Donne, whose son Edwin came into the business which became T. S. Donne & Sons. Since then, the family continuity has been maintained and the business was formed into a Private Limited Company in 1926, the original Directors being the late Captain William S. Donne, J.P., and our present Chairman, Thomas Salisbury Donne, who in this year of publication, 1947 (when we celebrate our 150th Anniversary of continued trading), although in his 70th year, continues to be very closely associated with the business which his forbears established in the days of Nelson.

Over a long period of years, the firm has built up a world wide reputation for the quality of its goods, and during the two World Wars did a worthy part in supplying its products in the service of the country. The Works are set in a very beautiful part of Somerset, and it is possibly unique to-day in as much that Twine making and the weaving of Narrow Fabrics are carried on within the same premises. For many years the firm has specialised in the needs of the Bedding, Upholstery and Allied Trades, and its reputation stands high in the manufacture of high grade Bedding, and Upholstery Twines, Chair Webbings, and all classes of Narrow Fabrics. Whilst we are giving prominence to these specialised products, all other classes of Twines, Ropes, and Cordage are manufactured at Higher Flax Mills, Castle Cary. Before the war the Somerset Chair, woven from fine flax cable laid cord, was famous. King George V accepted one for Buckingham Palace. It is hoped that production will recommence shortly.

To tell the story in a simple manner, a series of photographs were taken during 1946-47, and by following them a fairly clear picture of our activities will be obtained. The first gives a view of the Works, then an interesting photograph of our 80 years old engine, which has been superseded by electric power from the grid to every machine with an independent electric motor. It should be recorded, however, that the engine is a wonderful piece of workmanship, and the Company has arranged for this to be kept in perfect condition. It is started at regular intervals to ensure that any student of engineering can view should the occasion arise, it being felt that students might like to inspect from time to time.

Next come illustrations of an open-air Ropewalk where specialised Flax Cable Laid Cords (or "Railway Lines" as known in the trade) are still being made, then follow illustrations of Best Quality Cable Laid Cords.

Two operators are shown making Cow-spans, and all classes of Agricultural Ropes are regularly made by the Company, then you can see certain numbers of yarns being twisted together on a large Twisting Frame. The next two photographs show a scrubbing or Washing machine for Twines which are prepared, and wound on to large spools as illustrated on the following page. Following this come two photographs of the polishing machine where large spools of Twine are taken to be given the high glazed polish which is characteristic of "Donnes" Twines; and then follows a photograph of a girl operating a power balling machine. After this is shown an illustration of Flax Mattress Twine, Flax Cable Laid Cord, and Flax Tufting Loops as the finished product, and referring to Flax Tufting Loops it is interesting to record that during the most difficult period in 1945, the Company was called upon to produce millions of these Loops, to suspend springs which formed a very important unit of Tropical Containers, and which helped tremendously in safely dropping supplies to our men engaged in jungle warfare; similar Loops are now used extensively in the Bedding Trade.

We now come to the weaving section of our business, with illustrations showing a girl winding small spools which are used in the weft of the Webbing, and a weaver operating a ten multiple loom, and two close ups of a similar loom. Two illustrations of the Webbing now being manufactured follow, and finally we show an important photograph of the New Weaving Shed put into production during the early part of 1947.

The Works from the south-west – the rope walks, originally open, are here largely roofed over.

The steam engine, superseded by the use of electric motors.

Manufacturing Flax Cable Laid Cords.

Manufacturing Flax Cable Laid Cords, with the open rope walk beyond.

Examples of Best Quality Cable Laid Cords.

Making cow-spans.

Large spools of twine.

The Twisting Frame.

Views of the washing machine for twines.

The twine polishing machine.

A power balling machine.

Examples of Flax Mattress Twine, Flax Cable Laid Cord, and Flax Tufting Loops.

Winding small spools for the weft of webbing.

A weaver operating a ten multiple loom.

A similar multiple loom.

A similar multiple loom.

69

Examples of webbing produced.

The New Weaving Shed.

Twine being dried outdoors.

*Datestone on the eastern range at
Higher Flax Mills.*

A display of Donne's products.

[Somerset writer Monica Hutchings visited Donne's factory shortly after the end of the Second World War and in a chapter on Local Industry in her book 'Rural Reflections' published in 1947 recorded her impressions, including the following;-]

We arrived at the factory when the change from war to peace was being effected. During the war years a great deal of camouflage netting had been manufactured, but now the same part of the factory had been turned over to making plough lines, and cow-spans. We found that a great deal of the open-air floor space of the factory, formerly used for drying twine, had been taken by large Ministry of Food stores, but at the back of these shelter-like buildings we found a long 'walk' in the open-air where lengths of twine was being twisted into cords and ropes. Some of this, fine and white, with as many as two hundred and forty threads twisted together in it, had been used for making medical supplies, of which the little factory had a fair out-put.

The man who was engaged on this work was a native of Castle Cary, but was by no means a 'stick-in-the-mud!' He had left his native town when young; travelled abroad; been art editor on two well-known London periodicals; had migrated to Australia, and eventually returned to his home town, to make this rope-spinning his war-work.

The bulk of the twine, twisted and finished in this factory, is used in upholstery and mattress making, and besides seeing the thread for use in these industries, we saw webbing being made. It was being woven on looms that were reminiscent of miniature cotton-mill machinery, in plain colours and in two shades of black and white. Only a day earlier nothing but khaki webbing was being turned out, and the contract had just been completed. I visualised the journeys some of that khaki webbing must have made, and how twine woven in a little factory at Castle Cary must have found its way into many corners of the earth.

The main factory building was not large, and yet roomy enough to convey no feeling of overcrowding. There were about eighty employees in all, and five or six separate rooms to house the looms and other machinery. On the top floor we found webbing being made and twine turned out by machinery that was at once most ingenious and yet most simple. The power was all by electricity and steam now, though once the little River Cary had supplied it.

In one room on the second floor, we found the last of the camouflage nets and the first of the plough-lines with grease being rubbed into them by hand. The cow-spans were made of horse-hair, and are amazingly strong; they have to be, as farmers well know. I was presented with one as a souvenir - we happened to need a new one for a particularly awkward bovine!

In the other room on the same floor, was a woman sitting before something that looked very much like an old-fashioned spinning wheel. It was operated by hand, and as she turned, the twine was wound into neat balls. She explained that no machine-operated apparatus made quite such neat balls of mattress twine, and so she sits in the light of a large window and endlessly turns her spinning wheel!

She made a quaint picture, silhouetted against the golden afternoon light. Hers was a lonely and monotonous job, but she seemed cheerful enough.

Indeed the whole factory had a cheerful 'family' air. It was not so large that all individualism was lost, and my friend, who had some experience of great factories in wartime, sensed that atmosphere even more.

Here everyone patently knew everyone else very well. They were a community with a good wartime record, and each very proud of it. It seemed less a factory than one of those 'home-industries' in which Somerset abounds. So we came back to the ground floor and found perhaps the busiest room of all. Certainly it was the noisiest and most dirty.

Here the twine was finished and polished, going through a bath of size (above all things); being rubbed by rollers; teazelled with fine teazel brushes of wire mounted on leather to remove all the roughness and 'bittyness'; and then going over steam drying rollers in readiness for the balling room.

On our way out we were shown an old power-engine with the date 1866 on its glossy surface. Until a short time ago it was still in regular use. It still looked game for much more service, and it seemed a pity to us that it had to be discarded for a more modern one. In 1866 they apparently made engines to last.

The factory itself has an unbroken record of a hundred and fifty years, though it is believed that there was a factory on the site as early as 1717. The foreman who showed us round had been working for the firm since his boyhood and I reflected on my way out how such permanence, such continuity, is as much a feature of rural industry as it is of agriculture.

Castle Cary, for all its tucked away peace and quiet, has its share in world commerce, if only through its twine-factory. I thought of the hemp and flax coming from Holland and Scotland, and the kit-bags being dumped down all over the world - with their Castle Cary webbing, and the fisherman casting his lines of Castle Cary twine - no place is too small or too modest but that it makes its contribution to living.

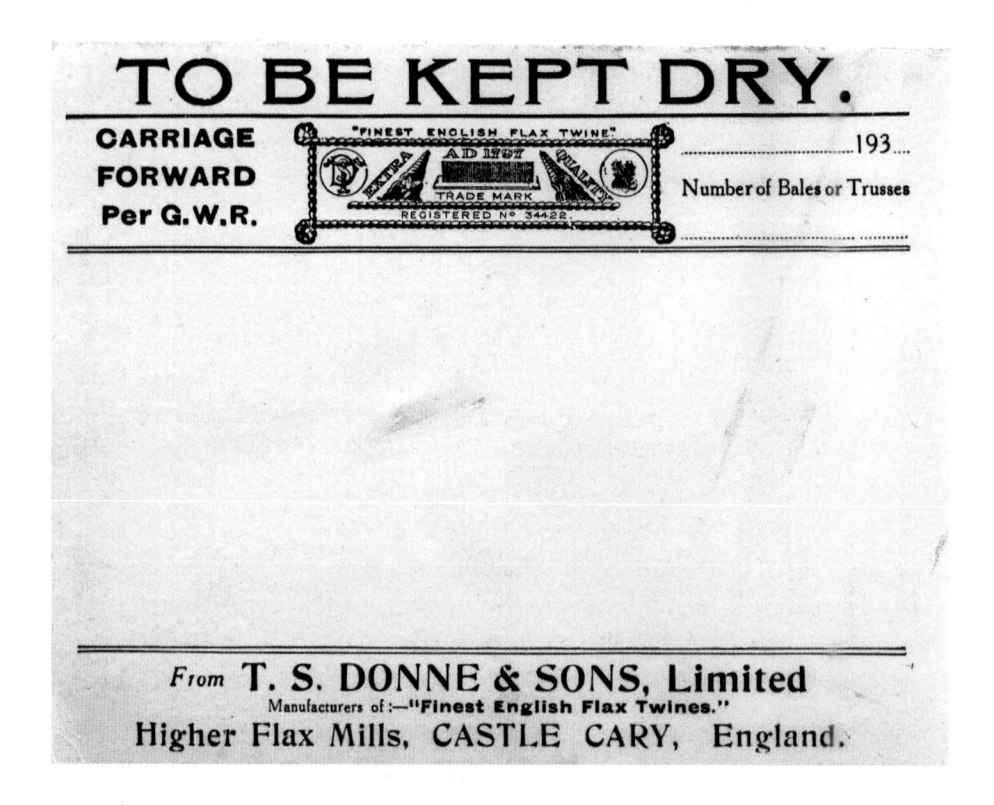

TO BE KEPT DRY.

CARRIAGE FORWARD Per G.W.R.

"FINEST ENGLISH FLAX TWINE"
AD 1797
TRADE MARK
REGISTERED No 34422

.................193....
Number of Bales or Trusses

From **T. S. DONNE & SONS, Limited**
Manufacturers of :—"**Finest English Flax Twines.**"
Higher Flax Mills, CASTLE CARY, England.

A view of the rope walk from the west.

The factory was originally powered by a waterwheel turned by the River Cary.

One of Donne's trademarks.

An advertisement for Donne's webbing from 1949.

Somerset FURNITURE
Made by Craftsmen

The three stools or tables are built to fit compactly over each other, and thus form an easily stored unit. First class craftsmanship—attractive colouring, and reasonable prices make this an outstandingly popular line.

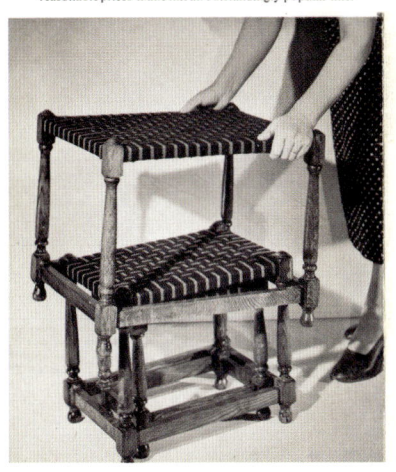

Somerset FURNITURE
Made by Craftsmen

"SOMERSET" Furniture is made by craftsmen employed by T. S. DONNE & SONS, LTD., who have been established for over 150 years in Castle Cary, in the county of Somerset, England.

DONNE'S Webbing, which is renowned throughout the world for its strength and durability is used in the manufacture of this furniture—and to give added strength, the one piece of Webbing is interlaced both above and below the surface, thus avoiding any possibility of pulling away from the sides.

It is easy to understand why such an attractive line, at such a reasonable cost should have achieved such a wide and steady sale.

T. S. DONNE & SONS, LTD.
HIGHER FLAX MILLS
CASTLE CARY, SOM., ENGLAND

PRINTED BY HAMMETT & COMPANY (TAUNTON) LTD.

Style Strength and Durability

Somerset FURNITURE
Made by Craftsmen

Somerset FURNITURE
Made by Craftsmen

The small chair and table present an attractive nursery setting. Dainty and colourful, but at the same time strongly built to withstand hard wear.

Somerset FURNITURE
Made by Craftsmen

The nest of three stools, and the miniature chair shown below, are available for immediate delivery.

This furniture has achived great popularity . . . the wide choice of colours of the webbing, and the dark or light hardwood frames enable it to blend harmoniously with any colour scheme.

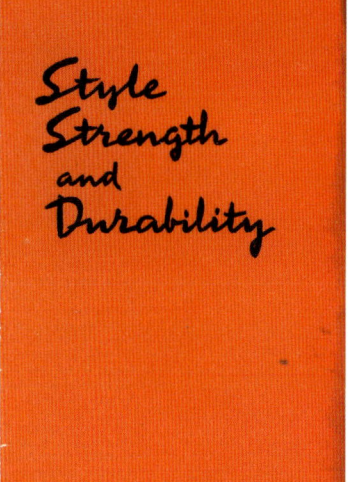

Somerset FURNITURE
Made by Craftsmen

There is a wide variety of daily uses in every home for three stools or tables of such convenient sizes, and the reasonable prices place them easily within range of a mass market.

A BRIEF ACCOUNT OF THE ACTIVITIES OF

T. S. DONNE & SONS, LTD
HIGHER FLAX MILLS
CASTLE CARY
SOMERSET

Manufacturers of Twines, Threads, Ropes, and Cordage of every description.

Specialists in Twines, Webbing, etc. for the Upholstery and Allied Trades.

KING GEORGE III to KING GEORGE V

OUR firm of T. S. Donne & Sons, was established in Castle Cary, Somerset, in 1797, by the great grandfather, and great great uncle of the present Directors, the firm for family reasons being incorporated as a Limited Company on 1st January, 1926.

The County of Somerset until more recent years always grew a large supply of the finest Flax, hence the productions of the firm largely emanated from the actual Flax grown in the immediate neighbourhood, and chiefly consisted of Canvas and Twines. These were supplied to the British Navy in the days of Nelson.

For very many years the industry was entirely associated with the Upholstery, Bedding, Mattress, and Allied Trades, which was always and still is the great speciality although Flax has now to be procured chiefly from Belgium and Holland owing to little or none being grown to-day in England.

DONNE'S "FINEST ENGLISH FLAX TWINES" have enjoyed world-wide repute. The firm has consistently and regularly exported to all parts of the world, to say nothing of the regular sales in the Home market.

From time to time up-to-date machinery has been required to take the place of the hand labour originally employed at Castle Cary, but there are still many products that can only be successfully produced by skilled hand labour which has been handed down through generations.

In addition to Mattress, Twines and Laid Cords for the Upholstery trade, all other items of Cordage connected therewith have received equal attention, together with Chair Webbings of all descriptions, Bindings and such like products.

1797 to 1934

More recently, it being appreciated that the big demand for Cordage of every description from the finest threads to the stoutest ropes was a product that could be produced nowhere better than at Higher Flax Mills, the Company is now in a position to cater for any requirements in the matter of Cordage from the lowest grades to the highest.

Inquiries large or small from any source are greatly valued, and it will be a pleasure to send samples and lowest quotations, having regard to the fact that about 500 different sorts and sizes are always in stock and during the course of twelve months we make specially to order a further 500, so it will be appreciated that to send out a quantity of samples will only further puzzle a prospective buyer. The necessity cannot be too strongly impressed when making inquiries:

(a) To send small samples or sample lengths of the Cord required, with an indication whether something stronger and better is wanted or to the contrary.

(b) To state precisely for what particular use the article or articles will be utilized in order that the most suitable product may be recommended.

(c) The quantity of each sort that is usually ordered at one time.

Terms to all traders are as follows :—

(1) A cash discount of 2½% on invoice amounts of £2 and upwards provided a remittance is received within 30 days of date of invoice.

(2) Carriage paid to any destination in Great Britain on 10 dozen lb. of Twine or 10 gross yards of Chair Webbing and on minimum quantities of 3 cwt. of heavy Cordage such as Ropes and the like.

77

The above illustration shows the usual form in which our twines and chair webbings are put up. Twines of the largest sizes are usually stocked in 16 oz. balls, cop or reel, as shown. Mattress twines and finer packing twines in 8 oz. balls. Whilst the upholsterer prefers the twine put up in balls for many reasons, the cop or reel is an advantage, especially to those who use twine for packing purposes. Twines are always stocked in the most saleable weights, but any weight ball can be made to order, or the twines can be made in skeins or cut lengths.

The better quality Chair Webbings are put up in 18-yard pieces, 8 pieces to the gross yards. Cheaper Jute Chair Webbings and Bindings in 36-yard pieces, 4 pieces to the gross yards.

As explained in the previous pages, our products are of special interest to the Upholsterer, Bedding Manufacturer, and those engaged in Allied Trades, and we have 137 years of experience behind us to know what is required and what to recommend.

In order to suit all tastes and requirements we regularly stock five distinct qualities in Upholstery Twines in various sizes and make-ups, viz.:—

1. Finest English Flax Twines
2. Pure Flax Twines
3. Defiance Mattress Twines
4. Super Italian Hemp Mattress Twines
5. Special Italian Hemp Mattress Twine

We turn out **Laid Cords** for Spring work, etc., in endless variety at various prices to suit all tastes and requirements.

Cable Laid Cords
Sash Lines
Blind Cords
Piping Cords

Satin Finished Carpet Threads in all colours and sizes.
Hessians, Scrims and Tarpaulins.

CHAIR WEBBINGS

Just as important to the Upholsterer as a good Twine is good Chair Webbing, and for many years this has been a branch of our business to which we have paid particular attention.

We strongly advise users to buy a good webbing, and have every confidence in recommending our

Black and White Chair Webs

in the following qualities:—

1. All Pure Linen
2. Super
3. Special
4. Standard
5. Stanfast
6. Extra

All usually stocked in 2″ and 2½″ widths, but can be made to order in any width 1″ to 4″

Some buyers, however, must purchase a low price webbing to enable them to compete. In such cases

Our range of Jute Chair Webbings

in striped or plain are unequalled for price and strength.

We regularly stock three qualities, viz.:
"A"   "B"   "P"

but can manufacture any weight or width to suit customers' particular requirements.

BINDINGS

We manufacture these in endless variety and weights.
Plain Cocoa Bindings   Coloured Bindings
Fancy Matting Bindings   Carpet Bindings
Napier Matting Bindings

Tray, Straining and Coffin Webs of all descriptions

TO ALL USERS OF CORDAGE

1. Manufacturers of all Products
Packing Twines, Stitching Twines, Threads, Loom Cords, Box Cords, Baling Cords & Ropes.

2. Grocers & Provision Merchants
Shop Twines, Tea Twines, fine white Cotton Twines, Sisal Twines and Cords.

3. Ironmongers and Saddlers
Halters, Halter Reins, Plough Reins, Cow Ties, Hair Cow Spans, Seaming Twines, Roping Twines, Tar Twines, Bird Twines, Whipcords, Nets, Fishing Lines, Masons' Lines, Garden Lines, Clothes Lines, Sisal Cords, Box Cords, Gasken, Manila Ropes and Cords, Straining and Girth Webs.

4. The Horticultural Trade
Fillis and Twists of all descriptions. Our special Green, Plain, and Tar Tie, Hemp Tar Twines.

5. Ship Chandlers
Seaming and Roping Twines, Canvas and Webbing. Tarred Threads. Twine and Marline. Rope of all sizes and descriptions.

6. Stationers, Printers & Bookbinders
Cotton Twines, Hemp Twines, Sisal Twines, Bookbinders' Twines and Threads. Page Twines: coloured, fancy and small, 1d. and 2d. balls.

Every requirement for these Trades —in Cordage— of any description.
7. Drapers and Outfitters
8. Motor & Electrical Trades
9. Purveyors & Bacon Curers
10. Sports Outfitters—for Nets, etc.
11. Druggists & Chemists
12. Departmental Stores

THE "SOMERSET" CHAIRS
as supplied to His Majesty King George V

In 1932 we embarked on a new departure in our industry and the history of this is worth recording.

Having observed that there were on the market numerous types of Chairs, the seats and backs being woven in sea grass and other common types of material, the idea came to us that a much neater, more resilient, comfortable and very superior article could be produced by utilizing our Super Flax Cable Laid Cord for the seats and backs.

As our Cable Laid Cord is manufactured from pure Flax, there was no question as to strength, appearance and wear, to say nothing of being a much superior article all round, having regard to the fact that finest Malacca Cane is being used for the framework, the whole chair, including the cord, being produced by hand labour in the county of Somerset. Despite their strength these chairs are extremely light, and can be readily used without detriment in the garden, their appearance warrants them for use in the drawing room, and as bedroom chairs they will be found most useful.

The idea caught on from its very inception, and although only recently put on the market the repeat orders we have received are most encouraging. At the moment we are regularly stocking seven different types, as illustrated on the following pages, but we can manufacture to any particular pattern and also make Tables, Linen Baskets, Footstools, etc., to match.

We are proud of the fact that His Majesty the King has given the Chair his patronage, and under date November 19th, 1932, His Majesty's Private Secretary wrote us as follows:—

"The King and Queen desire me to express their thanks for the Chair, with which they are greatly pleased."

TYPE A

A most convenient "Tub Shape" chair—giving the maximum amount of comfort. The beading on the arms and framework being interlaced with coloured cane. The colouring can be supplied to suit individual colour schemes, i.e. dark and light blue, dark and light green, orange and black, gold, etc., or as required.

TYPE B

A most comfortable "Tub Shape" chair, built up on solid malacca cane. Natural in colouring, the chair will conveniently "fall in" with any colour scheme.

TYPE C

An ideal Café chair: square seat, built up on all solid malacca cane. Pulls right up to the table, taking the minimum amount of space and giving the maximum amount of comfort and convenience.

TYPE D

Truly, this is a "Royal" chair, exactly as supplied to H.M. King George V. Built up on solid malacca cane. Height from the floor level 35 in. The back from seat level 14 in., and the seating capacity 18 in. by 17 in

TYPE E

A medium height Easy chair, with all the characteristics of Type "D" but not so high in the back, obviously the lady's chair. Height from the floor level 31 in. The back from the seat level 17 in. Seating capacity 16 in. by 17 in. Built up on all solid malacca cane.

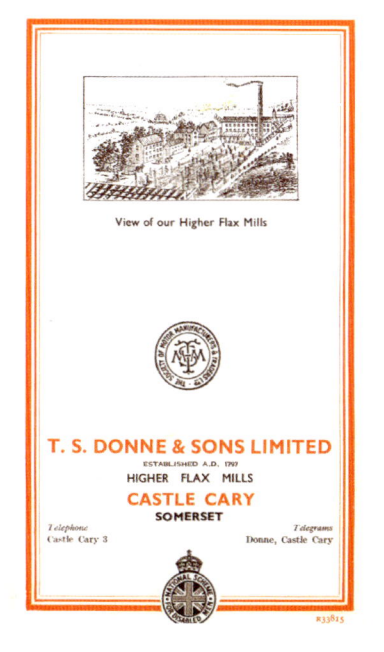

A Donne's leaflet advertising their products and illustrating the range of 'Somerset' furniture.

TYPE F

This chair is woven "singly," so giving a "firmer" seat and back where it is considered advisable. There is still that naturally sprung feeling—combining artistic appearance with utility. A really excellent chair.

TYPE G

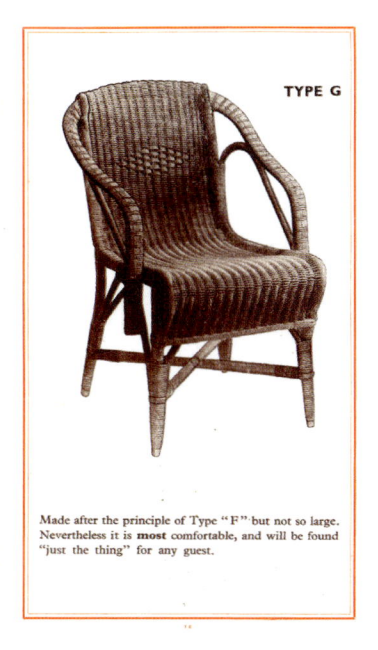

Made after the principle of Type "F" but not so large. Nevertheless it is **most** comfortable, and will be found "just the thing" for any guest.

View of our Higher Flax Mills

T. S. DONNE & SONS LIMITED
ESTABLISHED A.D. 1797
HIGHER FLAX MILLS
CASTLE CARY
SOMERSET

Telephone: Castle Cary 3
Telegrams: Donne, Castle Cary

79

David Stickland

David was born in 1938 in Poole, Dorset, and his parents, Robert and Lily Stickland came to Castle Cary with their young family from Wareham in 1942. His father worked for farmer Jack Barrett at Lower Ansford and in later years he cycled to work at Prideaux's milk factory at Evercreech. David went to the 'one room' junior school at Ansford (now a private dwelling) as did his two younger sisters, Janet and Susan. Children between the ages of five to eleven years attended this school. They were taught by Miss Jolliffe who covered all subjects for both boys and girls, while his older brother, Robert and his sister Ann went to Ansford Secondary Modern School. At the age of eleven years he too went to Ansford Secondary Modern School, his favourite subjects being maths, history and sport, at which he excelled under the supervision of the physical training teacher John Harrison: he was very soon playing for the school football and cricket teams during the 1950s. Schools in the area played competitive sports, e.g. football and cricket teams for the boys and hockey and netball for the girls. Football was always in David's thoughts and he played whenever he had a spare moment.

On leaving school in 1953 he joined the company of T.S. Donne and Sons at Higher Flax Mills in Torbay Road as an apprentice weaver, his weekly remuneration being £2.6.8d for a forty eight hour week, and under the guidance of the foremen, Frank Sweet and George Gower, he quickly absorbed the skills and expertise involved in weaving upholstery webbing and tapes, and also associated machinery maintenance. At the age of eighteen he was promoted to charge hand whilst still under apprenticeship and was given supervision of eight very large looms each having thirty six shuttles, producing approximately 45,000 yards of tape per week.

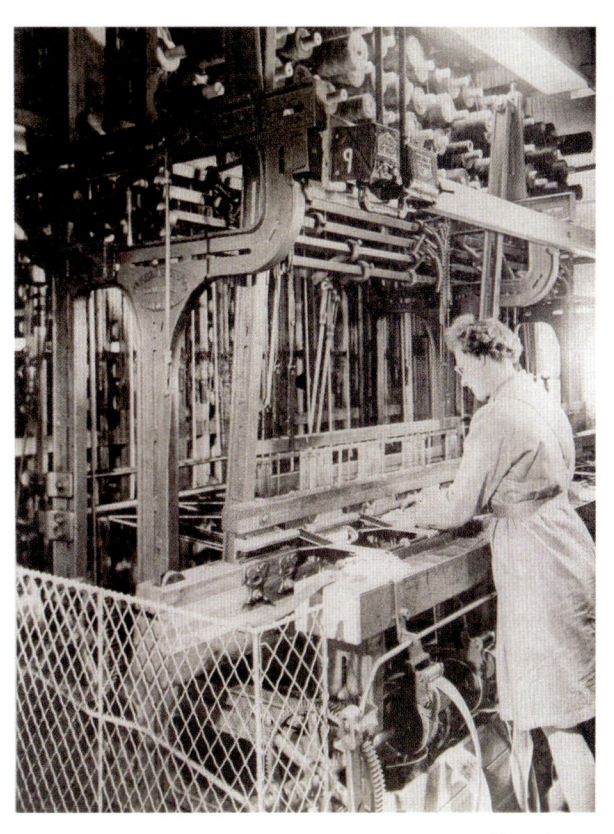

Lily Higgins operating a webbing loom.
LHG collection.

Ada Sweet making a ball of twine.
LHG collection.

During 1956 Boyd's horse hair looms were transferred from the Ansford factory to Higher Flax Mills, together with some of the weavers and their foreman, Mr. Jack Chamberlain. Many of the Boyd machines at the time of transfer were in the region of a century old.

In spite of serving apprenticeship and his duties of charge hand, David still found time to participate in his favourite pastime, football, playing his games for Bristol City Colts, and then for their Youth team, for which he was paid six guineas per game, almost treble his normal weekly wage. He also went to Bristol City Football Club for trials but did not like the routine of professional football and decided to leave while retaining the opportunity of rejoining them until he was twenty one years of age. Bristol Rovers, Swindon Town and Cardiff City also approached him to play, but he declined. However, he did play eighty games for the Yeovil League and over thirty for the county, winning some thirty medals, cups and plaques.

On completion of his five years apprenticeship in 1960, David had to fulfil his National Service obligation for at least two years, so joined the King's Shropshire Light Infantry and after basic training served in Germany, which frequently gave him the opportunity to continue his interest in playing football, as a member of his battalion team.

In 1963 on returning to civilian life he rejoined his old employers, T. S. Donne & Co., and was soon transferred to John Boyd's to understudy their then ageing foreman, Jack Chamberlain, a man of many talents. Not only did he know "weaving" but also the intricacies of the working of the machines and how to maintain them, including the making of spares, involving, for example, black

Castle Cary Football Club, winners of the Blackmore Vale Charity Cup, 1955-56 season. David is in the back row, fourth from the left.
LHG collection.

smithing and lathe turning, etc., assuredly a very difficult man to replace. Fortunately he was able to pass on his experience and skills to David, enabling him to take over with confidence when he retired aged eighty years, after 68 years service with John Boyd.

In 1965 David married Joan Brummel, who also worked for Boyd's. They had two sons Kevin and Gary. David was production manager for 50 years, facing the extremely exacting and often difficult task of keeping the ancient machines in working order, but one he enjoyed, especially when he viewed their beautiful and unique product, improved in more recent years with the addition of pastel shades, thanks to modern dyes which enable horsehair to be dyed in permanent colours, such as pink, mauve, pale blue, etc. Furthermore the use of silk instead of cotton on the warp for certain processes provides the hair cloth with a far softer and flexible finish. Horse hair fabrics are mainly used in the upholstery trade, and in the fashion industry for making handbags, purses, wallets, etc. Most of the production is exported.

In 1984 David was made works manager, a position he held until his retirement in 1999. He trained new workers to ensure that this Castle Cary tradition will continue for many years. He pays tribute to those colleagues who made up the Donne/Boyd's team during his working life, many of whom worked there for fifty years or more, namely: Ethel Cadman, Win Rowsell, Stella Sullivan, Mrs. Jeffrey, Walter Webber, Frank Fussell, Harold Higgins, Charlie Chilcott, Arthur Wade, Bill Peaty, Len Close, Frank Sweet and Albert Bryant. In October 1999 Boyd's held an Open Day with guided tours to enable the public to view the manufacturing process with the machines in motion and to discuss the procedure with the machine operators, indeed an eye opening event for the many visitors who took the opportunity to visit the factory.

The Higher Flax Mills complex included allotments and an orchard. John Bulley tends the vegetable patch, with the factory buildings in the background.
LHG collection.

Preparing the soil in the vegetable patch, with the beehives in the foreground.
LHG collection.

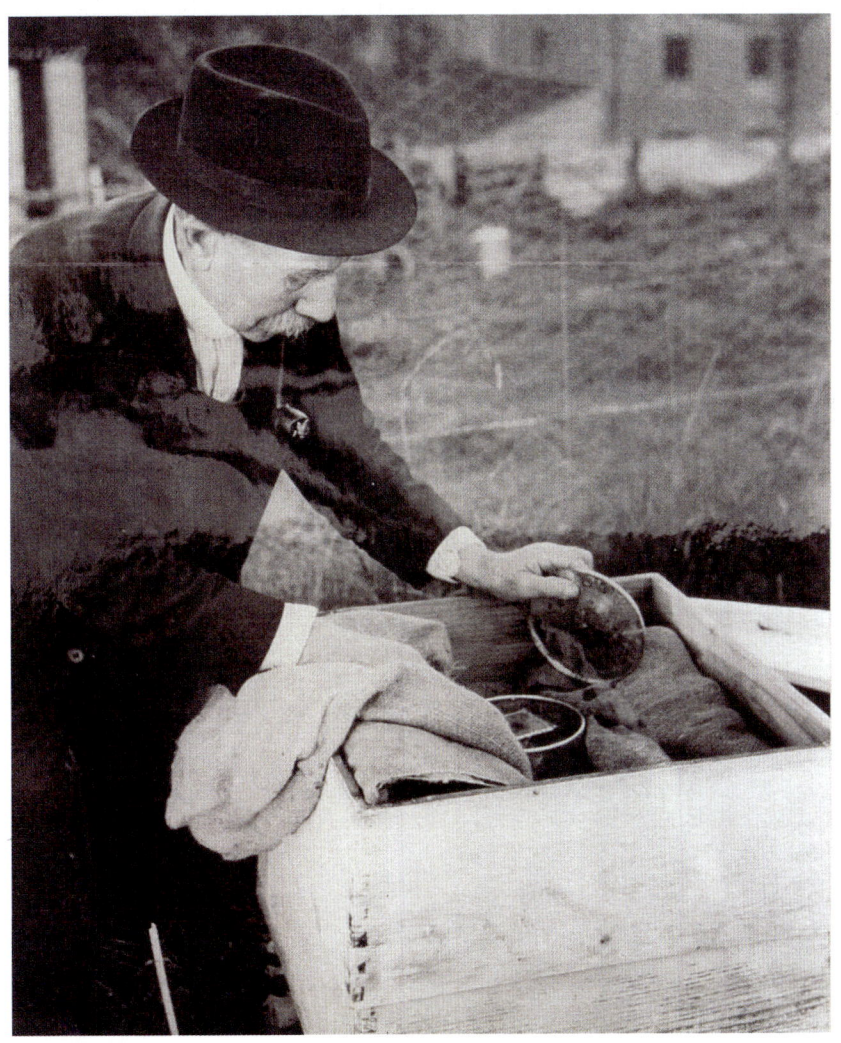

Arthur Webber tending the bees.
LHG collection.

David working on one of the Boyd's looms.
LHG collection.

The British Timber Trade; A visit to a Typical Country Sawmill
By Norman Hetherington

[Reprinted from "Monthly Pictorial" February 1929]

The many excellent qualities of English timbers are widely recognised. During the war, large areas of the wooded ground were denuded to meet the demand for timber for war purposes; and there can be no doubt that in many parts of the country, the work of afforestation might well be extended and accelerated, both as a means of providing work for some of our unemployed army, and also increasing the nation's real wealth.

The sawmill and timber yard at Clanville.

Those country concerns which are engaged in the preparation of home-grown timber for various purposes are exceedingly interesting. They provide a link between the old and the new, between rural pursuits and up-to-date production by machinery. Thus the visitor to the typical country sawmill of Messrs. Jonathan Cruse & Gass, at Clanville, near Castle Cary, in Somersetshire, can follow the progress of the wood from its felling until it leaves the mill prepared as planks, boards, scantlings, or for some other type of product.

For there the timber is handled through all its stages; the firm purchasing it where it grows, in the fields and woods, felling it, carting it to their own yard, and finally converting it in to planks, boards, scantlings and the like for collieries, railway companies, docks and various public works. The firm deals exclusively with the home-grown article. In addition to the supply of boards etc. to which reference has been made, fencing, gates and the many other articles required for the country estate and farm are made, together with articles designed to meet the requirements of builders, carpenters, and wheelwrights. Tinplate boxes, for the South Wales trade, are also supplied, the firm having attained a reputation for good workmanship and reliability, while the fact that the various products are manufactured from thoroughly sound English woods ensures durability.

Felling a park oak.

Felling park oaks.

Established somewhere in the late seventies, by the late Jonathan Cruse, this business has progressed continuously through its career. The late Mr. Cruse came from Kintbury, in Berkshire, and was one of the best-known and widely respected timber merchants in the West of England. On his death in 1909, the business passed into the hands of Mr. David John Gass, who had for many years acted as its manager, and who had thus gained a wide experience of the work. Today, Mr. Gass is still in control, having had an unbroken connection with the business throughout a period of more than forty years. He is a firm believer in the value of organised trade effort, both in the interests of the trade and indeed of the public; thus he has played a foremost part in trade organisations, and is Vice-President of the Western and Southern Counties' Home-Grown Timber Merchants' Association, and also one of its representatives on the Executive Council of the Home-Grown Timber Merchants' Associations. Since he has been at the helm the business has admirably maintained the high standard which secured its reputation early in its career, and he is assisted by a staff which is both loyal and efficient.

The Offices and Sawmill of the firm are very conveniently situated at Clanville, near Castle Cary, and quite close to the Great Western Railway Station, a considerable advantage from the distributive standpoint.

Hauling an oak home.

A wooden case bearing the firm's 'castle' branding.

The horizontal saw in the sawmill.

The tinplate-box making section.

JONATHAN CRUSE & GASS, Timber Merchants,
DAVID J. GASS.
Telephone No 12. CASTLE CARY, Som. 191

An Old Somersetshire Industry; John Boyd & Co. Ltd., Castle Cary

[Reprinted from 'Picadilly' July 1925]

One of the most interesting industries of the West of England is that of the horsehair manufacture carried on by the well-known firm whose name we take as the heading of this article. It is, moreover, an industry concerning which comparatively little is known by the general public.

The name "horsehair" must not be taken strictly to define the limits of the business. This really includes the manufacture of horsehair seating, curled hair, and prepared hair of all kinds, the raw material being supplied principally by three animals – the horse, the ox and the pig. The manes and tails of horses are used, the tails only of the ox, and the whole of the bristles of the pig. English and Scotch horses, we are told, are found to grow the most valuable hair, though large quantities come from South America and Russia; South America sends most of the ox tails; and nearly all the hog bristles come from the United States. The hair is manufactured into horsehair cloth for the use of upholsterers for covering furniture, tailors' linings for padding of all kinds, curled hair for upholstering furniture and motor cars, and for brushes, wigs, mattresses, fishing lines, whips and sieves.

The weaving shed.

Although horsehair manufacture is an old one, that of hair-seating dates back only about 100 years, and is said to have originated in Somerset. The firm under notice has existed since 1837, and several are known to have a much earlier origin. It is only about twenty five years ago, however, since the old hand-loom gave place to the power loom in this connection. The latter is a very marvellous piece of mechanism, or wonderful delicacy, on which the horsehair cloth which is one of the leading specialities of the firm may be produced in fine quality and without the slightest waste of time or labour; and it is interesting to note that it was a member of this firm who was responsible for the introduction of the power method of weaving into the horsehair industry.

It is impossible to go into the technicalities of weaving here, and to deal with how the methods used differ from those used in ordinary weaving. Some effort, however, must be made to trace the source of the raw material through the works, and to see what happens to it before emergence in the many forms in which it is used.

First in the process comes the sorting, which is performed with wonderful skill by men who first separate the short hairs from the long, and then take the latter and once more separate the lighter coloured hairs from the dark.

The second, which is very interesting, is the "drawing" or preparation of the hair for the use of Brushmakers and the weavers. The hair, which is in the raw state, contains all lengths from 4 to 40 inches, has to be separated into the various lengths and tied up into drafts levelled at both ends. The shorter lengths, up to 16 inches, are sold to Brushmakers, whilst the longer lengths are reserved for the firm for weaving their various cloths. The drawing is a most fascinating process, and a man is not considered an expert until he has had at least three years experience.

After leaving the loom, the cloth is pressed and calendered, operations performed by a single machine introduced by a member of the firm; and is then ready for despatch. In the meantime, the hair which has been set aside for curling is first devilled three or four time in a machine which takes all the refuse and tangles out of it; and is then twisted into loose ropes by a machine, a man walking backwards and adding fresh hair to the end that is not in the machine. These ropes are twisted into other ropes, and after boiling, baking and other processes, they assume a permanent curl and are fit for the upholsterer.

Such, in brief outline, are some of the processes and manufactures carried on at Messrs. Boyd's factory. The establishment, it is needless to say, is a large one, and it is a model of what such a concern should be in the matter of equipment, arrangement and management. A large staff of experienced and skilful workers is employed, and the resources are such that they are able to cope with any demands that may be made upon them. They have gained a high reputation, not only in this country, but in many others, for the excellence of their productions, and are universally recognised as holding the foremost place amongst those devoted to this industry.

The drawing department.

The loom department.

A loom.

Hair curling.

Horsehair manufactures.

The Horsehair Industry of Somerset

The Horsehair Industry of Somerset by Norman Wymer

[Reproduced from Country Life, November 29th 1946, by kind permission of Country Life Magazine.]

In the heart of the small Somerset town of Castle Cary, with a population of little more than 2,000, is a colony of hand craftsmen who are said to be unique. Here, in a cluster of old buildings - some little more than sheds - they may be found daily treating the hair of horses, pigs and oxen and making it up into various forms. Although the craftsmen are almost unknown outside their immediate neighbourhood, except by those who depend upon them, their work is sent all over the world.

Ever since small boys were set the task of tweaking single hairs from the tails of horses to make into rough-and-ready whips, the processing of hair has constituted an important rural industry, and this Somerset colony is believed to be the last survivor of its kind.

Craftsmen such as these provided the materials for stuffing the voluminous breeches of the country gentry, and for padding the broad-hipped dresses worn by the women in the days of Queen Elizabeth; they supplied the milliner Mlle. Bertin with the wherewithal for the tremendous head-dresses beloved of Marie Antoinette; they produced the stuffing for the crinolines of Victorian times.

Fashions change, yet the demand for the work of these craftsmen continues. Today the uses to which their products are put range from the stuffing of mattresses and upholstered furniture to the manufacture of hair-cloth for covering it; from brushes and judicial and theatrical wigs to whips, sieves, fishing lines and sporrans; from tailors' linings to window blinds for the railways of South Africa, India and Brazil. It was in Somerset that the idea of hair seating originated about 100 years ago.

Happy and contented is this band of craftsmen, as indeed were most rural communities in the days before industrialism. Retirement, it seems, is a word that has no meaning among them; rather is it longevity. Several men have seen 50 or more summers in the little workshops of Castle Cary, while a few can boast 70 odd, and one even 80. Not that this is an industry confined solely to old men, for sons still follow in the footsteps of their fathers as did their ancestors.

All types of hair are treated in these workshops; long and short, fine and coarse, white and coloured. The manes and tails of horses, the tails of oxen and the body bristles of pigs all provide material for some purpose and each varies in value according to the breed of animal. Though a great deal of the hair is imported to Castle Cary from the United States and Russia, it is from the English and Scottish horses that the finest quality is obtained.

When the hair arrives from overseas it is packed in enormous, matted, twisted, greasy bales, so clotted and clogged that it would seem well-nigh impossible to unravel it again, let alone sort it and weave it into cloth. That obtained from home-bred animals, on the other hand, is bought from marine store dealers in old clothes and scrap iron, junk men in fact, and reaches the workshops in smaller and slightly less forbidding consignments.

It is an object lesson in skill and dexterity to watch the craftsmen settle down to their unenviable task of sorting. When one considers that each of the hundreds of thousands of hairs that go to make up a bale has to be picked out by hand and placed into its correct pile it is not hard to appreciate that, in his way, the worker in horsehair is as skilled as any other village craftsman, and that it is only through long years of practice that he can expect to master the intricacies of his trade. For, as one man pointed out to me, they work not only by eye but by feel. A single misplaced hair will seldom be overlooked by the experienced man.

Pulling the hair through a spiked comb after washing.
(Fig.1)

Drawing the strands and sorting them into lengths, and using the hackle.
(Fig. 2)

Levelling a draft with a pair of clippers after drawing.
(Fig. 3)

Preparing a draft for dyeing.
(Fig. 4)

Curling hair into strands.
(Fig. 5)

Teasing the hair in a carding machine.
(Fig. 6)

The sorting is carried out in three distinct stages. First the long hairs are extracted and set aside for weaving, leaving the shorter ones for brush-making or for curling, a process to which all hair used for stuffing and padding is subjected. Next, the long are re-sorted into colour groups; the dark for dyeing and the lighter shades for bleaching for the wig makers and the like. Finally, all are regraded in their various categories into soft and coarse.

The sorting done, each batch is submitted to a rigorous - and much needed washing before being pulled, a handful at a time, through long steel combs fixed upright on the top of a bench, a process designed to straighten the hair and remove any broken strands (Fig. 1). Here the atmosphere is not unlike that of the old country tanyards, though the smell is infinitely more pleasant!

From the washing-shed the hair is taken upstairs for drawing, perhaps the most skilled of all the many processes. Here, seated before their benches and armed with short knives, a group of men pull the hair through two combs, one being turned upside down and spiked into the other to form a kind of cage (Fig. 2). With such speed do they work that it is hard to believe that they are not merely pulling the hair out again in the same form as that in which it was originally arranged. In fact, they are working with great accuracy, choosing the hairs which they pull, so that by the time they have finished they have a number of bundles the hairs in which may vary in length from 4 to 40 ins.

The drawing completed, the bundles are tied into drafts and levelled at both ends with clippers (Fig. 3), before being passed on to yet another man for washing and dye-ing (Fig. 4). Finally, the hair is sent to the weaving shed to be woven into various grades of cloth, ranging from window blinds at 130 hairs to the inch, to tailors' linings at 60. Although most of the weaving is carried out by power looms in these days, the old hand methods are still much in evidence at Castle Cary.

While one group of craftsmen is engaged on the longer hairs others will be no less busy on the short. Here, after washing, the hair is devilled; it is passed, in turn, through a number of machines - affairs of cogs, spikes and rollers, of grunts and groans, whose object is to tear the strands, toss them about, mix them all up and drive out any useless particles, which will be sent to the local farmers for manure. The newly devilled hair is then twisted into strands (Fig. 5) by a man who, in a manner reminiscent of the old rope-walks, moves slowly backwards from his bench, paying in more and more hair as he goes. After repeated doses of twisting and curling the hair is first boiled and then baked - processes which, together, help to give it more elasticity. For some purposes it is also teased on a carding machine (Fig. 6).

From first to last the manufacture of horsehair is a splendid example of continued importance of our old forms of country work in days of commercialism and uniformity.

Memories of Miss Longshaw

A rare view of the station c.1904 / 5, taken before the completion of the modifications required to accommodate the junction of the new line to Durston, opened in 1906.
A.V.Pearse collection.

Memories of Miss Longshaw

The Longshaw family came to Castle Cary during the First World War some time shortly after 1914 when she was about ten. Her father worked for the GWR railway all his working life and was working in Devizes when she was born. When her father was promoted they moved near to the tunnel at Old Sodbury. She can remember going to day school in Sodbury and walking the two miles and not thinking anything of it. It was also two miles to the baptist chapel in Sodbury. One of her first memories of chapel is of her mother standing with her arm around her as she recited a poem. At this time the Duke of Beaufort, who lived nearby, had the army guard the tunnels at Sodbury and Box since they were on the mainline to Ireland. The railway was building a new station and ferry port on the west coast. Her mother used to say that the guards, or rather soldiers on tunnel duty, always knew when lunch was almost ready for they would tap at the window of the railway cottage so they could get a titbit. She remarked on the fact that the Box tunnel always looked so beautiful in autumn covered in crocus. It was there in Sodbury that her little brother Gerald Durham died.

When they first moved to Castle Cary, another promotion for her father - this time to signalman at Castle Cary station, they lived in Salisbury Terrace. Dr. Price would visit them and being a keen ornithologist, would take the children to the woods behind Donne's factory to hear the nightingale sing. His wife came from a well-to-do family in Bristol and was related to the Wills Tobacco family. He would always say when she was away in Bristol. "when the cat's away the mice can play." Mr. Longshaw was not only a signalman at Castle Cary station but a very religious man. Before and after the First World War men were proud to work for the GWR; in fact if you wanted to get a job on the railways it was usually necessary to have a father or a close relative as an employee.

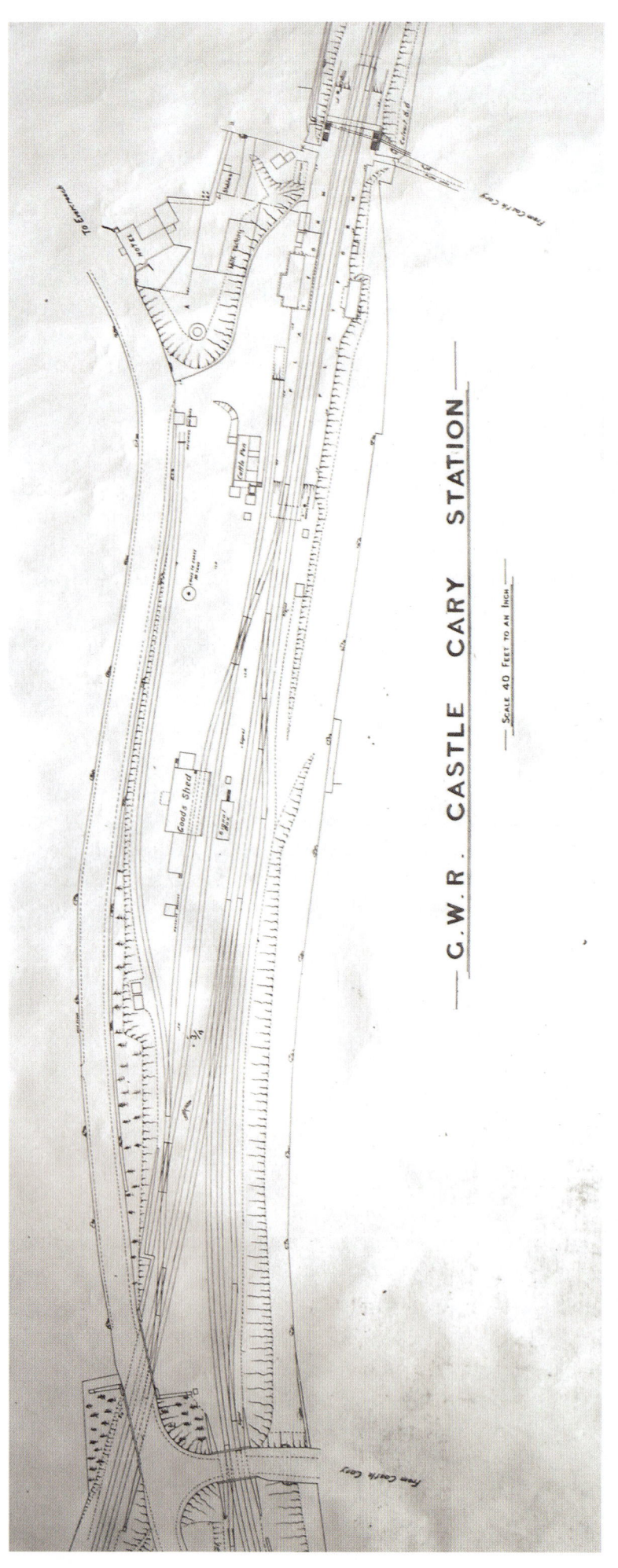

A plan of the station c. 1914, after the opening of the Durston line and construction of Prideaux's Creamery in 1910.

There was a railway strike in the 1930s. When at church, Mr. Longshaw was called to join the strike but refused saying that his duty was first to his God and then to his employers and his job. During the night there was damage to the railway points and also shots were fired outside his house but the culprits were never caught. After the strike, the men asked for their jobs back but were refused. Mr. Longshaw was offered £50 or £60 for the additional work he had done, which he did not take, saying that he was a Christian and he was only doing his job. He retired from the GWR in 1944 after 52 years of service.

Miss Longshaw remembers the glow worms that were by the signal box where the ashes were emptied out. There were also glow worms on Ansford Hill by the elm trees. The boys would put them on their caps and ride down the hill.

She also remembers the Jonathan Cruse and Gass timber wagon travelling down Ansford Hill and stopping at the Half Moon pub. The drivers, including a Mr. Guppy, would spend some time drinking. The horses, tired of waiting, would go on to the sawmills unaided and arrive in the yard complete with their load of trees. There was little traffic on the road and they knew where their food was!

Revd. Hastings was Rector of Ansford and lived in the Old Parsonage in Tuckers Lane. His housekeeper's son would put a white sheet over his head and put his head out of the window to frighten people in the lane.

She recalls a secret Wesleyan chapel in Pithers Yard in the High Street. She was taken and shown it one day. During the early years of the Wesleyan movement several secret chapels were built as its members were often persecuted. It is likely that this chapel belongs to this period.

She can remember Cornelius Martin running across the fields to catch the Weymouth train every day, as he owned property there. She also said that there was a wonderful cellar or underground place at Martin's and that there were tunnels going from Pither's to the front of Lush's shop. These small tunnels were visible a few years ago when the road was being dug up and revealed a tunnel crossing the road at this point and then going in the direction of the post office. It is possible that there was a tunnel from the premises which are now Parker's but which previously belonged to Pither's, to the post office.

There always used to be swans on Park Pond until the 1920s. She can remember them flying away and taking a thousand years of history with them. There were about twenty pairs of swans and one day she saw them go off in twos, including one who had been injured in the eye by a mink, first to Slimbridge where you could see them eating the corn and preparing themselves for flight. She thinks that they went on to Abbotsbury. Later there were two black swans on the pond which were moved to a bird sanctuary. The swan on the weather vane above the town hall she said belonged to the days of the castle in Cary. She said that it was Joseph of Arimathea who brought the lar that was found on Lodge Hill to Britain and also a jewel that is now in Glastonbury. This shows, she believes that there was Christianity in Cary from a very early date. Also on Lodge Hill there used to be a seat of healing but one hot day the spring gave way. It had been a place of refuge.

She talked about the Gospel Hall. It was built in 1925 and registered as a place of worship for Christian brethren. Although it was only a temporary building it was always well looked after. It closed in 1977. People came from a ten mile radius and there were 173 children in the Sunday School when it closed. They went to chapels in Street, Sparkford, Glastonbury and Sherborne.

Park Pond, one of the oldest features in Castle Cary, was 'improved' in the nineteenth century, but is now somewhat overgrown and neglected.

The Gospel Hall closed in 1977 and has been used for storage. It is due for demolition in 2012.

The Delaware Veterinary Group

The Delaware Veterinary Group - Over 100 years at Castle Cary

The practice was founded by Reginald Lydford who had trained at The Royal Veterinary College, London, and was admitted to the membership of the Royal College of Veterinary Surgeons in December 1905. He practised from his parents' home in Castle Cary, at Montague and Delaware House, that formed the builder's yard owned by his father Thomas Lydford, with a surgery in a large wooden shed with access from Woodcock Street. In 1924 Reg Lydford became seriously ill and Richard Tazewell, who had recently been admitted to membership of the RCVS, also training at the Royal Veterinary College, London, was employed to help out until Reginald recovered. Sadly he never did so, dying in October of the same year.

Edwin Richard Tazewell, having taken over the practice, continued as a single hand practitioner until the early 1950s. 'Taz' as he was known, came from a farming family in Norton Fitzwarren. His father was a dealer in remount horses for the army, which probably explained why Taz was such an accomplished and fearless rider. His first motor transport was a Brough motorcycle and sidecar, soon moving on to a Trojan motor car which had, for that time, an impressive top speed of 30 mph. He always liked smart cars, owning a succession of Jaguars, Sunbeam Rapiers and finally a black and white Vauxhall VX490. In the early days the practice was entirely devoted to horses and farm animals. Taz, a pioneer in dehorning adult cattle, initially used chloroform as a general anaesthetic. However, he soon became proficient in the technique of using a local anaesthetic. He used this to good effect travelling well outside the practice area to dehorn herds of cattle, taking with him some strong young men to do the sawing, most notably Robin and Trevor Bartlett from Galhampton.

Reginald Lydford.

Montague and Delaware House in Woodcock Street, with yard and outbuildings behind. LHG collection.

The 1950s was a time when the practice began to expand rapidly and the range of animals treated now included companion animals. Paul Greenough joined as an assistant in 1951, soon to be followed by Bill Harrison. They both became partners in 1955 and purchased the builder's yard at Delaware House and had it converted to a state of the art veterinary premises, which received national acclaim. The move from the old tatty shed to the new premises took place in 1961. By this time Paul Greenough had become an expert in lameness in cattle, travelling widely to lecture on the subject. The practice continued to expand and a number of assistants were employed. Ian McNab joined the practice in 1961 and Taz retired due to ill health in 1962 after 38 years, continuing to live at Delaware House until his death in the early 1970s. Ian McNab became a partner in 1964 and soon after Paul Greenough left the practice to pursue a career in academia, teaching at Saskatoon Veterinary School in Canada where he still lives.

A Thomas Lydford billhead from 1898. A.V.Pearse collection.

Dick Tazewell.

The outbuildings at Delaware House before and after conversion to veterinary premises.

The new premises were unique for their time in that they had facilities for hospitalising cows. Much of the building work constructing the loose boxes was done by the partners and the then office manager Len Jeffrey. Non urgent operations were often performed after evening surgery, the cows being kept in to recuperate for up to a week. The after care of these, some with dubious temperament, was left to the two stalwart nurses, Isobel Bray and Alison Oborne, who coped without complaint. The new office had a large dispensing area, for the preparation of powders, medicines and lotions and there was also a small drug store, injectable and intramammary antibiotics were in their infancy but their use was growing rapidly. The weekly drug order was delivered by Bond's Chemists of Castle Cary but Paul Greenough, together with Jack Walsby from Midsomer Norton and Philip Brown from Chippenham, had the idea that they could obtain better terms from manufacturers if they could buy as a group. With the help of Ken Youings and J. O. Bond Chemists, they set up what was to be the forerunner of Centaur Services, a veterinary co-operative, now one of the major veterinary suppliers in the UK. The warehouse was set up in the old milk factory at Castle Cary station and the first manager moved from Castle Cary Veterinary Practice. After Paul Greenhough left for Canada, Bill Harrison became one of the Centaur directors continuing to hold this post until he retired. During that time the wholesale company moved to the old cheese store in South Cary, which it outgrew and then moved to the current site on Torbay Road.

Before Paul's retirement from the practice Arthur Llewellyn and David Gregory had joined as assistants and soon became partners, with the practice trading as Harrison McNab and Partners. This brought a period of expansion to the practice with an increase in companion animal work. A number of very able assistants were employed at this time, swelling the number of vets to six.

The next milestone was the purchase of the practice owned by John Hall and Alan Hughes at Yeovil in 1976. They practised from premises in Market Street that had been custom built for Mr. Gollege in 1907. They held morning surgery for pets from 9 until 10 and then visited farm clients at a fairly leisurely pace. John Hall retired immediately and Alan Hughes three years later. However his wife Pat was a very able nurse and secretary and she continued to serve the practice with great diligence for many years. There was clearly scope for expanding the Yeovil practice. Bill Petheram, who had previously been an assistant at Castle Cary, was invited back as partner to take the practice forward. Ian McNab moved to Montacute to provide some back up for the out of hours service. It soon became apparent that the premises were not ideally situated for pet owners and that the access was poor. New premises on Hendford Hill were purchased and after a complete refurbishment the practice moved in 1978. The Yeovil arm of the practice now houses 6 vets, mainly employed with companion animals.

Bill Harrison.  *Ian McNab.*  *Paul Greenough.*  *Arthur Llewellyn.*

David Gregory.  *Bill Petheram.*  *Don Collick.*  *Mike Kerby.*

Nick Perkins.  *Peter Luscombe.*

At the same time as developments were taking place in Yeovil, Don Collick joined the Castle Cary practice as an assistant. He soon proved to be an asset and joined the partnership. He had a keen interest in dairy cattle and studied for a diploma in Bovine Reproduction to further his career. Ian McNab had already set up the first dairy herds to use the 'Daisy' computerised management system in the UK, in collaboration with Reading University and Don soon took over and was able to utilise it to great effect. He also continued the practice tradition by becoming an authority in lameness in cattle, striking up a friendship with Paul Greenough. In the early 1970s as part of the Daisy package the practice also obtained an innovative computerised accounting system and although very basic by today's standards, it ran very well for almost ten years. The Castle Cary practice continued to expand and the need to hospitalise cattle and horses increased. The access to the Castle Cary premises became a problem for stock vehicles. Don Collick moved to Royal Oak Farm at Clanville and the practice purchased the adjacent paddock to build a large animal hospital facility which functioned well for a number of years.

In the 1990s the older partners were approaching retirement age; Bill Harrison was the first to retire followed two years later by Arthur Llewellyn, who decided to retire at the age of 55. David Gregory followed a year later and Ian McNab completed the exit in 1996. In turn they were replaced by Mike Kerby, Peter Luscombe and Nick Perkins. It was decided at Bill Harrison's retirement that the practice name should be changed to the "Delaware Veterinary Group".

Fulford House, the purpose built premises on Torbay Road, opened in 1999.
A.Brittain collection.

The premises at Castle Cary had become very cramped as more office staff were employed to deal with the ever increasing amount of paperwork. With a team of young partners in place, this was the ideal opportunity to move to a green field site, to build a modern veterinary centre and to reunite all the practice facilities under one roof. Don became the team leader and project manager of the new premises, eventually to be called Fulford House. The move from Delaware House to the new premises took place in August 1999. The new building incorporates a dedicated large animal reception area to facilitate farming clients and a drive through large animal unit with stalls down one side for hospitalised cases. Each stall is fitted with double gates for ease of loading and unloading, plus equipment within the stalls to facilitate examinations and surgical procedures. The unit also features piped gases, a padded equine box, a dedicated embryo transfer room along with laboratory and post mortem facilities. Fulford House also has everything the modern small animal practice could want - ample car parking, a welcoming reception area, air conditioning, good sized consulting rooms, a dispensary, a laboratory and X ray facilities. The operating facilities are built around a large preparation room and there are separate hospitalisation facilities for dogs and cats. Upstairs there are offices for partners and assistants and ample room for administration staff and two flats for nursing staff and vets. Just when the practice was settling down to a period of stability and growth, it suffered two severe setbacks. Sandra Honor the office manager, died after a long battle with cancer, and very shortly afterwards Don Collick died suddenly on 23 November 2002. Following his death the large animal unit at Castle Cary premises was named 'The Don Collick Large Animal Unit' in his memory. Don had been the managing partner after Ian McNab's retirement and with the loss of Sandra, plans were in place for a practice manager to assume much of the day to day running of the practice. Fortunately Nicky Creed had already been appointed but had not yet taken up her post. However, Nicky, with some help from the partners, has fulfilled this role admirably in very difficult circumstances.

The partnership continued to expand, with the addition of Roger Lewis and Richard Hill. However, finding a veterinary successor to Don has proved to be more difficult, few recent graduates having an interest in dairy farming or understanding of the agricultural community. The Delaware Veterinary Group celebrated its centenary in 2005 and in 2008 another setback was encountered when partner, Richard Hill lost his battle with cancer and died at the age of 36.

Today at Castle Cary there are 7 farm animal vets, 2 equine vets, 4 small animal vets, a nursing team of 5 and 12 support staff. Overall in the group there are currently 5 partners with Owain Jenkins joining the partnership in 2012 and 51 employees, which is a far cry from one man in a wooden shed in 1905!

Roger Lewis.   *Richard Hill.*

[All pictures courtesy of Delaware Veterinary Group unless otherwise credited.]

Robert John Norris

Robert John Norris, always known as Jack Norris, was born on 8th October 1900 at The Bakery, Barnet, Hertfordshire, where his father, also Robert Norris, was a master baker. The family later moved to new premises at 1, The Parade, Belmont, Surrey where Jack sang in the Church Choir and attended the local school until leaving at the age of fourteen. He was then apprenticed to Sir Howard Smallman's Garage in Sutton where he learned to drive both cars and charabancs (coaches), which was quite a feat for a young man in those days. After Robert Norris, senior, took very early retirement, the family moved to Devon and young Jack soon followed and took an engineer's job at Trivett's Garage near the sea front in Seaton. Jack came from a very musical family and played the flute and clarinet in local productions such as The Pirates of Penzance and H.M.S. Pinafore, whilst living and working in Seaton.

After arriving in Castle Cary in the 1920s Jack Norris made new friends and contacts. He enjoyed entertaining and formed a small dance band which toured around the local villages playing at their weekly dances. Jack played the clarinet and flute, other players included Gordon Macmillan on the banjo and Jack Weeks on the drums. Evidently the players were quite popular with the local girls wherever they played and one well remembered event was when Jack Norris disappeared with a young lady who worked in the bakery at Street and eventually emerged covered in flour! It seems that Jack Otton who ran the local radio shop, also went along with the band, not to play an instrument, but to 'play the field'! During the war Jack Norris, being just too old to join the forces, did war work at the Cathedral Garage in Bristol and whilst there helped form a concert party to entertain troops based in the area. Again he played in a band and with other members of the troup, performed amusing sketches on stage.

Jack Norris's Central Garage in Fore Street in the 1950s.
LHG collection.

In 1923 Jack applied for a job at the Central Garage, Fore Street, Castle Cary. He got the job and this was the beginning of the rest of his life which was spent in Castle Cary. His first lodging house was at No. 1 Upper High Street, his landlady being Mrs. Mary Pitman who was also destined to become his mother-in-law. He met sixteen year old Ivy in the hall of his new lodgings and it was love at first sight. After starting to 'go out' with Ivy it was decided that he should find pastures new and so he moved into new lodgings in Ansford Road at the home of Mrs. Bartlett. The courtship was a long one and it was not until April 20th 1931 that Ivy and Jack were married at All Saints Church, Castle Cary.

Ivy was born in 1907 at No. 1 Upper High Street. Her father, Harry James Pitman, was the gardener and coachman to the local G.P. Dr. Coombs who lived in the large house known as Beechfield House. There was only one local doctor earlier in the century and if he was needed to attend a patient in the middle of the night the coachman had to saddle up the horse and take the doctor to wherever he was needed. Sadly, already suffering from asthma, and succumbing to the terrible 'flu epidemic of 1918, Ivy's father died in November 1918. After the terrible conditions in the Great War, people were very weak and vulnerable and easily picked up the virus. Harry Pitman was not the only one as apparently whole families were wiped out in Cary and throughout the British Isles. Mary Pitman was forced to take in lodgers and to do dressmaking as there was then no Widow's Pension and no children's allowance. Ivy at sixteen was apprenticed to Tulletts, who were ladies and gents' outfitters, the shop being next door to the Central Garage in Fore Street. The apprenticeship lasted three years and quite a few other local ladies took part in the same training. Working hours were long and pay was very low, but the employees of Tulletts were very happy in their jobs and loyal to their employer, who rewarded them each year with a special outing. When a young lady married she was normally no longer allowed to continue in a paid job, so in 1931 Ivy had to retire from Tulletts.

Central Garage in Fore Street, Castle Cary, which is now D. Marsh, Hardware, was a very old building, reputedly having been a coaching house in the 16th and 17th centuries. A local myth was that it was where King Charles II disguised himself as a groom and escaped from Cromwell's men through a secret passage to the castle on the hill. In the 1930s several mechanics were trained and worked in the Central Garage, which Jack Norris had purchased a few years previously. One was George Willcox, but when war was declared he and the others were forced to enlist and even Jack himself had to take off so he was reluctantly forced to close the Garage. After the war, in 1945, it was re-opened with new staff, including Tom Moores and Bert Harrison.

Jack Norris' special friend in Cary was another Jack - Jack Pike. Whilst Jack Norris' great passion was cars and motor bikes, Jack Pike's was bicycles. He built, sold, and raced them - his silver trophy filled cabinet was proof of his success in this field. Jack Norris had also always loved speed and raced his motor bikes on Lodge Hill in the 1930s. His very special thoroughbred car was his Graham Paige, built in the U.S.A. in 1920 and well ahead of its time. It was very luxurious with feather-filled separate cushions in the back seats which when the car was driven over a hump in the road, would make deep hissing noises when the occupants, (usually Win Pike and Ivy Norris) having been raised into the air, came back to earth again, with loud protests of 'Oh Jack!' After the war Jack Pike had considered buying himself a car but it was eventually decided to continue sharing Jack Norris' vehicles for their weekly trips to the coast and use his bicycle for local trips. Jack Pike had actually 'eloped' on his bike when he married the local butcher's daughter Winifred Lush. His family had opposed the marriage so the couple got up very early and tied the knot. In those days he and Win. rode a tandem. Their house overlooking the Horse Pond was built in 1936 (recently demolished) and the stones which spelt out 1936 were gathered by the two Jacks and their wives on one of their trips to Portland Bill. Win came from the local Lush family - her father, Eli boasted that he had fathered 21 children - 18 with his first wife and three with his second. The last three were Reg Lush, who produced seven children and took over the local butcher's shop, Nell who became Nell Dill and had six children and Win who was childless, but a very popular auntie. The house, with the cycle shop adjoining, was always full of young visitors and Eli lived there until his death in his late nineties.

 Both Jack Pike and Jack Norris were kind and generous men - they had very little, but gave a lot. Jack Pike would help young people out when their bicycles gave trouble and likewise Jack Norris loved helping people in a quiet way. An example of this is when he was left £10 in the will of a local lady - Ada Hallett, who used to play the piano in the local cinema in the silent movie days and whose head almost touched the ground when she walked. It transpired that Jack always drove her to her home at the top of the hill after doing her shopping, but never charged her a fare.

Jack and Ivy Norris outside their home in upper High Street.
LHG collection.

Jack on his motorcycle in the 1920s.
LHG collection.

Jack Pike in the doorway of his shop overlooking the Horsepond, in the 1940s.
LHG collection.

Life as a Wartime Evacuee

A view looking north along Lower Ansford lane in October 1936, and as it remained until the early 1960s when part of the thatched farmhouse was demolished and bungalows constructed in the orchard.
A.V.Pearse collection.

Life as a Wartime Evacuee at Ansford by Keith Crane

Due to air raids, I and my mother and her sister left our home in north-west London and came down to Castle Cary. The first house where we stayed - in Ansford - had a large bedroom which was divided in two by a curtain - on one side the owner and his wife slept in a double bed, on the other my mother and her sister with me as a six year old sleeping between them. My mother wasn't happy with this arrangement, and asked the lady who lived in the next house if she could help us. Very kindly she offered us our own bedroom, and so we moved next door.

This family ran a small-holding; there was a large vegetable plot and an orchard where a dozen sheep lived, while on the right hand side there was a large chicken house with a big run. To reach the lavatory one had to walk through the vegetable plot and then through the orchard to the hedge right at the bottom of the plot where there were two upright slabs of stone through which you had to pass in order to reach the shed where the lavatory was located. I hated having to go through those stone slabs because I thought I was going to get stuck between them.

I was surprised how rough the fleece of the sheep was - not a bit like the wool my mother used to knit my pullovers.

The owner of the small-holding had a 1930s Austin Seven car which he kept running during the war with a mixture of paraffin and methylated spirit. The little car ran quite well on this mixture, although it had to struggle up hills. When we reached the top the driver switched off the engine until we almost reached the bottom of the downward slope, when he re-started the engine. Thus we made trips to shops in Somerton.

During my stay at Ansford I had whooping cough, and had to sit with my head over a steaming jug of Friar's balsam, a towel covering my head, the intention being to make it easier for me to breathe. Once the doctor called to see me and gave me an injection - in those days the syringe was made of steel and it and the needle had to be boiled in water. Unfortunately when he removed the syringe the needle was left sticking in my leg, and he then had to find a pair of pincers to pull it out. Since then I have had many injections, but always knew that the needle could be pulled out. I eventually recovered from whooping cough, but it left a weakness in my lungs.

Every morning a milk girl called round the village with a trap/milk float containing two large milk churns. She dipped a long handled ladle into a churn and then poured the contents into the china jugs which the women from the local houses held up to her.

Every week a man selling household goods came round the village with a van - he also sold paraffin which people needed for their lamps and "valour" heaters.

I didn't go to school during my stay in Ansford but my mother used to take me on nature walks and in this way I learned the names of wild flowers and how to identify the trees by their leaves and cereal crops by their seed head - barley, wheat and oats, etc. Sometimes we went to the railway cutting to watch the steam trains.

The row of cottages in Lower Ansford where Keith stayed, seen here in the early 1950s.
A.V.Pearse collection.

Childhood Memories of Ansford by Gordon Groves

Number Three, Fir Tree Cottages, Lower Ansford is where I spent my childhood. These cottages were not then the desirable countryside residences they have now become - in fact they were condemned by the Sanitary Inspector, Mr. Padfield, who (so the story was told) promptly purchased them and set about "modernising" them! The 'one-up and one-down' cottages each had an extension added to the back consisting of a kitchen and upstairs bedroom. The thatched roofs were removed and replaced by slate tiles whilst the cottages were still occupied, and I remember lying in bed at night and looking up at the stars! Electricity was added sometime in the 1930s and we only had an electric connection in the living room, as money was short. At least I could now read in the evenings without having to sit close to the table where the oil lamp gave out a very poor light. We continued to use the oil lamp, along with candles, in the rest of the house for some years to come. The outside flush toilets did not arrive until 1947, prior to which buckets were used and the front garden served as the repository, with my father digging holes in rotation.

Gordon in 1940.
G.Groves collection.

Milk was delivered daily to the residents of Ansford from Barrett's farm which was situated near Fir Tree cottages. A two-wheeled horse drawn vehicle with rubber tyres carried three milk churns and delivered the milk door to door. The milk was dispensed from a pail and ladled into a customer's jug by either Len Helps or Frank Fussell. Most household requirements were delivered door to door in those days, including bread, weekly groceries and coal, etc. Mr. Barrett also made cider, mostly for the family's own consumption, and that of his labourers. I had an uncle in Bristol who worked in a reserved occupation, and one year at haymaking time he came down and joined the labourers in building the hay ricks. The cider was duly passed round, and my uncle, not being used to it, before long, was as drunk as a lord!

I remember Mr. Baker who was the caretaker of the Mansion (now known as Florida House, situated at the top of Florida Street). Mr. Baker suffered from respiratory problems, as he had been 'gassed' in the First World War, but liked his cigarettes and I would fetch them from Martin's Stores. Incidentally, there were two large ornate gates at the top of Florida Street which disappeared during the Second World War, along with an old cannon that was in the field opposite Yew Tree Cottages. They were probably collected by scrap merchants to be turned into armaments, along with the Nation's unwanted pots and pans and prized wrought-iron fences, etc.

When the Second World War started the Green Howards were stationed in a building near the Mansion, which overlooked the playing fields and I remember hearing one of them had shot himself, rather than face being sent abroad to fight for King and Country. When the Americans arrived in Castle Cary, their headquarters were situated in the Mansion, with huts billeting the men in the surrounding grounds. There was a sentry box at both the Florida Street and the

Transferring apples to the cider loft at Lower Ansford Farm in October 1936. This image has been frequently published, and is here used on the cover of The Farmers Home supplement for 10th. Nov. 1936.

A.V.Pearse collection.

Greenway Road entrances. I befriended one of the sentries and every time the ration of cigarettes arrived from America, he gave me two cartons of either Lucky Strike, Chesterfield or Camel cigarettes which I distributed free of charge to friends. On one occasion, another sentry gave me a pair of brown leather shoes. I remember one of the troops had a different coloured skin from the rest of the men, and when I queried this with the sentry was told he was a genuine Red Indian, I was enthralled.

Food was in short supply, and we boys would often arrive at school with our pockets stuffed with Morgan Sweet apples pilfered from Joyce's orchard. There was a wonderful food bonus one day as I was walking up Ansford Hill, when a Supply Convoy went by and the last vehicle suddenly started shedding half-pound blocks of margarine. I collected as many as I could and triumphantly took them home!

I was one of the first pupils to attend Ansford School when it was newly opened in 1940 - I thought it was marvellous, despite running around the playground and tripping over a piece of wire left by the builders, resulting in painful injury to my knees! Sadly, a pupil was killed in a road accident shortly after the school was opened, which led to the hedges being cut back to improve visibility. We had to make sure we had our gas masks with us at all times and when the air raid sirens sounded, three bells were rung at the School and we all had to go to our allocated Girls or Boys cloakrooms. I could never see what safety there was in that - a direct hit would have eliminated so many of us - the only benefit was that we were all together for teachers to check numbers!

The Goods Yard and Signal Box at Castle Cary Station before the buildings were destroyed by German bombs in 1942.

I realised the utter seriousness of the War on Thursday the third of September 1942, when Castle Cary Train Station was bombed and machine-gunned by a German bomber. I remember the house shaking and the noise of the bombs exploding. The rattle of the machine guns added to the melee. I ran upstairs to see if the bedroom walls had cracked and from the bedroom window I could see the Station wreathed in thick smoke. As soon as my parents allowed me out of the cottage, I made my way to the road bridge to see what had happened. The Signal

Box was completely destroyed and the Goods Shed was wrecked, along with many goods wagons, and a steam engine lay on its side. The Signalman, Arthur Sibley, did not stand a chance and was blown out of the Box and landed in the farmer's field the other side of the railway line. The lever frame of the Signal Box had been blown across the railway track. One of the engine crew had also been killed, but Tom Whittle, the Engine Driver, survived as he was thrown out of the cab as the bomb exploded. A fourth bomb bounced over the road and into the river - exploding and drenching the field with water. One lad, Ken Weeks, found a bullet which turned out to be live, and he blew off the top of his thumb. Following this incident, we all received lectures from our school teachers instructing us to leave such things alone. The Railway Inn had also suffered serious damage, as a bomb had bounced through it and shortly after, the Inn had to be completely demolished.

Air-raid damage on 3rd. Sept. 1942 – showing the destroyed Goods Shed and remains of the Signal Box, from the south-west.
The National Archives.

Damage to the Goods Shed as seen from the north side.
The National Archives.

A destroyed truck alongside the Goods Shed.
The National Archives.

Damage to milk vans.
A.V.Pearse collection.

When I left school in 1943 at the age of fourteen years, I first worked at Donne's factory in Torbay Road, making rope. Huge military camouflage nets were also made there, and I remember seeing the nets stretched over a large frame, and the women stitching in the different colour camouflage pieces. Part of the factory was used by the Ministry of Food as a storage depot and I was selected to help collect or distribute food as required. There were big huts also used for storage in the grounds of the preparatory school at Sparkford. There was a certain amount of wastage, as storage conditions were not ideal. The sugar for instance, became congealed and rock hard when it got damp.

A year later I was able to join the Railway, starting as a Telegraphist in the rebuilt Signal Box at Castle Cary. I clearly remember the ambulance trains passing through on their way from Weymouth or Plymouth. Each train comprised of six carriages with beds and one carriage for sitting-up patients, giving a total capacity of about three hundred patients. In addition, there were two carriages for medical officers, nurses and attendants, along with two catering carriages. A further carriage was equipped with an operating theatre and pharmacy, and brake carriage incorporated boiler-heating facilities and finally another brake end vehicle and stores section brought the total to fourteen coaches - a complete hospital on wheels. A red cross was painted on the tops of the carriages and the ambulance trains always stopped at Castle Cary Station to take on a banker (extra steam engine), in order to get it up the steep incline between Castle Cary and Brewham. When the train reached Brewham Signal Box, the banker would drop off and return to Castle Cary Station as quickly as possible. The only freight trains which didn't need a banker were the occasional ones hauled by the big American Baldwin 2-8-0 locomotives.

Castle Cary Train Station was extremely busy with goods, troop, and supply trains regularly passing through it. Ammunition trains came directly from Dimmer Dump. Jack Pike was the Signalman there. He owned the bicycle shop that stood behind the Horse Pond (in later days it became a very popular cheese shop until its demolition). On reflection, there must have been at least thirty-five people employed and associated with Castle Cary Train Station, including a Station Master, three signalmen, two telegraphists, parcel and goods office staff, shunters, two booking clerks, two porters, a road van driver, a lamp man, two drivers and two firemen for the banker, four linesmen plus the gangers who kept the lines in good order.

In 1947 my call-up for National Service came, and I duly went away for two years serving in the RAF. When I had completed my service, I applied for the post of Signalman and worked at the Brewham Box, cycling there in all winds and weathers, more than once landing in the hedge when the roads were icy. I worked a three shift rota until my promotion took me away to Challow, nr. Wantage in the 1950s.

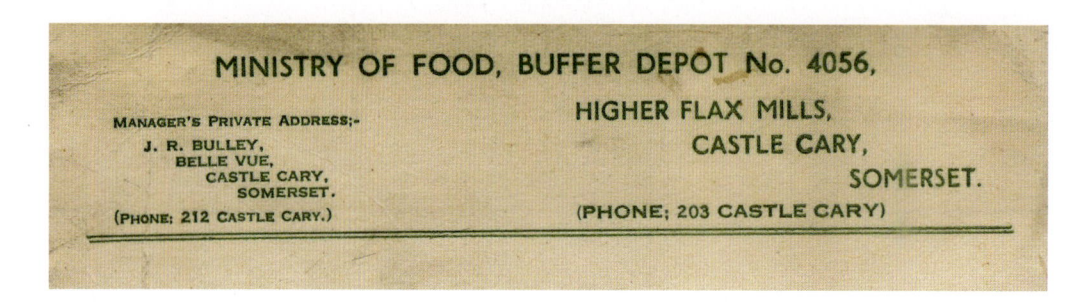

```
                MINISTRY OF FOOD, BUFFER DEPOT No. 4056,
    MANAGER'S PRIVATE ADDRESS:-           HIGHER FLAX MILLS,
         J. R. BULLEY,
           BELLE VUE,                        CASTLE CARY,
             CASTLE CARY,
               SOMERSET.                                    SOMERSET.
        (PHONE: 212 CASTLE CARY.)       (PHONE: 203 CASTLE CARY)
```

Views of the interior of Castle Cary Signal Box after it was re-built.
LHG collection.

A busy rural railway junction – Castle Cary station in the late 1950s, from a painting by John Cordon. R.Rathbone collection.

Yvonne Francis

Yvonne was born in St. Peter Port, Guernsey in 1925; her family moved to Brighton when she was four years old and later to Southport, Lancashire, where her father was employed making tarpaulins. All the moves were necessitated due to her father seeking employment - times were hard and her mother was kept busy caring for four children and making ends meet. Many of the children's clothes were hand-me-downs. Sadly her father died in 1942 when she was 17. By then Yvonne was employed making gas masks and haversacks for the war effort.

A recruiting poster for the Women's Land Army.

Land Army girls and the farm workforce at Steanbow Farm, Pilton, in 1943.
Pilton Village History Group collection.

The workforce at Steanbow in 1944.
Pilton Village History Group collection.

In 1945 as the war was drawing to a close Yvonne was called up to serve the country, she was given a choice of munitions, or the land; she chose the land so aged just nineteen, she and a friend got a train from Southport to Somerset, which must have seemed a million miles from home in those days. On arrival she was sent to Steanbow Farm, Pilton, which had been taken over by the Government to billet Land Army girls. There were also some Italian prisoners of war there but they never came into contact with them. At Steanbow she did not work on the land but was put in charge of breakfasts and caring for the rooms, etc., and making hot drinks at night.

After the closure of Steanbow Farm, Yvonne chose to do market gardening and was sent to Castle Cary to work at Porter's Nursery in Upper High Street, and was billeted with the Dill family in West Park. She was given the downstairs front room as a bedroom but after the war ended and Norman Dill came home from Wales with his new bride Gladwys, they needed the room, so Yvonne had to share a bedroom with Joan Dill. Mr. and Mrs. Dill still had their school age youngest son John and daughter Barbara at home, so conditions were crowded. Porter's was a nursery and market garden producing tomatoes and cucumbers and cut flowers, in large greenhouses. Three young men, Bill May, Ernie Dill and Ernie Drew were employed there. Mrs. Porter made wedding bouquets and holly wreaths at Christmas, and they also owned a shop in Weymouth and Yvonne sometimes took the train from Cary to help out there.

The travelling fairs used to come regularly to Coles' field at the top of Torbay Road. One evening when Yvonne was there enjoying the roundabouts and swinging boats she met a young man named Norman Francis. They began going out together and were married in 1948 at All Saints Church. Yvonne married from the Dills' home in West Park, she wore a dress she had managed to buy secondhand from Len Close's wife, Freda, as the restrictions on clothing using coupons had not yet been lifted. The wedding reception was at the Britannia Hotel and they went on honeymoon by train to Norman's aunt and uncle at Bradford-on-Avon, but not until Norman had played his usual Saturday afternoon football game for Cary.

On returning from honeymoon they began their married life living with Norman's mother in her cottage at Wyke Road. Norman's father had died at the age of thirty six, leaving five children and when Norman was thirteen he used to go milking after school for George Clothier, whose farm was nearby; this helped to bring in some extra money. The cottage was owned by Mr. Clothier, it had no electricity, no bathroom and no toilet, the only one being outside at the top of the back garden. Yvonne hated having to go out there on cold, dark nights.

Yvonne remained in the Land Army at the nursery for two more years, then became pregnant with their first daughter Linda. Shortly after, they were allocated a house in Victoria Park. Norman, by then, was employed by George Clothier's son Tom; he worked long hours, milking began at 5 am, he went home for breakfast at 6.30 am and worked all day, milking again at 4 pm. He generally finished between 6 and 6.30 pm. He worked some Saturdays which brought in a little extra money, needed as their family was growing; they had a further five children and his wages were £16 a week. There were no free school meals or benefits - Norman grew all the vegetables in their large garden and Yvonne cooked substantial meals; the children said no one made stew like their mother. Pea soup and suet puddings were also produced and the children ate what was put in front of them. There was no choice or asking what they would like. This was no different to every one else's lives at the time when the country was recovering from the war and things were not readily available or mass produced.

After the war Yvonne received a letter from Buckingham Palace thanking her for her work in the Land Army and has recently received the medal which she was entitled to. Sadly Norman died in 2000 but the family has increased and Yvonne now has fourteen grandchildren and ten great grandchildren.

Italian prisoners of war were also based at Steanbow, and one of them named Rossi produced this cartoon featuring the Land Army girls and other personalities at the farm, now preserved at Croscombe.
Bull Terrier Inn, Croscombe.

Women's land Army arm band, shoulder patch and badge.

By this personal message I wish to express to you

MRS. N. FRANCIS

my appreciation of your loyal and devoted service as a member of the Women's Land Army from 11th September, 1944 to 7th January, 1950. Your unsparing efforts at a time when the victory of our cause depended on the utmost use of the resources of our land have earned for you the country's gratitude.

Elizabeth R

The letter of thanks Yvonne received in 1950.
Y. Francis.

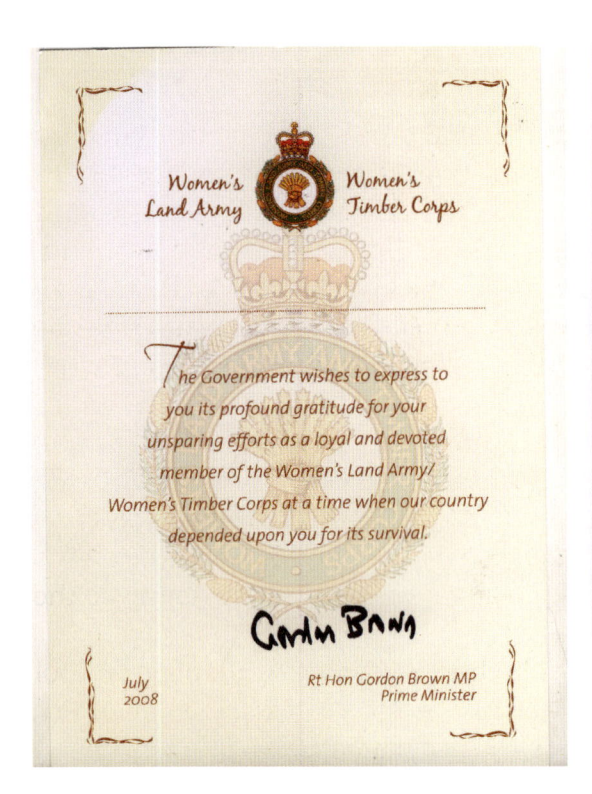

A letter of appreciation and medal issued by the Government in 2008 to WLA members.
Y.Francis.

A recently produced tin featuring a WLA poster.
Y.Francis.

Raymond Boyer

I was born in 1928, the only son of Percival and Rosa Boyer of Orchard Farm, Cockhill. My father served in the First World War, and moved to Orchard Farm a year before I was born. He was a member of the Home Guard and later of the British Legion, where he served as branch chairman and with my mother took the Legion flag to the Royal Albert Hall for a Festival of Remembrance. He also served on the Parish Council for over 30 years until he passed away soon after retiring. My mother lived into her nineties, spending her last few years at South Cary House.

I was christened in All Saints, Castle Cary, by the Rev. Reginald Lupton, and when old enough, taken by my sisters to Sunday School - I remember being taught by Sister Higgins of the Church Army. Every summer we went to Weymouth by train, and I remember the tea party we had at the Dorothy Café on the sea front. I attended evensong regularly - we always sat at the back because the front pews were reserved for the gentry.

I went to Castle Cary Primary School when I was five, walking to school with my two sisters and getting a lift home in the afternoon with Parsons Bros., the local milkmen who fetched milk from Charles Coward at Cockhill. The headmistress was Miss Ames, who came by train each day from Frome; there was also Miss Lydford who became Mrs. Parsons. The senior part of the school was supervised by Arthur Gomm, whose son was a Somerset County cricketer, and also played football for West Bromwich Albion.

I took the 11-plus exam and passed for Sexey's at Bruton, to be told that Sexey's was full with paying pupils, and as my parents could not afford the fees I went instead in 1939 to Ansford School, then still being built, with Mr. Gomm as headmaster. In 1940 he was followed by Mr. Gough - very strict but respected, and the arrival of over 100 evacuees from Deanery and Freemantle schools at Southampton, who amalgamated with the locals surprisingly well. Local pupils attended in the mornings, evacuees in the afternoons. A house system was established, named after four local landmarks - Butleigh, Cranmore, Tor and Stourton - pupils were allocated to each with a house master - I was in Butleigh. Pupils were separated according to gender - this applied to PE, and the girls learnt cooking, needlework and house-keeping, even having a 'flat' to look after. I remember the Misses Cutler, King, Blackmore and Parslow. The boys were taught by Mr. Tindall for woodwork, and Sam Steer for gardening. Mr. Stickland taught arts and crafts, Mr. Reed geography. My house master was Tommy Charlton from Southampton, also the sports master. He was well liked and also a friend of my parents. The gardening class provided all the vegetables for the kitchen.

During my second year I was made head boy, with Stella Pinder as head girl. At that time most of the pupils either walked or cycled to school - a few came by bus driven by Mr. Smith of Pylle - the firm still operates today. Over 70 years later I was invited to cut the tape for a sponsored walk by about 600 Ansford pupils to Lovington school - the methods of teaching have greatly changed, with computers rather than blackboards. The garden has been replaced by a fitness centre, and the bike shed seems redundant. Amongst many friends were Trevor Bartlett from Galhampton. I remember going to the famous football match at Huish Park, played in the fog on the sloping pitch, with Yeovil winning by the odd goal against First Division Sunderland.

When I left school I worked for my parents; as this was during the war years the only available labour was Italian POWs who were brought daily from Wells - they could not speak English and we could not speak Italian but it was surprising what a bit of home cooked English food did! My mother was a good cook and always gave them some lunch. I missed the call-up because when I came of age this was suspended for a year because a large number of the forces were coming home - I was too young to join the Home Guard though most farmers and farm workers were members and spent many nights training and guarding the railway system. My father was a corporal in the North Barrow division and was issued with a sten gun, which it was my job to reassemble after practise. The country owed a great deal to the men who spent their evenings in the Home Guard.

I remember one morning being in the yard at Orchard Farm with my father, and we saw a German bomber flying very low overhead and then the explosions when the bombs landed on Castle Cary station. There was an anti-aircraft gun in one of our fields, but as no officers were on duty it could not be fired. During the war several planes crashed in the parish, including one in Mr. Powell's field off South Cary Lane, while a few bombs were dropped in the lane and across the fields near Donne's factory. A plane on a training flight from Yeovilton crash landed in a field at Thorn - embedded itself in a hay rick being thatched - the thatcher left in a hurry!

At the end of the war Ansford and Castle Cary held a horse show in the field opposite Ansford School, then farmed by Fred Phillips of Clanville. The British Legion held concerts in the Drill Hall for the returning forces, and a large fireworks display was to take place in the Vicarage field but a stray firework landed in the back of the lorry containing them, resulting in a huge explosion.

It was at this time I began to be involved with playing skittles as a member of Dimmer Farmers' team, run by Mr. Hutchings, and one year we won the Bruton Labour Party cup. In later years I played in the NFU League at Galhampton, captained by Alan Bartlett and later by Dick Biss and Claude Wadman. The team still plays today - when the Harvester closed we moved to Lydford Cross Keys and then to Charlton Adam. I also put my name forward to play for the Consti Colts, but was never asked so on enquiry was told they didn't want council school kids, so I immediately cancelled my membership!

During the late 1940s Miss K. Maddever was the local Ministry of Agriculture dairy inspector, and also appointed as Somerset Young Farmers' Club organiser. She was a wonderful person and did a great deal for Somerset farmers. In her job she met many of their sons and daughters and persuaded them to join the local YFC - I was one of the lucky ones and joined the Mid-Somerset Club at Ditcheat. During petrol rationing coupons were available for YFC talks, so the Annual Ball was held after a talk on grassland. Mid-Somerset was a thriving club, with a peak membership of over 140, and where I made many good friends, some of whom I often see today. After several years I became Chairman, and a highlight was a visit to London with Jim Doble and several others including Len Creed, club leader at the time, to receive a trophy from Princess Elizabeth - so I can say I have shaken hands with the Queen! However, the highlight of my years with the young farmers was meeting Olive, who became my wife. The YFC movement was very active - in addition to meetings we always had a pantomime visit combined with a factory tour at Bristol. We produced our own variety show at Ditcheat with Jim Clothier, Cliff Cary and Ernest Dyke as vicars, but one example of many. We also helped with county rallies and I remember competing in stock judging at local shows including Shepton Show, of which I became a member and cattle steward, helping to erect the cattle lines for many years. I was always Jersey steward, and Olive and I gave an annual trophy and continue to attend the show.

Mid-Somerset YFC at its peak in 1953.
R.& O.Boyer collection.

After our marriage in 1955, Olive and I started farming on our own with a small mixed herd, some given by our parents, and a few Jerseys we purchased. In 1958 foot and mouth disease struck the farm and the entire herd was destroyed and buried the same day - fortunately we were not allowed to see the actual slaughtering, but we could not leave the farm for a while, which was then cleaned by prisoners from Bristol. As a result of a visit to Jersey we were able to contact Francis Le Rue, who sent over 20 pedigree Jersey cows direct from the island. By this time our son David was born, and we were milking the cows in a small bail in the yard. The milk was sold to the MMB, but to increase our income Olive made some into clotted cream, sold in Phillips grocery shop in Castle Cary and also by a baker in Weymouth, where it was sent by train several days a week. This output worked admirably, but an eventual decline in the demand for Jersey milk led us to sell the herd in 1973, which as we had successfully exhibited at local shows, sold very well. Consequently we increased our Friesian herd, mainly with cattle purchased through George Coombes, a well known buyer at Banbury market, and over the years established a pedigree herd.

Our first Jerseys entering the milking bail.
R.& O.Boyer collection.

Our son David and a Jersey cow examining each other.
R.& O.Boyer collection.

In the early 1960s we sold our milk to T. W. Clothier at Wyke, and delivered it using a tank behind our truck; the milk being paid for by the MMB with a supplement because it went to a cheese maker. Then the government under Mrs. Thatcher decided to disband the MMB, which had served us so well and given farmers a guaranteed market at a price they knew six months in advance. I had been milking for 40 years, so decided to give up, and in November 1980 we had a sale of surplus Friesian heifers on the farm and invested the proceeds in some Charolais cattle purchased at Neilson's Overhall herd sale in Herts. The dairy herd was sold profitably, and a beef herd established, with many calves coming from Mr. Clothier, fed by automatic calf feeding machines. At this time the Carnival club collected waste paper which was stored at Orchard Farm. However the bottom fell out of the trade leaving a lot of surplus paper which we started to use for stock bedding. The cattle would eat some and one day the press who had come to photograph a carnival float took a picture of the cattle eating the paper, which appeared on page 3 of The Sun. This brought in the local TV, and a few days later I was contacted by Radio Tokyo to give an interview.

In addition to calves, we bought store cattle from the Welsh hills, mainly from Brecon, Knighton and Builth Wells, finding the Welsh farmers very trustworthy and the transport first class. We expanded the Charolais herd until one afternoon Olive was knocked down by one of the largest cows, and we thought they were getting more than we could manage. A herd sale was held on the farm and because we had exhibited at several shows and won prizes the sale attracted a good number of buyers, with the top cow making £3,000. We then kept beef cattle for some years and then sold the herd privately and let the grass keep locally.

We also started to grow vegetables in Barretts Field - mainly potatoes, cabbages, cauliflowers and brussels sprouts which were sold at Cary Fruit and Greens, and also by Alan Mullet in Cary.

The birth of Philip completed our family – he was needed as a tractor driver at an early age!
R.& O.Boyer collection.

The herd of Friesian heifers and a couple close to calving
R.& O.Boyer collection.

The Charolais herd, with Orchard Farm in the background.
R.& O.Boyer collection.

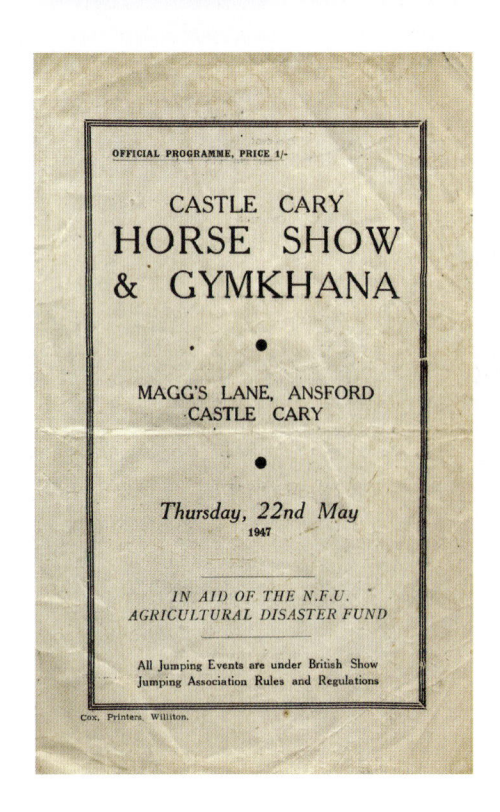

I remember before I left school the Hutchings brothers of Dimmer turning swaths of hay by hand with hand rakes - each person turning a single row. Then came the horse-drawn turner which turned two rows at once, followed by the iron-horse - a contraption which enabled the turner to be towed by a tractor. The next step was to have a tractor mounted turner which was powered by the PTO and could be lifted on corners, and the side rake which put two swaths into one. Today machines are available capable of gathering up to 30 feet at a time. We started with a single swath mower which was mounted under the tractor, then came the wider mower with three drums cutting eight feet at a time - today mowers are mounted on both sides and one on the front.

When I was a boy the hay was ricked loose with men from Cary coming in the evenings to help, often on an annual basis. I call to mind George Woods who was the local road foreman and his son-in-law Norman Kirby, both of Torbay Road coming to help and after an evening's work they would have a farmhouse supper, usually of cheese. As a boy my first job in the evenings was to make sure the cider jars were full.

My father purchased a second-hand baler from another farmer - it was made in America and worked very well for many years, eventually replaced by a new Welgar when I was farming on my own. Not being happy with the result we tried barn hay drying, firstly in stacks in the field and then in the barn where we had built a false floor. The dryers were hired from Jack Sherborne who lived on the outskirts of Bristol - these were a large fan driven by a Lister diesel engine built into a trailer, so they could be towed by a Land Rover, and fuelled by diesel direct from a drum. If the weather was fine they were kept running all night, and produced a first class product. Bob Falkingham, the Somerset machinery officer, was a great help, and supervised an open day we staged at Cockhill to show other farmers what could be done.

The Alvan Blanch grass drying plant set up in 1973.
R.& O.Boyer collection.

A prize winning Charolais.
R.& O.Boyer collection.

Irrigating cauliflowers, cabbages and potatoes, grown to supply local shops in the 1970s, and for which the sandy loam here was ideal.
R.& O.Boyer collection.

Prize cards and rosettes won at Yeovil Fatstock Show.
R.& O.Boyer collection.

David Adams round bale silage wrapping – wilted grass is compacted in bales which are held together by a plastic mesh and covered in black plastic film to exclude oxygen. A popular alternative to clamp silage and haymaking.
R.& O.Boyer collection.

In 1973, after buying dried grass nuts from Philip House at Cloford near Frome, we decided to install our own grass drying plant. Fuel was cheap, and substantial machinery grants were available from the government, so we purchased an Alvan Blanch machine and two self loading trailers, producing loose dried grass which we baled satisfactorily though dust was a problem. The addition of a mill and mixing machine made the unit more automatic, though careful management was necessary to avoid blockages.

Unfortunately the 1979 fuel crisis increased the cost of diesel from 8p to over 30p per gallon, which made grass drying un-economical - luckily we sold the plant to a nursery in Suffolk for drying herbs.

We started silage making with a small single swath harvester and after several years hired David Adams who had a large self propelled machine. Initially the clamp was housed in a small shed, but we later laid a concrete area and covered the silage with a polythene sheet held down with old tyres. After David Adams moved to the north of England, Targetts of Dimmer took over the silage contracting.

When we started farming we managed on our own, with the help of casual labour and contractors. We then employed Allan Kightly, followed by Vic Cornick and Martin Flower, who stayed with us until we gave up milk production, and reluctantly had to make him redundant. Martin was a great asset to us and managed the farm when we were away and helped us with showing the Charolais cattle and winning shows. He bought a cottage from my mother, and we sold him an adjoining barn, now converted as a house for his daughter and her husband. Girls were employed to help with the calves and lighter jobs - Jean Baghurst and Rita Collard were both from Bristol. Rita came to us on leaving school and stayed until she married Cecil Kingston at Castle Cary church. He farmed at Babcary with his brothers.

Over the years we used the AI Services provided by Horlicks, who had an office at Castle Cary, and built up a friendship with John Allen who also taught us ballroom dancing. Chris Wingrove and Jim Parry were also employed by Horlicks.

Animal feed supplies were manufactured by several large companies based in Bristol such as Silcocks, BOCM, Pauls and also Bibbys who had a factory at Bridgwater and a depot at Castle Cary station. A new mill was built at Sparkford by Longmans. There were also smaller companies such as Sheldons at Wells and Jones at Bruton who later amalgamated and more recently Mole Valley Farmers who have built a new mill at Bridgwater. We have dealt with them for farming requisites for many years.

Veterinary products were bought from travelling salesmen representing such firms as Pinkstones of Bristol and Day, Son and Hewitt from London. The government prohibited the sale of these products other than through a vet, subsequently Centaur Services at Castle Cary was formed. A lot of feed additives are sold by MVF and other small companies.

We built a poultry shed and for many years kept chicken for fattening, buying them as day-olds and selling them fat to Quantock Poultry Packers and later to Waldens at Trowbridge. Colin Law of Silcocks was our main feed supplier.

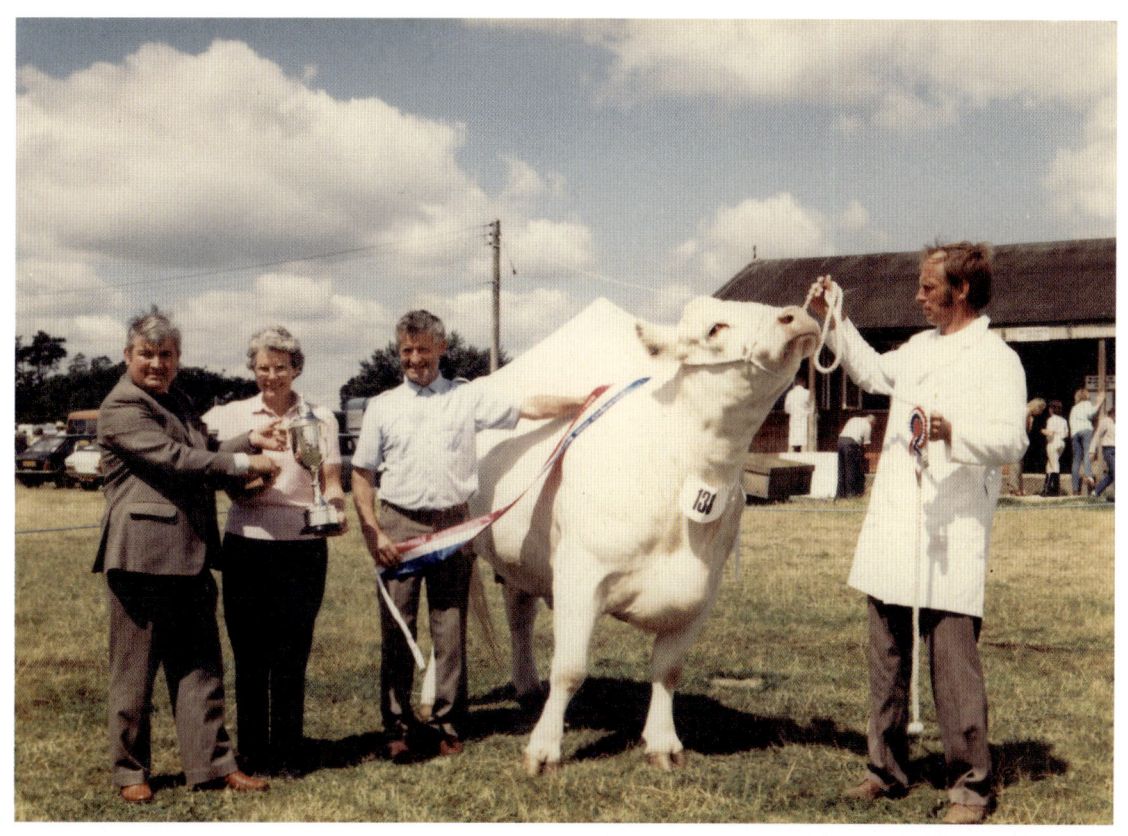

A prize-winning Charolais at Yeovil Show, with Harry Pursey of Wincanton awarding the cup to Olive.
R.& O.Boyer collection.

 The first new tractor I ever drove was bought by my father, it was an Allis Chalmers without a self starter and without a cab and was supplied by my uncle Jack Gilson of Stoke St. Michael. The tractors were mainly Fordsons, Fergusons, with a few American made ones during the war years. Most implement repairs were carried out by the local blacksmiths; at Castle Cary we had Parsons Bros., whose main work was shoeing horses. Before I left school my Saturday job was to ride a horse to Cary to have it shod. Also at Castle Cary T. White and Sons sold implements from outside the Market House with Maurice Herman as salesman, he later moved to Galhampton to set up on his own and later sold the business to Tinknells of Wells.

 The first new tractor we had was a Fordson Dexter supplied by Swaffield of Yeovil. We then bought a new Zetor from Cloford engineering of Bruton and years later another one from Nick Heal of Redlynch.

 I joined the NFU at Wincanton after being taken to a meeting by my father, and became Branch chairman the year before it was combined with the Langport and Yeovil branches, with an office in Yeovil. Some years later I became Chairman of Yeovil branch and was appointed to the County Executive which held monthly meetings at Taunton. I had the opportunity to go to the AGM in London, with a dinner in the House of Commons arranged by the MP Robert Boscawen.

 I was chairman of The Land Tenure committee for two years, and met some of Somerset's finest farmers including Fred Golledge of Hadspen, John Montgomery of North Cadbury, Metford Jeanes of Nether Stowey and Bert Hopkins of Horsington. Two great men on the staff were Harry Wilson and Charles Evison - Paddy Ashdown, the Yeovil MP., was a frequent visitor to the office.

While local NFU chairman I was asked to form a local branch of the Agricultural Training Group, and helped by NUAW member Ted Marsh this ran for many years until the abolition of the ATB and demise of the smaller farmer. As a member of the Lydford Agricultural Group we formed a buying group, with Philip Eavis, better known as founder of Living Homes, as secretary. After several years we amalgamated with Somerset Group Traders of Yeovil, which is now under the wing of Mole Valley Farmers.

The holiday cottages at Orchard Farm, converted from old cowstalls.
R.& O.Boyer collection.

An additional business enterprise commenced in 1991 with holiday cottages and bed and breakfast. Using tiles purchased in Evercreech, we re-roofed the old cowstall, which was gutted and converted for holiday accommodation. Rooms in the farmhouse were altered to enable use for bed and breakfast guests, and we were fully booked by summer of that year. In 1992 we joined the Somerset Stay on a Farm Group, of which I was later chairman, and successfully ran the holiday business until we retired in 2004.

Two years after my father passed away I was asked to join Castle Cary Parish Council, on which I served for 37 years until ill health forced me to retire. I was honoured to be on the council and made many friends there, and witnessed the closure of Donne's factory, BMI and Avalon Components and the moving of Boyd's. I served as chairman of the playing field committee for several years, during which time the Bowls Club was established and other improvements were made. Recent years have seen approval for the Crown Pet Food factory, and efforts to regenerate the Market House. I also represented the Council on a twinning visit to Remelard, and presented them with a red telephone box - evidently the only one in France.

When I was courting Olive my church going was at Lovington, but after our wedding we attended All Saints at Castle Cary, where both our sons were christened. We used to take part in the Rogation Sunday serices, which in later years were always held on a farm; on two occasions at Orchard Farm, with the farmer and his wife always providing refreshments after the service. For many years we also helped with the Harvest Festival and decorating of the church - our most ambitious effort was using a complete hay elevator placed in the centre of the church and decorated with flowers, while the porch was transformed into a rick with a thatched roof by Ted Marsh and his helpers. That evening there were nearly 500 people in the church, which at that time still had the galleries. Today, alas, with a big reduction in farmers and farm workers, and health and safety regulations, only a much smaller service is held. The produce was for many years sold at the George Hotel, and later at the Post Office, and currently it is taken to a homeless shelter in Yeovil.

Olive and I joined Cary Comedians Carnival Club the year after they were formed. The first float I drove for them used our trailer and tractor, with the generator carried on the tractor, and we also went that year to Shepton Mallet. The next float was built in the old gasworks, used as George Stockley's builders yard - the float roof was too high so we had to let the tyres down to get it out. Over the years the Comedians floats have got bigger and gone to many more carnivals - I think the record number during our time of involvement was 14, in addition to the Castle Cary appearance. Orchard Farm became the float building site, and the larger tractors needed were provided by Richard Longman and Nick Heal until the club purchased their own tractor. The float 'Tiger Feet' lost a tiger on the way to Yeovil carnival and a roof panel on the return trip, but it was one of the best floats we produced. The 'Who Gives a Buck' float won the county comic championship. Len Fennon was for many years our electrician, and owned the generator. Floats are now massive in size and often their complexity has to be seen to be believed. We made many friends in the carnival world and still support Cary Carnival as vice-presidents and band sponsors. Gordon Stockman has been head of Cary Comedians since its formation and also head of Castle Cary Carnival Committee for many years and without him there would be no carnival at Cary.

A family group at Shaftesbury Show in the early 1960s.
R.& O.Boyer collection.

Running the farm and our other enterprises left little time for holidays, and we never missed milking and feeding the animals on Christmas Day for over 50 years. But we have managed some interesting trips, notably to Olive's cousin near Vancouver and other relatives in Canada, and also to Austria and Israel, the U.S.A., Thailand, Burma and Slovenia, as well as to our son David in South Africa.

Our two sons David and Philip were pupils at Castle Cary Primary School, either walking to school or being taken by local garage proprietor Fred Chancellor's taxi. Both passed their 11+ exams. David went to Crewkerne Grammar School as a boarder, and then moved to Sexey's at Bruton with Philip. David progressed to London University's Wye College for a degree in agriculture, and Philip to Fitzwilliam College at Cambridge to study veterinary science. David met and married Helen in Guernsey and worked in Kenya, South Africa and Namibia, before returning to take up residence at Orchard Farm on our retirement to Ansford. Philip joined veterinary practices in Market Harborough, Wilmslow and Castle Cary, and is currently a partner in the Kingfisher Group at Crewkerne, while his wife, also Helen, works at a practice in Yeovil.

One of the Cary Comedians' carnival floats built at Orchard Farm called 'Pussy Galore' leaving for Bridgwater Carnival.
R.& O.Boyer collection.

Farming around Castle Cary by Raymond Boyer

Originally Castle Cary Parish included farms at Thorn, now in North Barrow, and several farms at Galhampton. Our journey starts at Foxcombe Farm, home of George White, which became part of the Longman Group, and then reaches a small farm occupied by Mr. Gould, followed by Sportsman's Lodge, run by Mr. Hayward and later by Thomas White until he retired - it is now a private house. Smallway Farm was farmed by Mr. Perry and his son Jim. Heading towards Cary was a small turnpike house which was demolished. Turning left towards Cockhill there was on the left a small cottage occupied by 'Manuel Gibbs, the local rabbit catcher who lived alone. Descending the hill, Higher Farm was the home of the White family for many years until Norman White moved to Sportsman's Lodge and Bert Adams became the tenant, followed by Gilbert Lee, whose wife was a White. On his death she and her daughter carried on, the latter married Colin Targett from Dimmer who now runs the farm.

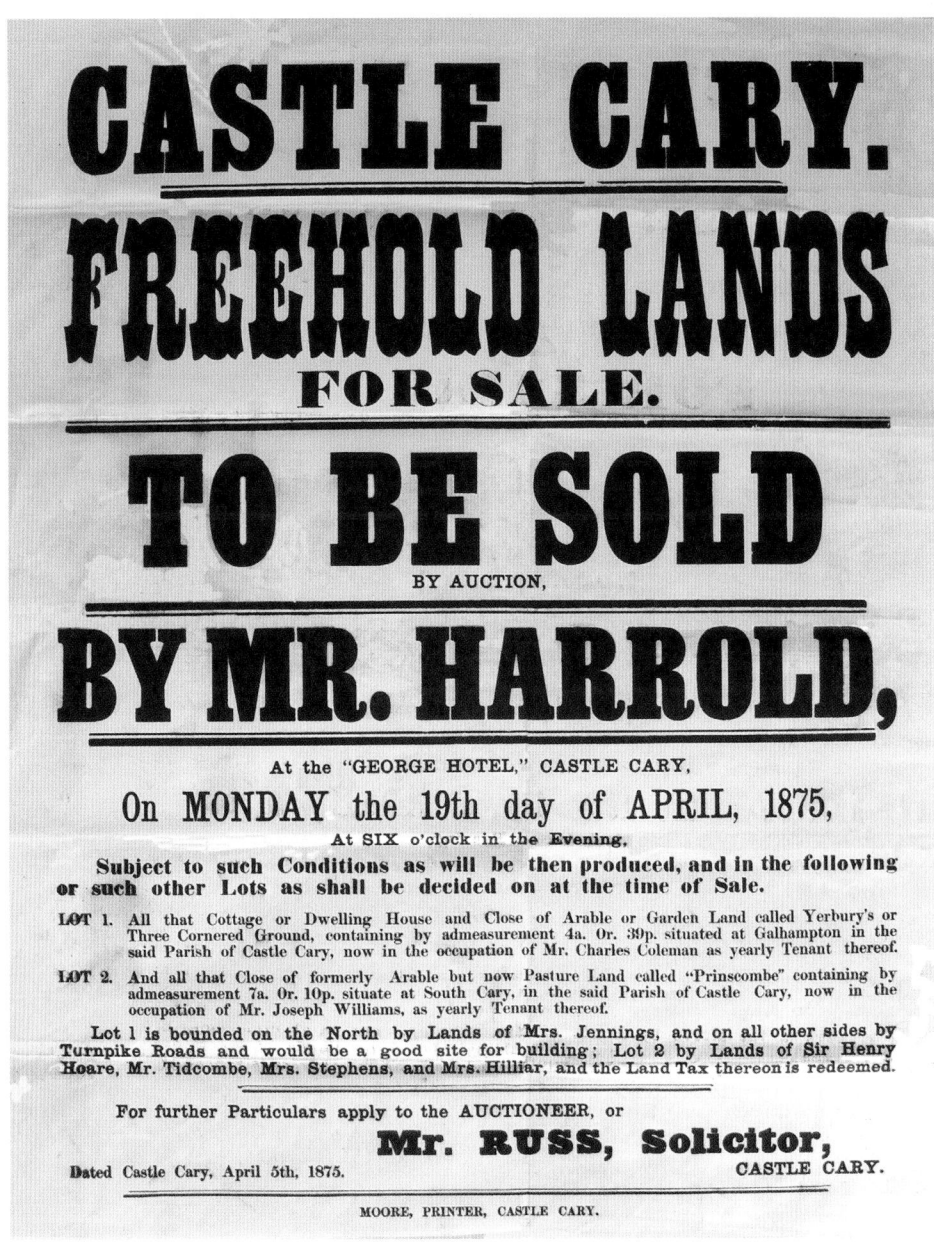

CASTLE CARY.

FREEHOLD LANDS

FOR SALE.

TO BE SOLD

BY AUCTION,

BY MR. HARROLD,

At the "GEORGE HOTEL," CASTLE CARY,

On MONDAY the 19th day of APRIL, 1875,

At SIX o'clock in the Evening.

Subject to such Conditions as will be then produced, and in the following or such other Lots as shall be decided on at the time of Sale.

LOT 1. All that Cottage or Dwelling House and Close of Arable or Garden Land called Yerbury's or Three Cornered Ground, containing by admeasurement 4a. 0r. 39p. situated at Galhampton in the said Parish of Castle Cary, now in the occupation of Mr. Charles Coleman as yearly Tenant thereof.

LOT 2. And all that Close of formerly Arable but now Pasture Land called "Prinscombe" containing by admeasurement 7a. 0r. 10p. situate at South Cary, in the said Parish of Castle Cary, now in the occupation of Mr. Joseph Williams, as yearly Tenant thereof.

Lot 1 is bounded on the North by Lands of Mrs. Jennings, and on all other sides by Turnpike Roads and would be a good site for building; Lot 2 by Lands of Sir Henry Hoare, Mr. Tidcombe, Mrs. Stephens, and Mrs. Hilliar, and the Land Tax thereon is redeemed.

For further Particulars apply to the AUCTIONEER, or

Mr. RUSS, Solicitor,

CASTLE CARY.

Dated Castle Cary, April 5th, 1875.

MOORE, PRINTER, CASTLE CARY.

LHG collection.

CASTLE CARY.

Sale of Standing WHEAT.

MESSRS.

WAINWRIGHT, LAVER & CREES

have been instructed to SELL by AUCTION at the Allotment Feild, at South Cary, near the Old Toll Gate, about

26 ACRES of CAPITAL WHEAT

in Lots, which will be marked out, on

THURSDAY, Aug. 15, 1907

at 5 o'clock in the Evening.

The Wheat will be found good, and a rare opportunity to those who wish to procure some good Straw.

The Auctioneers will meet their friends punctually on the Field at 5 o'clock.

A. BYRT & SON, PRINTERS, SHEPTON MALLET & WELLS.

LHG collection.

Further on is Middle Farm, lived in by Mr. and Mrs. Tolley, followed by the Colberts and Clarkes, and then David and Jean Adams, who moved to a farm in the north of England, after which it became a private house. Opposite are Orchard Farm buildings, partly converted to holiday cottages and a workshop and housing for the Cary Comedians' Carnival Club's floats. Orchard Farm was the home of the Allen family until bought by Mr. Palk, who let it to Mr. and Mrs. Percy Boyer, followed by Ray and Olive Boyer until they retired. It is now occupied by their son David and his wife Helen who have converted some of the land to a conservation area, including a lake, wetland and woodland, attracting many rare birds including swans. Another part has been developed as rented allotments.

Lower Cockhill Farm was run by Messrs. Higgins and Kimble, with Charles Coward as an employee, until they retired and he and his wife took over. The Boyers bought the farm from them, with Ray and Olive Boyer moving in. Percy Boyer's widow lived in part of the old house for many years, and during this time mediaeval wall paintings were discovered in the older part of the house, which was parted off and sold to Mr. and Mrs. Vaughan who restored it and converted some of the buildings to holiday cottages. Cockhill Cottage was sold to Mr. and Mrs. Martin Flower, who are restoring one of the barns. Other buildings are let to horse owners. Mr. and Mrs. Curtis bought the northern part of Cockhill Farmhouse, and converted a barn to a picture gallery, open to the public on occasions.

CASTLE CARY.

SALE OF CAPITAL CLOVER FOR MOWING.

MESSRS.

WAINWRIGHT, LAVER & CREES

have been instructed to SELL by AUCTION at the Allotment Field, at South Cary, near the Old Toll Gate, about

26 ACRES OF FIRST-CLASS

CLOVER

in Lots, which will be marked out, with full liberty of Removal, under conditions which will be given at time of Sale, on

TUESDAY, June 9th, 1908,

at 5 o'clock p.m.

The crop is very heavy, and affords a good opportunity to those wishing to get some good Hay.

The Auctioners will meet their friends punctually at 5 o'clock to start.

A. BYRT & SON, PRINTERS, SHEPTON MALLET & WELLS.

LHG collection.

In the High Court of Justice—Chancery Division.

ASTON *v.* GOULD.

Particulars and Conditions of Sale
OF
FREEHOLD PROPERTY
Known as
"France Farm,"
Situate at
DIMMER,
In the parish of Castle Cary, and North Barrow,

And a parcel of **MEADOW LAND**, in the Parish of East Pennard,

IN THE COUNTY OF SOMERSET.

Which will be sold by Auction,
IN NINE LOTS,
By

MR. T. O. BENNETT,

AT THE
"**GEORGE HOTEL**," Castle Cary, Somerset,

On Thursday, the 5th of May, 1881.
At THREE o'clock in the afternoon.

With the approbation of the Judge to whose Court this Cause is attached.

CROWDER, ANSTIE & VIZARD,
55, Lincoln's Inn Fields, Middlesex,
London, W.C.

'France Farm' has in more recent times been known as Franks Farm, and was sold during the last decade by Somerset County Council to Mr. and Mrs. R. Targett.
LHG collection.

Higher Dimmer Farm in the 1920s, now owned by the Targett family.
LHG collection.

Members of the Foote family at Higher Dimmer Farm in the 1920s, from left to right;- Annie; Sabina; Hilda; Sylvia; Annie.
LHG collection.

Left to right;- Hilda; George; and Sylvia Foote.
LHG collection.

After the First World War the County Council set up a number of small farms for ex-servicemen to start farming - six of these were at Thorn, and amongst the tenants were Messrs. Ireland, Carpenter, Powell, Toop, Bush, Dilling, Down, Biss, Clarke, Atwell and Sexton. Desmond Sexton was deaf and dumb, but was a member of the local NFU Farmers' skittle team, and a good player too. Mr. Carpenter organised the local Ministry machinery depot, and his son Donald ran the local threshing outfit during and after the last war.

At Dimmer a Munitions Camp was established during the war, which is now the Council waste disposal site for this part of Somerset. Franks Farm was also a Council smallholding, first the home of Reg. Bond, followed by the Frys, Adams, and then Mr. and Mrs. Drake, until the Council sold it as a private house. Park Farm was owned by the Hutchings family, followed by Mr. Parsons and the Targett family. Mr. Foote was at Higher Dimmer Farm, and later the Targetts, while the Hutchings family occupied a since demolished Middle Farm. Mr. Hutchings was captain of the Local Farmers' skittle team which won the Labour Party skittle cup in the 1940s. Dimmer Farm was the home of Ernest Creed, captain of the bell ringers at Castle Cary church for many years, and even photographed on the top of the spire with a pint of cider in his hand. He was succeeded by his son Harold, also captian of the bell ringers. Dimmer Farm was the site of local threshing days held during the war years: local farmers brought their corn during winter months and a team of ten or more undertook the threshing, partaking of liquid refreshment in the barn when it rained. Close to Dimmer Farm was a group of cottages called Dimmer Hobby, now demolished. Norman Stone, who worked for a local farmer collapsed and died on the railway bridge at Dimmer, and is buried on the adjoining hill where a monument marks his grave. Another small farm was occupied by Mr. and Mrs. Tony Adams.

Closer to the town at Torbay Road there was a farm at Torbay House occupied by Walter Martin. Over the bridge at Blackworthy a holding was farmed by Eli Lush, founder of the Lush butchery business. Blackworthy Farm on the top of the hill was run by the Kynaston family. Beyond, Clanville Manor has been in the Snook family for many years, and today they provide farmhouse and cottage accommodation. Eastwards, the first farm was occupied by Fred Phillips, the next by Leonard Gibbs, then Alan White, with Mr. Pierce in the large farmhouse. Clanville Sawmills was founded by Jonathan Cruse and David Gass, a well known west country entertainer, and retains their names today. Dorset House Farm was occupied by Mr. and Mrs. Coward, originally from Cockhill and then by Mr. and Mrs. Bush from Thorn.

Tank Cottages were mostly occupied by railway employees; the nursery on the main road was run by Mr. Yeabsley, a well known councillor. At the station was a milk factory owned by Messrs. Prideaux of Evercreech, milk was also sent direct to London in 17 gallon churns. The factory closed shortly after the demise of the Milk Marketing Board.

On Ansford Hill was Hillside Farm, run by the Williams brothers, who retailed their milk in Ansford and Castle Cary, and near Ansford School was Ansford Farm belonging to Mr. Clothier. Reached by Maggs Lane and overlooking the wide valley to the north was Park Farm, also occupied by a Mr. Clothier. Opposite Cumnock Terrace is land left to Cary Museum by Donald Mullins, and in Wyke Road a farm run by Tom Clothier, now a poultry unit. On the hill towards Wincanton is Grove Farm, home of Peter Wyatt, whose father John farmed with Fred Golledge, one of the best known farmers in Somerset, and Chairman of Somerset NFU. During the war he persuaded many farmers to plough land for corn growing and was known for his white hair and open top car.

In Lower Ansford was the farm of Jack Barrett, who was well known for his cider from apples grown on his land. William Derrett, the local butcher, farmed land in Tuckers Lane, now mostly built on.

In Castle Cary a Mr. James had a holding above the Methodist Chapel and operated a milk round, as did Roy Brake of Silver Ash Farm in South Street. The Parsons brothers at Mill Lane, off Station Road, also had a milk round, fetching their supply from Charlie Coward at Cockhill. They also operated a vegetable nursery and had extensive glasshouses.

Manor Farm in the centre of the town was formerly run by the Corp brothers, their sister being the local district nurse. It was then acquired by the Longman Group, and farmed by Guy Churchouse, sometime chairman of the Parish Council. During the 1950s it was struck by foot and mouth disease and the entire herd of over 100 cattle and 500 pigs slaughtered. For many years cheese was made on the farm, the whey being used to feed the pigs. The original farm buildings, behind the Horse Pond, were demolished to make way for the Castle Rise development.

CASTLE CARY
SOMERSET

PARTICULARS

OF A

VERY VALUABLE

FREEHOLD ESTATE

KNOWN AS

"CLANVILLE FARM"

SITUATE IN THE TITHING OF CLANVILLE, DIMMER AND COCKHILL

COMPRISING—

52A. 3R. 24P.

OF RICH

GRAZING AND DAIRY LAND

TOGETHER WITH SOME

ARABLE LAND

A CONVENIENT FARM HOUSE

WITH GOOD

FARM BUILDINGS

AND SUNDRY CLOSES OF

ACCOMMODATION LAND

Within One Mile of the Town of CASTLE CARY, and the Railway Station

Mr. HARROLD

has received instructions from the Trustee under the Will of the late Reverend JAMES DAUBENY, to offer the above important Property

FOR SALE BY AUCTION

AT THE

GEORGE HOTEL, CASTLE CARY

On THURSDAY, AUGUST 17th, 1882

At 3 for 4 o'clock in the Afternoon in the following Lots, or otherwise, as may be determined at the time of Sale

The Estate may be Viewed on application to Mr. WHITE, the tenant, at Clanville Farm.

MESSRS. WINTERBOTHAM BELL & CO.
SOLICITORS, CHELTENHAM.

W. STEVENS, ENGRAVER, AND PRINTER, CHELTENHAM.

LHG collection.

CLANVILLE,

near **CASTLE CARY**, Somerset.

Particulars and Conditions of Sale

OF A VALUABLE

FREEHOLD ESTATE

known as

LOWER CLANVILLE FARM

IN EXTENT

87a. 2r. 11p.

with a well arranged and suitable

FARM HOUSE & OUTBUILDINGS

MR. F. W. HARROLD

will offer for Sale by Auction,

at the GEORGE HOTEL, CASTLE CARY,

On THURSDAY, 16th of MARCH, 1899,

At 6 o'clock in the evening.

THE ABOVE VALUABLE FREEHOLD ESTATE.

Mr. J. O. CASH, Solicitor,
Castle Cary and Wincanton.

J. H. ROBERTS, Printer, etc., Market Place, Castle Cary.

LHG collection.

CASTLE CARY,
SOMERSET.

Sale of a Very Valuable and Desirable Freehold Estate,

COMPRISING

27A. 3R. 9P.

Of Rich Grazing Land together with Convenient Outbuildings and remains of Farm House (lately destroyed by fire) known as

"SOUTH CARY FARM"

Messrs. MOODY & SON

HAVE RECEIVED INSTRUCTIONS TO SELL BY AUCTION,

At the "Britannia" Hotel, Castle Cary,

On TUESDAY, January 24th, 1888,

At 6 for 7 o'clock in the Evening, subject to such conditions as will then be produced and either together or in the following or such other Lots as may be determined upon, the undermentioned

VALUABLE FREEHOLD

PROPERTY

VIZ:—

No. on Tithe Map.	DESCRIPTION.	CULTURE.	QUANTITY (more or less) A. R. P.	ADJOINING OWNERS.
	LOT 1.			
116	Dwelling-house and Offices, (in ruins), Outbuildings, Yard, Barton, and Garden,	Homestead	2 38	J. Hellyar, Esq., Sir H. A. Hoare, Bart., and Mr. C. Thomas, Junr.
172	Townsend-field, Orchard, and Cider-house,	Orchard	1 2 22	J. Hellyar, Esq., and Mrs. Stephens.
203 204 229	Summerleaze, Nursery, } in One Close, Strip,	Pasture	9 0 26	T. S. Donne, Esq., J. S. Donne, Esq., Mr. C. Allen, Mrs. Stephens, and J. Hellyar, Esq.
			11 2 6	
	LOT 2.			
201	Cockhill Elm and Implement Shed,	Pasture	5 3 19	T. S. Donne, Esq., Dinder Glebe, S. R. Dampier, Esq., and Mrs. Stephens.
234	Boleswell,	Pasture	10 1 24	Mr. C. Allen, Mrs. Stephens, S. R. Dampier, Esq., and Dinder Glebe.
			16 1 3	

The Property comprises some of the finest Pasture land in the County. It is situate close to the important Market-town of Castle Cary, and the Farm Buildings, which are very extensive and well-arranged, have an extensive Frontage to the Main Street.

To view apply to the Tenant, Mr. Thomas Bartlett, and for further particulars to the Auctioneers, Pylle, Shepton Mallet; or to

Mr. Randolph Woodforde,
SOLICITOR, CASTLE CARY.

Dated Castle Cary, January 5th, 1888.

MOORE, PRINTER, CASTLE CARY.

LHG collection.

Ronald Allen produced concrete products for local farmers after the Second World War for several decades at his works at Torbay Road. The business is now sited at Galhampton. Seen here is an example of a prefabricated Dutch barn, and a concrete gatepost.
A.V.Pearse collection.

CASTLE CARY BULL SHOW

Castle Cary Bull Show was first held in March 1901 at Millbrook and was an annual event attracting entries and buyers from a wide area.
A.V.Pearse collection.

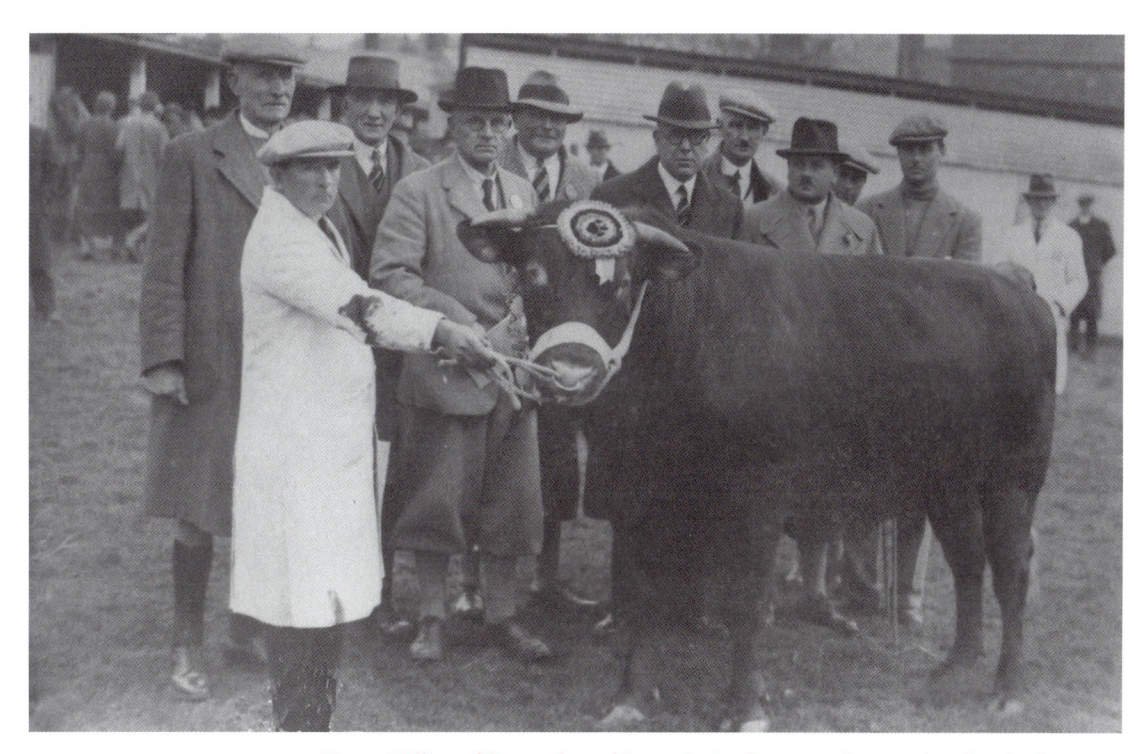

Henry Hillier, of Stone, shows his entries in these two photographs taken in the 1930s.
The last Bull Show and Sale was held in 1940.
H.& A.Gifford collection.

Jack Barrett hauls his milk to Prideaux's Creamery by the Station from Lower Ansford, with Rachel Oakes and Richard Rathbone, in the 1950s.
A.V.Pearse collection.

Veronica Stickland

Veronica Stickland

Veronica, second daughter of Sam and Winifred Perrott, was born in February 1935 in their little cottage in Upper High Street. Dr. Price walked up from his home just down the road in Highfield House to deliver Veronica; it was during the night with snow on the ground and he arrived wearing his dressing gown over his night shirt and slippers!

Veronica attended Ansford Primary School located within Ansford School as Cary School was taken over by troops during the war, and later Ansford Secondary Modern School, where she enjoyed participating in sport. Their home was opposite the nurseries owned by Mr. and Mrs. Porter and Veronica started working there after school when she was only twelve years old. She left school at fourteen and was then given full time work at the nursery alongside Yvonne Francis and Ernie Drew.

There were large greenhouses in which tomatoes and cucumbers were grown during the summer and large bloomed chrysanthemums and pot plants for the winter and Christmas. Christmas was a busy time making holly wreaths and crosses; it was hard on the hands and made them very sore: they had to dip them in disinfectant every now and then to avoid infection. Work began at 7 o'clock in the morning and sometimes went on until 10 or 11 o'clock at night. The nursery gardens were dug by hand and manure pushed in wheelbarrows was dug in. There was nothing mechanical to help with this, and Veronica worked hard at these tasks. Red and black currants were also grown, the fruit had to be picked and the bushes pruned.

Dr. and Mrs. Price at their son's wedding in London in the 1920s.
LHG collection.

Veronica, back row, sixth from left, in an Ansford Old Scholars versus the School Team, netball game, in 1949.
LHG collection.

The entrance to the Nursery from the High Street when it was owned by Mrs. E. Wheadon, in 2000.
LHG collection.

When Mr. and Mrs. Porter left to live in Weymouth, Bill May took over. In those days everything was delivered by bicycle with a carrier on the front. Veronica cycled to the station to collect big boxes of flowers for wedding bouquets, posies or wreaths; it was nothing to make 50 to 100 wreaths for a funeral. It was also Veronica's task to cycle to Bruton or Wincanton with a delivery, if the order was large a van was hired. Bill May left to become steward at the Constitutional Club with his wife Evelyn, and for a short time a retired naval commander took over, but it was soon sold to Mr. and Mrs. Wheadon. Mrs. Wheadon and her son Roy ran it until its closure in May 2000.

Veronica's father served in the 1914-18 war and was later employed at Boyd's Horsehair factory at its original site in Upper High Street opposite their cottage; he was in charge of dyeing the horsehair. He enjoyed playing rugby and would walk to Yeovil if there was an opportunity to play, he also played football and cricket. During the war he helped with haymaking for Clothiers at Wyke as well as tending his allotment in the nursery grounds; he also did the lawn mowing at Beechfield House and gardening and shoe cleaning for Dr. Patenall at Highfield House.

Veronica's mother Winifred, was one of sixteen children of John and Mary Meaden. The whole family lived in a two bedroomed cottage next to the Alma in South Cary. Mr. Meaden had an allotment on the opposite side of the road in South Cary and Mrs. Meaden carried all the water up in buckets from their cottage; much of the food for the large family was grown there. Mr. Meaden was also in charge of winding the church clock but his principle occupation was his own painting and decorating business. His equipment was stored in the shambles of the Market House. All the girls in the family went to work in service at the age of twelve and when sons Walter and Reg returned from serving in the war in India, they carried on their father's business and could be seen pushing their ladders, paint, etc., around Castle Cary on a hand cart.

Veronica also remembers Mrs. Simpson and Miss Boyd living in Beechfield House. Mrs. Simpson was Jane Elizabeth Donne Boyd, daughter of Alexander and niece of John Boyd. Scottish officers were billeted in Beechfield House during World War II and Veronica remembers them marching from Salisbury Plain to Castle Cary. The Ricardos lived in Phelps House and the Donnes at The Pines next to the Methodist Chapel, while the Macmillans lived at the top of the hill. Mr. and Mrs. Cleal lived in one of the elevated houses known as Mount Pleasant - Charles Cleal had a shoe shop and repair business opposite the fish and chip shop. Mr. and Mrs. James lived in the cottage beside the entrance to the nursery, they had a smallholding opposite and lost all their cattle to a foot and mouth disease outbreak. A cottage at the back of the nursery on the left was the home of Mr. and Mrs. Pounds - he was a policeman.

An aerial view showing the Nursery bordering Clarks Ansford Factory, with the glasshouses and other buildings. Veronica's family home is opposite the High Street entrance.
LHG collection.

I was an Evacuee

I was an Evacuee by Stella Clothier

In the summer of 1940 after Dunkirk it was decided to evacuate the town children to the safety of the countryside away from the bombing and the threat of invasion by the German army. I was then a pupil at the Deanery School for Girls in Southampton and most of us were evacuated to Castle Cary. We travelled by train from Southampton Central Station and although our parents were asked not to come to the station lots of them did. Most of us were very excited, but there were a few tears as well, and as we travelled along things got quieter and quieter. This was not just a day out in the country; it could be for a very long time and as it turned out in my case for the rest of my life. We all had labels attached to our clothes and we were only allowed to take one small suitcase with a change of clothing and of course gas masks in their little cardboard boxes and our identity cards. I still have mine and my number was ECAD44/8. When we arrived at Wincanton we were taken by bus to Castle Cary to the Old School in the town and from there by car to our new homes by Miss Mary Mackie who later arranged for us to join the Girl Guides. I and another girl were billeted with Mr. Walter Martin and his housekeeper Miss Gibson at Torbay House. It was a lovely old farm house but it had no electricity and the rooms were lit by beautiful oil lamps. Mr. Martin kept a few cows and some chickens and I loved to watch the cows being hand milked by Mr. Howard who worked on the farm. Sometimes I helped collect the eggs. Mr. Martin did not have a car - he had something much better, a pony and trap and he would sometimes take me for a ride, and occasionally I was allowed to drive it around the field.

A re-union of evacuees from Southampton, outside of Castle Cary Church.
S.Clothier.

The new school at Ansford was not quite finished and our teachers took us for long walks when we picked blackberries and rosehips. We started school in September, Mr. Gough was the headmaster and Miss King headmistress. Digs Parslow, Miss Blackmore, Mr. Spens, Mr. Strickland and Mr. Charlton were our Southampton teachers, and I was in class 3A with Mr. Charlton. The school was divided into four 'houses' Cranmore, Butleigh, Tor and Stourton. I was elected games captain for Cranmore and also a prefect and later head girl. All the local children also came to the new school but the infants and juniors had their own headmaster, Mr. Gomm.

In 1941 my home in Southampton was bombed and my mother came down to Castle Cary and stayed with Mrs. Fox in North Street until my dad managed to find another house on the outskirts of Southampton and she went home again. It was lovely having her and I missed her very much when she left. Unfortunately, Mr. Martin died and we girls had to move on. By now the town was full with evacuees and the wives of soldiers, I eventually went to stay with Mr. and Mrs. Derrett at Abbey Gardens. He was a butcher with a shop in Fore Street and Mrs. Derrett worked in the office of Woodforde and Drewett solicitors. It was through her that I too went to work there. Firstly I went after school and Saturday mornings for which I was paid 3s 6d until I left school at 15, and then worked full time for 7s 6d a week. I had shorthand lessons from Mr. Chilcott until he was called up. Mrs. Derrett had to go into hospital and I was on the move again. This time I went to stay with Mr. and Mrs. Bush and my friend Marjorie, until in 1944 I returned home. I worked in another legal office but it was mainly court work which I did not like. I stayed there for a year but when l was offered my old job back with Mr. Drewett, I returned to Cary and lodged with Mr. and Mrs. Bush again. So now I was no longer an evacuee - I was a lodger.

Stella (sitting) with, from left, Lorraine Pope and Jennifer Cox, in the office at Drewett's solicitors, on Bailey Hill, at the time of her retirement in 1991.
S.Clothier.

Stella at a W.I. cake stall outside the White Hart.
S.Clothier.

In 1950 I married Edwin Clothier whose family has lived in Castle Cary for several generations. For the first year we lived with Ed's parents until we moved to 8 Park Avenue, I was still working for Mr. Drewett and Ed was working at Cary Station. We had two daughters, Sally and Barbara and when I was asked to go back to the office part time, Ed's mum looked after the girls. In 1965 we bought a newsagents business from our friend Hetty Barber and we moved to the shop in Fore Street now occupied by Palmer and Snell. Of course, I had to stop work but it did mean that I was at home all day for the girls. Ed by then was working in Yeovil, but he helped me with the papers in the morning, while I ran the shop. It was very hard work and the hours were long giving us very little free time to ourselves, but I had two very good assistants, Joan Sweet and Joyce Close.

Both our girls were married in 1976 and we decided to sell the shop, and went to live in a house we had built in the Park. Ed took early retirement and I went back to the office yet again. By then I had worked for three generations of the Drewett family, R. B. Drewett, R. J. Drewett and John Drewett. I retired in 1991 and at first was utterly lost - I just did not know how to fill in my days. However I had joined young wives and W.I. of which I have been a member for 54 years. I also helped with the teas when the team played at home.

In 2010 we celebrated our diamond wedding and had a lovely lunch at Holbrook House for our family and friends, and our girls took us on a trip on the Orient Express, which was a wonderful experience. We now have 6 grandchildren and 5 great grandchildren. Mine has not been a very eventful life, but it has been a wonderfully happy one and l am very grateful to everyone who helped to make it so.

Stella with her husband Edwin at their Golden Wedding Anniversary in January 2000. Standing behind, from left, are Alan Biddiscombe; Barbara Biddiscombe; Sally Dauncey; and Timothy Dauncey.
S.Clothier.

Memories of Castle Cary

Memories of Castle Cary, by a wartime evacuee Jack Yockney

I was born and brought up in Southampton surrounded by railways, docks, rivers, boatyards and factories, it was no surprise that Castle Cary was a major environmental step, both mentally and physically, and what a wonderful change it was to be. My brother and I were billeted with Jim and Ruth Squibb at Keniston House in the High St.

What a wonderful environment it was with the Squibb family as a whole! My experience of a warm home, to be accepted into the family wholeheartedly with open arms, the home atmosphere experience, meals, conversation, relaxation, winding down after school, dress and 100% acceptance were unforgettable. Squibb family meals at the Heart & Compass public house are again unforgettable, all sitting around one table, the wide range of vegetables, etc., brought to me an experience never forgotten following my background up to then. To me to see everything growing on their allotment was an eye opening experience.

Keniston House, the Squibb's family home, at the junction of Ansford Road and the High Street. Jack stayed here as an evacuee. It was formerly Fowles' drapery shop.

Squibb's Garage in Station Road, built on the site of Cary brickworks. The family began a coach-building business here, which evolved into a motor garage. LHG collection.

These memories were revived by a visit to Castle Cary recently; it has been some 66 years since I have had the opportunity to step upon the wonderful surfaces of the town and what a day - I met Mr. & Mrs. E. Lush; Ted was one of my best pals when I was at Ansford Secondary school and what times we had. Ansford School I really enjoyed - initially Cary pupils were there one half of the day whilst our teachers and us evacuees had the other half of the day. My school and its teachers were evacuated as a whole, however we soon integrated, and we also had some evacuees from London but we all got on together and l have no memories of any problems. Some teachers' names I remember, Mr. Gough was the headmaster, Miss King, the headmistress, came from Southampton with us, I remember she wore crepe soled shoes so as she walked the soles of her shoes squeaked on the floor so we always knew when she was approaching. I also fondly remember Mr. T. Charlton, he told us he was called Tommy but wanted us to treat him with respect. He usually joined us at sports or games as did Mr. Gough when we played cricket. Other names that comes to mind are Mr. & Mrs. Strickland; I think Mr. Strickland was our art teacher, and I have fond memories of the other teachers, but their names are lost to me.

Of my school pals Ted Lush stands out - l shall never forget the enjoyable times in the orchard at the back of the shop, games at school and times in the classroom. My introduction to gardening was walking behind a plough dropping potatoes into the furrow in the bit of spare land adjacent to the school, ultimately picking the grown potatoes to be stored for the school meals, also walking the green lane adjacent to the school as a class, picking blackberries, etc., again for school meals. Class subjects were enjoyable, art I loved; PT in the gymnasium; use of the library to list a few of my favourite subjects. Other activities involved were rehearsing for plays and l thoroughly enjoyed the choir, which gave me a life long love of vocal music as well. Mr. Gough implored us all to behave outside the school because we were representatives of it, and our behaviour reflected the atmosphere at the school, and there were no problems. Classroom discipline was enforced by way of having a boy sit with the girls if he misbehaved, and if it were a girl who had misbehaved, she would have to sit with the boys. There were times when we had mixed teams of boys and girls when we played rounders, what fun!

Castle Cary Scout Troop, 1941-42, with contemporaries and friends of Jack. Miss Warren, the Leader, is seen in the back row, near the centre, and in the inset.
LHG collection.

Activities outside school included Scouts. Miss Warren was our leader, firm and friendly. Apart from the usual activities, I remember weaving coloured strips of material into netting to form camouflage netting for the soldiers and assisting in salvage sorting on Saturday morning in a hut adjacent to the entrance of her residence. I was also a simulated casualty, strapped to a stretcher being lowered down a ladder to assist in the training of first aid volunteers. We went camping once, each patrol taking their tent, etc., on a trek cart; we had to pitch our tents under the shade of the trees out of the view of any passing aircraft, albeit German. We had one blanket each but it was so cold we all slept together.

In winter there was tobogganing down Lodge Hill on a duckboard converted into a sledge and evenings going around in a small number, visiting various houses singing carols in the evenings leading up to Christmas. At Sunday School, prior to the dear old vicar arriving, we played leapfrog over the gravestones with the choirboys, followed sometimes with an appropriate chastening. This was usually followed by an evening attendance at the church with the Squibb family which was no problem to me....I enjoyed the singing.

Wartime memories include aircraft flying overhead at night, the vision of night-time attacks on the towns and cities on the west coast, etc., the bombing and machine gun attack on Castle Cary station on a Saturday morning, and a policeman cycling down Bailey Hill blowing his whistle and shouting 'air raid'. One morning, seeing a cluster of soldiers and a jeep outside on Bailey Hill, I slipped outside to see what it was all about and noticed that there was something in the back of the jeep that was causing all the interest, I managed to approach the object and touch it, it was an unexploded German bomb! Sometimes roads were shut up due to unexploded bombs and only opened when they were removed.

A few years ago we were invited by our next door neighbours to have a Christmas drink, we started talking about past times and I mentioned Castle Cary and the unexploded bomb, the husband's eyes lit up and questioned me again about it, then in a surprised tone he told me that he was the officer in charge of bomb retrieval and disposal in that area at that time. The Guards Division was reforming after Dunkirk and based in the vicinity, and we were conscious of the presence of soldiers and their vehicles. Some soldiers were ex boy scouts and they would come along to our meetings and talk to us about scouting, etc.

To sum up, the Castle Cary experience was a major episode and experience in my life, and it had a major effect; it developed my love of the countryside and my attitude to life as a whole. Apart from initially working in Southampton and training in a shipyard, I have spent the majority of my life in country surroundings (the Cotswolds), and my late wife was a country woman and a herdswoman. I am eternally grateful for the time spent in and with the lovely people I grew up with in Castle Cary, and will never forget my experiences there.

National Service Years by Julien Nicholls

[Editor's note:- In common with most young men not in reserved occupations or medically unfit, Julien Nicholls was called up for National Service during the post-war decade, and as a result witnessed the war-ravaged state of central Europe, as well as acquiring the discipline and skills that served him well in later life. As with both the world wars, National Service brought new and otherwise unimaginable experiences to many who might otherwise never have ventured far from such a relative backwater as Castle Cary.]

Early in 1954 I was notified by the Ministry of Defence that upon reaching the age of eighteen years I would be called up to do my National Service. After various medical examinations, written tests and interviews I joined the Royal Air Force in April 1954. This was the first time I realized that I was no longer a boy, when my father shook hands with me, as I bade farewell to my parents on Castle Cary railway station, with a rail pass to take me to Bedford via Paddington and King's Cross. As the journey progressed more and more young men of my age appeared to be aiming for the same destination. At Bedford Station we were met by numerous RAF police who directed us to RAF coaches to travel the last few miles to RAF Cardington, (the one time home of the English airships). We were kitted out with complete uniforms, great coats, best blue and working battle dress uniforms, boots and shoes, caps and berets, underclothes, towels etc., and lectures on hygiene, etc., and the purpose of our duties in the Royal Air Force and which trade we could choose to perform. When all that was completed, we were sworn in to be loyal to Queen and Country.

From Cardington we were selected into groups of about two hundred and fifty men and sent to various basic training camps in and around the Midlands. Our intake was sent to RAF West Kirby, the most God forsaken place in the north of England, an old Military hospital on the end of the Wirral looking out over the mudflats of the misty and murky Mersey. Here I did all my basic training. This was an extremely tough and exhausting experience. We were taught and disciplined to look after ourselves and our fellow men, we were drilled, marched from 6 a.m. until 9-10 p.m., in between having lectures on all aspects of health and how to keep ourselves free of ailments and diseases (as we could be sent to anywhere in the world). Physical fitness training involved route marches of up to twenty miles in full battledress and equipment and five and ten mile runs. We were also taught how to use and look after rifles, Sten and Bren guns. Our clothes and living quarters were always immaculate and ready for inspection by 6 a.m. each day. It was eight weeks of continual verbal abuse and humiliation from the corporals, sergeants and the NCOs, who were in charge of each platoon of about twenty men. It certainly sorted out the very few boys from the men, and we were all respected by our seniors at the end of Basic Training.

I was sent to RAF Weeton near Blackpool, where I had been selected to train as a Motor Transport Driver. This took a further six weeks training, and though I had a full civilian driving licence I had to take a course on driving large vehicles up to 20 tons unladen weight. This course included general servicing of vehicles and their maintenance. We used Hillman Minx saloons and the original Bedford Q.L.s (Quadra Lateral) 4 wheel drive and Austin Six ton tilted lorries. We had civilian Ministry of Transport driving instructors, and also lectures on safety, etc. I learnt a great deal for my personal knowledge on this course which has helped me in later years. I was also sent to Lichfield in Staffordshire for a ten day course on the heavy vehicles, i.e. A.E.C. Matadors and Leyland Hippos, which included driving with long load trailers and reversing trailers into small and difficult positions and driving and reversing articulated vehicles.

I was then posted to RAF Honington in Suffolk, HQ of 94 M.U. commonly known as a bomb dump, which had numerous satellite stations at Barnham, Old Buckenham and Hockering in Norfolk and Great Ashfield in Suffolk. These were disused WWII airfields with thousands of tons of bombs stacked and stored on the runways and standings. From these satellite stations we supplied and tested bombs for the RAF bases throughout the world. We delivered to the docks at Tilbury, Southampton, Portsmouth and Liverpool. We also delivered to and collected for the underground bases such as the quarries at Matlock in Derbyshire, Chilmark and Dinton in Wiltshire. These journeys always took place in the hours of darkness. They were also very long journeys at slow speed with the RAF police escorts, usually using twenty ton Leyland Hippos with a twenty ton trailer or twenty ton A.E.C. Matadors. It was very tiring as there were no motorways in the 1950s. We also took live ammunition to the Royal Ordinance Factory at Altringham in Cheshire, making overnight stops at Hindustan Barracks in Leicester, home of the Leicestershire Regiment. I travelled most of England and Wales during the short stay at RAF Honington; 94 M.U. was a very busy base and covered most of the UK. At the age of eighteen years we were driving vehicles of a capacity that was unheard of in civilian life.

*Julien on his bed at RAF Weeton,
near Blackpool,
in September 1954.
V.Nicholls collection.*

Late in 1954 a rail strike took place and we drivers of 94 M.U. were given the task of delivering mail to the big towns and cities which normally went by rail. I did overnight runs from London to Bristol and Bath, sleeping during the day time. This went on for about two weeks.

In January 1955 I was posted to the B.A.O.R. (British Armies of the Rhine) in Germany. My journey went as follows: by train from Castle Cary to Paddington, Paddington to Harwich in Essex, troopship to the Hook of Holland (Hoek van Holland), train again through Holland into north west Germany to RAF Eioch intransit unit, from which I was posted to RAF Geilenkirchen. Travelling alone I arrived at Geilenkirchen village by train complete with my belongings in a kit bag, a back pack and two suit cases; all that I needed for six months. Geilenkirchen station (Banhoff) had been very damaged during the war and I noticed all the bullet and shell pit holes in the building itself and it looked a very war ravaged place. I was met by an airman driving a Volkswagen Kombi, khaki in colour and marked 2 TAF. Geilk. The driver was L.A.C. Frank Edwards, a Welshman from Tenby who became a very good friend. We lived in the same billet and he was still at Geilenkirchen when I returned from my tour of duty in Cyprus after the Suez crisis in 1956/1957. At the base I had to book into all the departments, i.e. Guardroom, Medical, Mess, Living Quarters, HQ, Transport, etc., to notify them I was there. Collecting all new bedding and finding my living quarters was a hard task in a completely new land. I was glad to have a shower and a good night's sleep as I had been on the move for about five days and nights.

The first job I had at Geilenkirchen was to drive the RAF Regiment Guard around, mainly to its fuel distillations and bomb dump on the far side of the airfield which bordered no-mans land; also the planes and hangers, and the complete boundary of the base, including the married quarters. Duty consisted of four hours on and four hours off – it lasted seven days and also gave me an insight of driving on the other side of the road without going on main roads. The nights were about sixteen hours of darkness and with only eight hours of daylight I really had no idea what the base looked like other than it was so very flat and sparsely covered with fir trees, the ground was very marshy and it was not long before I realised the base was built on a bog. There was a continuous gurgle of frogs that lived there in their millions.

Julien with an English Leyland Hippo at the Motor Transport Yard in March 1957. V.Nicholls collection.

Julien, at left, with some of his pals at the Geilenkirchen base.
V.Nicholls collection.

My first journey outside the base was when I took the short bus ride to Geilenkirchen village to have a look around and to see what Germany was like. In fact I was not very impressed; the village was drab and dirty and required a lot of rebuilding. The second time out was with Flight Sgt. Jones, (he came from Bristol) and was the Sgt. c/c of our motor transport section. He took me to Wuppertal in one of the fuel tankers which required specialist work done. We spent the day looking around the town, riding on its overhead rail system. I was beginning to like Germany for the first time.

To get me used to driving on the right hand side of the road I was next given the privilege of driving a 6 ton Magirus Deutz covered lorry, together with four other similar lorries to RAF Butzwielerhof near Cologne (Koln) on what was known as the "ration run". This was an early start, 4 am, we went on the 100 mile round journey to collect rations for the day, returning to base around noon. This daily journey, which I did for about four weeks, gave me a lot of experience of driving on the open roads of the continent and also in the city of Cologne.

Everything at Geilenkirchen was mobile, i.e. on wheels; mobile medical centre, mobile cookhouse, mobile offices, mobile aircraft contact tower and a mobile oxygen producing unit (which in some way involved me). Geilenkirchen supplied most of the B.A.O.R. and TAF with oxygen, therefore this gave me the opportunity to see a great deal of Germany, Belgium, Holland, Denmark and France. I visited most of the RAF and Army bases in the B.A.O.R. Often when delivering to RAF Gatow in Berlin, having to pass through the Russian Zone of eastern Germany we were held up by the Russians, sometimes up to three days, insisting our paperwork was out of order, but it was always in perfect order. The oxygen cylinders we hauled on Leyland Hippo lorries and twenty ton trailers, a total weight of about 60 tons at a max. speed of 48 kph, (30mph). We drove thousands of miles weekly to keep our British aircraft on 24 hour Red Alert.

Between our long distance journeys we had to do spells driving tankers, refuelling aircraft on the base at Geilenkirchen. As we operated 24 hours a day, our aircraft Hunters, on No. 3 and No. 234 Squadrons and Swifts on No 2 Squadron flew patrols continuously. We who were on the refuelling of aircraft, and ground crews, all worked 13 hour shifts every day or night, with every 8th day off. Wherever the squadrons were on exercise we went with them, and operated in the same manner as we did at Geilenkirchen, working with whatever NATO force we were involved with in Germany, France, Belgium, Holland or Denmark and our American allies. We all worked extremely hard and long hours. With self imposed discipline, we kept ourselves clean and fit and we did most of our laundry. Our food was good and plentiful; this was prepared by RAF chefs and German outworkers as servers and peace was kept in Europe during the very difficult days of the Cold War period.

Between 1956 and 1957 was the Suez crisis and I was with others called from duty in Germany to serve in Cyprus, where drivers for refuelling aircraft were needed. We grouped together at RAF Wildenrath which was about 20 miles from Geilenkirchen and here we were fitted out with khaki drill uniforms and flew off in old Sterling troop carriers to RAF Nicosia in Cyprus, stopping on the way to refuel in Malta. Some of us had a quick look around Valetta harbour and if I remember correctly, we had a 24 hour stop. The ground crew I worked with was mainly made up from men who were serving in B.A.O.R. and/or recalled from civilian life, as we all had a reserve period to be called upon. I worked as a tanker driver refuelling aircraft, which I had done frequently at Geilenkirchen, together with my old pals Ted Green and Bill Hill. We returned to Portsmouth in March 1957 on the aircraft carrier HMS Bulwark after a rather stormy cruise which I did not enjoy. From Portsmouth we had to return to base. I returned to RAF Geilenkirchen in Germany together with Ted Green and Bill Hill. We were all overdue for demob, and I finally returned to England in a similar way as I left, just over two years previously, travelling by train from the old Geilenkirchen Banhof to the Hoek van Holland via Harwich to RAF Innsworth in Gloucestershire where we were finally demobbed. I was still on a reserve call-up period for three years for which I was paid one shilling a day. I also had a choice of whether to accept a suit of clothes and overcoat etc., or £8 in cash. I took the cash as the clothes looked very similar and cheap.

Julien's RAF badges and a uniform button.
V.Nicholls collection.

The National Service Medal awarded to Julien. These medals were made available on application in recent years in recognition of the tremendous contribution made by National servicemen and women to the defence of the realm.
V.Nicholls collection.

Clarks at Castle Cary

Clarks at Castle Cary by Julien Nicholls

Footwear component manufacturing in Castle Cary was conducted under various names:- Avalon Leatherboard Co. Ltd, Strode Components Ltd, Avalon Components Ltd, and Clarks International but always owned by the Clarks Shoe Company of Street. It was one of a group of companies known as Avalon Industries, which was set up to manufacture most of the requirements needed in the footwear trade generally; the factories were established in seven local towns on eight sites.

In 1955 the Avalon Leatherboard Company needed extra space to increase their production of blended insoles and insole strips, and rented the old mill buildings at Higher Flax Mills, owned at that time by T. S. Donne and Co. In April 1956 production started and by the end of the year twenty five people were employed in rather cramped conditions. By 1959 the purchase of the then vacant John Boyd & Co. Horse Hair factory in Upper High Street was being negotiated, and in June 1960 the complete factory set in two acres of land including Ochiltree House was purchased for £8,000, and by August production started. With the ever increasing demand for insoles, insole strips and heel stiffeners, even more production space was required, so in 1964 the Company was able to rent the covered rope walk at Higher Flax Mills at Torbay Road to make stacked heels, some stiffeners and heel fillers, concentrating on insoles and insole strips at the Ansford factory.

By 1967 the final phase of moving board component manufacturing from Street to Castle Cary was completed; machinery and tooling etc., and the conventional stiffener manufacturing was also relocated to the Rope Walk factory.

Now under the name of "Strode Components", Clarks was supplying most footwear manufacturers in the United Kingdom, and exporting throughout the world including Russia and south east Asia.

Heel stiffeners were made from materials mainly suplied by the Avalon Leatherboard Company; they were cut with press knives in right and left foot shapes from flat sheets of board, the edges of the stiffener were 'skived' (i.e. to make thinner) to facilitate suppleness on the top border edge, while the bottom edge was crimped to make it easier to mould; some stiffeners were waxed, but the majority were coated with latex which could be re-activated when the shoe/boot was partly assembled and moulded under heat to the shape of the last.

A product display panel depicting soles, insoles and heel stiffeners, together with examples of shoe designs, from 1986. LHG collection.

The Insoles were made mainly of two types:-

(a) 'Through insoles' were cut with press knives from a sheet of insole board, also mainly supplied by the Avalon Leatherboard Company, and used in men's and children's boots and shoes.

(b) 'Blended insoles' were much more complex, and made from two types of insole board, one hard and one flexible, jointed in the waist of the foot, and then moulded according to the height of the heel, with a steel shank attached to give it strength; fashion and colour always determining the eventual finish.

By 1970 the combined workforce on both sites was nearing 200 men and women, and was using in the region of 180 tonnes of insole and stiffener board weekly, together with some 300 gallons of various adhesives/latex, approximately 5 tonnes of steel shanks, which made a weekly output from both factories of 100,000 pairs of blended insoles, 40,000 pairs of through insoles, 50,000 pairs of stiffeners, 20,000 pairs of resin soles, plus 10,000 insole strips for the outside customers, supplemented by a factory at Great Harwood in Lancashire supplying most of the small boot and shoemakers in the Rossendale Valley under the control of Castle Cary, with some of the Castle Cary workers moving to work at Great Harwood and a few others travelling to work there on a weekly basis.

A new factory named the Crendon Building, mainly constructed by local builder, Chas H. Clothier, was built at Ansford in 1971 - 1972 to cope with production of the many new types of insoles in various materials, styles, colours and finishes required to keep up with fashions of that period.

In 1972 as a result of industrial disputes and strikes causing problems with the power supply to homes and industry throughout the country, the Government under the leadership of Edward Heath put all industry on a three day working week; within a few days Avalon purchased and installed two generators (one mobile on an old Albion lorry) both with an output of electricity sufficient to run most of the machines required to keep production almost uninterrupted on both sites, or when general power failures occurred.

The wooden last store in the Crendon Building at the Ansford factory.
LHG collection.

Staff and visitors at the open day in June 1986.
LHG collection.

By 1979 - 1980 the recession in the United Kingdom generally had forced many footwear manufacturers out of business; Avalon was also under pressure mainly caused by cheap footwear imported from eastern Europe and economies had to be made. The Great Harwood factory was closed completely with its production transferred to Castle Cary, which together with rationalization between the Rope Walk, Donnes and Ansford factories, permitted the use of the comparatively new Crendon Building for the last and model making production, relocated from Street on a greatly reduced capacity in August 1981. Even so it filled the Crendon Building with very complicated and expensive machinery, and the men were very skilful in their own right. Hard Rock Canadian maple was used to make the original last models, these were made by hand, and from them bulk production lasts were copied, turned on copying lathes from specially moulded polyethylene (plastic) blocks, pale blue to identify their manufacture by Clarks. The lathes on which they were turned were of Italian origin and were capable of turning two left and two right foots in one simple operation. There were eight of these lathes in daily use, all the material turned off the plastic block was automatically extracted from the lathes to be recycled into future blocks, and when the style of any of the lasts went out of fashion these too were returned from the shoemaking factories to be dismantled and the plastic recycled.

In 1981 Ochiltree House was completely restored to be used as offices and showrooms for the marketing arm. Avalon Shoe Supplies also relocated from Street, and the Company was renamed Avalon Components. For several years business stability was achieved, and in the early 1980s Avalon Components purchased the covered rope walk at Higher Flax Mills from Donnes for £75,000; concentrating on the manufacture of resin soles for ladies shoes, heel stiffeners, and insole strips to be used at Ansford, and other non company manufacturers.

On the 12th June 1986 a public 'Open Day' was held to demonstrate how the company was run, with guided tours provided for groups of visitors to see employees at their work and machines in operation. Several hundred attended and were evidently most impressed with all they saw on both sites. By the end of the decade, however, the company as a whole was able to obtain its own branded footwear made far more economically in Portugal, Italy, Brazil and India where overheads were far cheaper than in England.

In July 1990 all manufacturing at the Rope Walk factory ceased and many employees were made redundant from both the Ansford and Castle Cary sites. The marketing division was also closed, and the supply of outside customers discontinued. During the following two years, decline of the business now trading as 'Clarks International' was rapid, and in 1993 footwear component manufacturing transferred to the actual shoe making factories, and the last making department re-located to Street where it originally started. The old John Boyd Horse Hair Factory and the new Crendon factory at Ansford were then sold; the covered Rope Walk factory at Higher Flax Mills being retained by Clarks, the parent company, and used as a machinery store. The other member companies of the old Avalon Industries were either sold or closed during the late 1980s and 1990s.

The covered rope walk, off Torbay Road. LHG collection.

Julien at his desk in the purchasing office at the Ansford Factory, shortly before its closure in 1992. LHG collection.

A Cary Childhood by Graham Wheelan

I first came to Castle Cary in 1948, as my mother was employed as cleaner, cook and bottle washer, looking after Miss Ricardo at Phelps House in the High Street. We soon made friends in the town, amongst the first were the Ashers at the bakery in the High Street, where Jean became a close friend of my mother. I used to play in the garden at Phelps House, riding my bike with solid tyres and spoiling the flowers. Ray Collings' father didn't smile much and didn't like to see me on my bike. One of my friends, Douglas Paul, had a summer house out the back and it used to go round on balls; it would go round and round. One day I put Douglas in the summer house and shut the door - I thought he would like to go round in it - and I moved it round gently, then a little faster and then pushed it round and round. Then when I stopped it I couldn't see him, and there he was on the floor with all the chairs!

Graham, back row, fourth from right, at Castle Cary Primary School in Mrs. Hill's class.
G.Wheelan collection.

I used to go to Cary School and on the way home there was a stream that used to go down through Fore Street. We used to try to walk up there with our shoes on without the water going up over the top of our shoes. That wasn't easy and I didn't manage that very well. My mother wasn't very pleased as I got my feet soaking wet. My mother got ill and one day she said to me, "I've got to go away, I'm not very well, you'll have to go to Mrs. Asher's and then you've probably got to go away to a home". I suppose I was about 6 to 6 1/2 years old. So I said goodbye to mother and went to the Ashers'. Someone came to collect me the next day and I went to Cardiff.

The home was a largish place, lots of children did like you did in those homes, and Saturdays used to come round and we all had to go into the playroom and stand up, and a man and a woman would come in and walk up and down and pick somebody out - I'd think, that's funny - perhaps they smiled. So the next Saturday I smiled and they picked me. I was really chuffed! They took me out for the whole day, I couldn't eat all the sweets. I was taken to the park. We wouldn't go out of the home otherwise. I was there about 4 months at that time.

Then Matron called me into her office and she said, "I've got some bad news for you, your mother has died". Well, you know what it's like if you say that to a child - it breaks their heart, and that's what it did to me. Then within a few minutes she said, 'the people who brought you here - Mrs. Asher - have offered to have you home for a week's holiday.' Well, the tears just stopped - like bang - so they came and picked me up. There was no bridge then across the Severn, just the ferry which used to take about 4 - 5 cars and you went down this slope to get onto it. Well we managed to get on to it and came to Cary. Lovely! They showed me to my room - it was like heaven, lovely to be in a room on my own. During the week I heard someone say, "We ought to keep him, didn't ought to send him back". I didn't say anything, so I really behaved myself and didn't do anything wrong and made sure everything was right. Then it came to, "We're going to keep you another week", and I said, "Oh, that's lovely, thank you". So I stayed another week. The weeks went on and next time they said, "We've decided you're going to stay". So that was it then. It was wonderful. So I had to join Cary school. All my mates were there and we went back to playing in the stream. I called Mr. and Mrs. Asher mother and father in the end. They used to ask me to go down to Parsons' - they'd run out of milk for the cafe. I had a bike with pumped up tyres and that was lovely, so I'd have a basket and ride the bike. Of course in those days there weren't many cars on the road, which was a good job. I cycled on down Fore Street and the stream was there which we used to try and walk back up. Well, my basket caught under my knee. Where did my bike land? Down in the stream and there I was laid in the stream with the bike on top of me. Someone in one of the shops came out and picked me up and took me in, and they must have rung up Ashers. Joan Sampson used to work in the shop and she came down to get me, bike as well.

Graham, aged 15, on holiday in Castle Cary.
G.Wheelan collection.

Graham at Dr. Barnardo's at Southborne.
G.Wheelan collection.

After some time Mr. and Mrs. Asher were no longer able to look after me, so I was taken to Castle Cary station, where a label was tied on me and I travelled to Paddington station. Here a kind lady met me and took me across London and put me on a train to Kent, where another lady met me and took me to Dr. Barnado's at Southborne - it was a big house at the end of a drive with many other boys staying there. My education was not very good, but I got on well with the other boys and stayed there until I was sixteen, when I was told I must get a job.

I said I wanted to work on a farm in Somerset, but was sent to Burton Bradstock in Dorset, and settled in quite well. One day the farmer asked me if I could drive a tractor - I couldn't, so he said he would teach me. We went out into the yard, and there was a Massey Ferguson tractor, and the farmer showed me the gears and how to start it. Next day I took the tractor up the track, and when I had to come down thought I would cross the track as it was quicker, but got stuck, and had to tell the farmer - he wasn't very pleased, but I managed to get it out alright.

One day he wanted me to spread some fertilizer - it was basic slag, so I went out in the field and threw it about, not being very particular because I thought it wouldn't show. A week or so later he asked me what I had done with the fertilizer, and called me out to the field to look, as the grass and weeds were growing in patches, while in the areas I had missed there was nothing, so he was not very pleased.

Later he said that I had killed his cockerel, which I denied, but he insisted and the Welfare Officer came to mediate, saying I should have admitted I killed it, but I insisted I had not. The upshot was that he had to find me another job, this time just outside Chilcompton. Here I got on quite well, and eventually bought myself a BSA 125 motorbike, something I had wanted for some time. One day, coming back to the farm I overshot the gateway and finished up in a ditch. I stayed on this farm for several years, and then moved to a farm near Evershot - this looked alright but I was working all hours, sometimes finishing cleaning out the cows at midnight.

I moved on and got a job with a builder in Castle Cary, and was happy to be back in the town, later changing my job and working in Clarks factory until made redundant, when I returned to the building trade and also helped with the bingo at the Constitutional Club.

One day my wife and I were going to Cardiff on the coach to do some Christmas shopping when we got as far as Evercreech and were diverted, as there was an accident on Prestleigh Hill - the road was blocked and the Air Ambulance had been called. I said to my wife that was going to spoil some ones' Christmas; we continued across the bridge to Cardiff and had a good days shopping and had only been home a few minutes when the 'phone rang, it was my eldest daughter, who had been trying to contact us, as her husband had been in a van involved in the Prestleigh accident, and had been taken to Taunton by Air Ambulance and was in intensive care. Fortunately he recovered. As a result of this incident I became involved in fund raising for the Air Ambulance service.

Several months later I had a big birthday and my wife and I said we didn't want any presents, so we had an evening at the Constitutional Club and asked people to put some money in the box - we raised a lot of money and then thought about holding a Bingo event at the Club - we were overwhelmed with help and raised over £1,000 for the Air Ambulance. My wife and I joined the organisation and took a stand at many shows selling raffle tickets and signing up new members. At one of the open days at Henstridge Aerodrome a young lady in a wheelchair came up to me - I didn't recognise her but she remembered me working for a builder on the Unique factory at Evercreech. A lorry had shed a load of blocks on her at Shepton Mallet, and it was thanks to the Air Ambulance she had survived. She was but one of many examples that make me proud to help the organization.

Taking part in a three-legged race up Lodge Hill, from the Two Swans, Graham is sixth from the left. G.Wheelan collection.

Dimmer Tip by Ray Boyer

The land which the present tip occupies was commandeered by the government at the outbreak of war because of the type of sub-soil; the idea was that in the event of bombing the clay would prevent explosions from spreading and any bombs falling away from the bunkers would go into deep clay. The land taken was farmed by Charles Foot of Dimmer Farm and by P. D. Boyer of Cockhill. Well Farm at Alford was acquired at a later date. There were about 30 bunkers, each split into 4 sections served by a roadway at one end and railway at the other, connected by a link to the main line, where a signal box was built. Yeovilton airbase was built at the same time.

After the end of the war a consortium of local farmers tried to buy the site but on government orders the local council at Wincanton were given the first option, and used it for rubbish dumping; this was taken over by SCC who established Wyvern Waste.

Bronzeoake purchased a site adjoining for the purpose of burning cattle, suspected of having mad cow disease, and in the long term converting it to a wood burning electricity generating station. The burner ran for about 3 years and then closed down when the government contract was not renewed, and the long term plan to install a wood burning plant did not take place because of lack of any government support.

Alastair Todd who had negotiated with local farmers then retired and the local liason committee was wound up.

A pair of ammunition storage bunkers, built of brick during the early part of World War II, and provided with rail and road access.
LHG collection.

In front of the bunkers was a brick blast wall.
LHG collection.

Brick water tanks were constructed for the immersion of flare and phosphorus bombs.
LHG collection.

The solidly built brick side walls of ammunition bunkers were retained and incorporated in a new depot for building materials by Wyvern Waste.
LHG collection.

A presentation by Martin Ellis, Wyvern Waste manager, of a cheque to Castle Cary Children's Playing Field Fund, with Graham Asher and Judith Pullen from the Town Council.
LHG collection.

Mill Lane Dairy by Eileen Pattle

My grandfather Arthur J. Parsons started up as a dairyman selling milk around Castle Cary by the old method of dipping it from a churn with a measuring ladle into people's jugs.

The milk was fetched from Mr. Coward's farm at Cockhill. I sometimes went down with dad to get it.

After a while the milk was collected from Prideaux's milk factory by the station and later my grandfather was the first to establish a milk bottling plant at the dairy. My brother and I used to watch the milk going down into the bottler from a container on top of the machine, then the bottles were taken off and cardboard tops pressed on by a hand held machine. We used to pinch some of the cardboard tops to make wool pompoms.

The returned empty bottles were washed on a revolving brush and then put into a tank of sterilising solution, while the empty churns were steam sterilised. This all came to an end when milk had to be pasteurised and the bottled milk came delivered by lorry from Oakdale Creameries in Poole. There were 3 grades of milk then - Channel Island being the richest - gold top; red and silver top (Tuberculosis Tested), and silver top.

When we were young we sometimes went to help on the round on a Saturday, if we got up in time for a 6.00 a.m. start. Dad did the Galhampton round, through South Cary and on round to Greenway Road and Victoria Park and then home.

We had to deliver the little milk bottles to the school for the childrens' elevenses and when we reached the Britannia (Horse Pond Inn) dad always had a cup of coffee while he delivered their milk and I would get an iced bun.

In those days dad delivered the milk every day of the week - no lie in on Sundays and I would receive 6d for my help.

A milk bottle from Mill Lane Dairy.
Museum collection.

Memories of Lower Cockhill Farm House

Memories of Lower Cockhill Farm House by Olive Boyer

I was married to Ray Boyer in 1955 and lived in the farmhouse, a place of doom and gloom. It was to me a very old building with no comfort; furniture you bought when you could afford it. From one end to the other seemed a mile, our bedroom was at one end and the bathroom at the other, with this kind of chapel to pass on the way. A couple of bedrooms en-route and at the top of the stairs was a great area which was useless but you had to remember to duck your head.

Downstairs was still a mile long, or so it seemed. There was the larder, then a room with a cold stone floor, big enough for our present kitchen to fit in three times, then a living room with a wooden floor and a hall with a stone floor containing the phone and stairs to the bedrooms. The lounge beyond the hall was rarely used.

Olive found one good feature about the old house in that the cold stone floor quickly cooled heated milk allowing her to skim the clotted cream.
R.&O.Boyer collection.

Between the living room and the kitchen was a closed in area, giving us a dark passage to walk through, we wondered what was inside until one day Ray was told a wedding had taken place many years ago, the two families had fallen out and the remains of one family were in that wall. When fitting a Rayburn cooker in the kitchen the ceiling began to creak, so having no mobile phone at that time I had to go and find Ray who was working with his father - both came and decided something must be done and as a result a big iron girder was fitted to support the ceiling.

Ray worked for his father for a while, then the great day came when the land was divided and we had our own little farm. Grandpa Boyer gave us a few cows and my father who farmed at Lovington did likewise, so we had a very mixed herd. As we had been to Jersey for our honeymoon we fancied the Jersey breed and a Jersey farmer who we had met sent us over enough for a complete herd.

A few years later we had foot and mouth disease suspected at the evening milking. Ray had a job to milk several of the cows as they had blisters on their teats, we had a sleepless night wondering what was going to happen in the morning, when we found things were much worse - the cows that were housed in the shed nearest to Castle Cary all had blisters. We rang the vet who told us Mr. Churchouse of Manor Farm had foot and mouth and they would notify the Ministry immediately. A ministry vet came by 8 am. and confirmed it. We then rang a valuer, Mr. Dare, of Yeovil who soon came. We were advised to go indoors and stay there, so that was the last we saw of our animals, they were all killed and buried by the afternoon. A gang of prisoners were brought from Bristol and the entire farm buildings were scrubbed clean. A policeman was outside to make sure no one came to the farm and we didn't go out - we had a very old television set, so Jack Otton of Castle Cary brought us a new one. After a months quarantine we were allowed to restock and purchased an entire herd from Jersey, sent over by Francis Le Rue.

A few years later we moved to Orchard Farm and sadly my father-in-law died soon after retiring. Grandma Boyer lived in the newer end of Cockhill farmhouse, leaving the older end empty. Gran. would keep the old end tidy and one day she noticed that plaster had fallen off the wall in the old chapel, leaving some sort of painting showing. The milk recorder who came monthly, being interested in older buildings, called and got a specialist from London to have a look at it; soon the house was 'Listed' and Gran. decided to put it on the market. The Land Agents said they had customers from London who would be interested. Mrs. Peppin came to see the house and was very interested, then Will Vaughan arrived with her. This worried Grandma and she didn't want any hanky panky going on in Cockhill, but all turned out well and Gran. was pleased to have Will and Pek in the old end.

Olive with some of the original Jersey cattle – never did she think they were all to be slaughtered because of foot and mouth disease.
R.&O.Boyer collection.

Once again dairy farmers: Mr. and Mrs. R. Boyer, of Cockhill Farm, Castle Cary.

Restocked from the Island

So this is Somerset! Some of the Island-bred Jersey cattle being unloaded at Cockhill Farm, after their long journey by boat and lorry from the Channel Islands.

LIKE many other people, Mr. Raymond Boyer lost his whole Jersey herd in the f-and-m outbreak in Somerset in February. All his 34 head of attested Jerseys went on his 50-acre farm at Castle Cary. With the help of Island breeders he has now stocked up again, with 28 head acquired from 16 herds. Among the 20 in-calf heifers, 5 cows and 3 calves are one G.M. and five S.M. animals.

The change in methods of management to which the Island-bred Jerseys must become accustomed was something they were being broken to gradually. Mr. Boyer still left the headstalls on the first batch to arrive till they had learnt to be driven rather than led.

Since all the cows imported by Mr. Boyer were in-calvers and close to calving there was not a lot of milking to be done at first. This cow, Maureen Revival G.M., was, however, still giving a little milk although due to calve within the month to a 5,000gn bull recently sold for export to Canada.

Following the loss of their herd to foot and mouth disease in 1958, Ray and Olive re-stocked from Jersey.
R.&O.Boyer collection.

A contented Jersey cow and calf in front of the old farmhouse c. 1960.
R.&O.Boyer collection.

The Old House at Lower Cockhill Farm by Pek Peppin

When you leave central Cary along Station Road and then go down Torbay Road you come to Fulford's Cross. If you then head along the North Barrow Road for about a mile you come to Lower Cockhill Farm, a small cluster of buildings facing west. The old farmhouse at Cockhill is a remarkable survival from the middle ages, saved from destructive alterations largely by the addition of a substantial new wing probably in the 18th century. The farming family who lived there would have moved into this warmer and much more comfortable accommodation and the old house was used as over-flow space and for storage. In medieval times the old house would have had three rooms and a cross passage, on one side of which was a two-bay floor-to-roof hall with a central hearth, a store room perhaps used for cattle and on the other side a smaller more private space that may have been a kitchen. The timbers of this original building have a tree-felling date of 1435. Around 1480 the north end of the house was upgraded. An upstairs was either added or improved, and a small timber-framed room was 'jettied' out over the front door. This was a very grand, highly decorated room and with carvings and wall paintings some of which survive to this day.

Around 1600 a first floor was inserted into the open floor-to-roof hall and a chimney was built to replace the central hearth. Serious modernisation of the old house seems to have stopped at this point, apart from the thatched roof which was replaced with asbestos tiles around 1920.

We first saw the house in the summer of 1982 - we drove from Sandford Orcas where we were renting a flat, and spotted it as we crossed the railway bridge over the Castle Cary to Weymouth line at Cockhill. We made an appointment to view, and as soon as we both stepped over the threshold we knew that this was 'the one'. We had been house hunting for ages - my father had brought me up to regard Somerset as 'the garden of Eden' from which he had been cast out at the age of 13 and where he yearned for the rest of his life to return. In fact he might have seen Lower Cockhill Farm in the years before the First World War when he travelled by train from Marston Magna where he lived, to Kings School Bruton every day. However those were the days when the trains had no corridors and he and his brother had become the victims of some older girls who used to get on at Castle Cary - and tease the little boys mercilessly. So the brothers had taken to hiding as the train came into Castle Cary Station - either under the seats or in the luggage racks - in the hope that the girls who ran up and down the platform looking for them would fail to spot them; so it is likely that he rarely saw the old house.

When we found it, the house was owned by Mrs. Rosa Boyer and the old part had not been occupied for many years. There were nettles growing up between the flagstones - indoors, and there was damp running down the walls. Mrs. Boyer's son Ray and his wife Olive remembered living in it in the 1950s. Olive particularly did not like it - finding it cold and dark with a spooky corridor between the old and newer wing, and there were stories of a massacre at a wedding feast and it was said that there were bodies bricked up in the old chimney. We knew about this story when we opened the chimney up and were very relieved only to find builders rubble and mouse droppings.

John Peppin, left, with his brothers in 1907.
P.Peppin.

We did not have a survey done. Norman Cant, the local architect who helped us with the conservation work advised us in no uncertain terms that a survey would be a complete waste of money. 'The house has dry rot, wet rot, wood worm, death-watch beetle, rising damp, leaking roof ....' the list went on and on. He added 'Just assume the worst!' and we did.

The main problem was the room that had been added over the front door in around the year 1480 - which Mrs. Boyer had told us was known as 'The Monk's Room'. This was interesting because when we gradually uncovered original wall paintings in this room they turned out to have Christian iconography. In fact it was the discovery of the paintings that decided the Boyers to sell - after a lump of plaster had fallen off the wall in this room revealing primitive paintings underneath, Mrs. Boyer recognised that here was something most unusual and showed it to the man who came monthly to record the milk yield and who was interested in historical buildings. He in turn contacted an expert and the house was 'Listed'.

Structurally this room had major problems - the front wall had fallen off and the area projecting over the front door was supported with screw jacks and railway sleepers. When we entered the room we could actually feel the floor shifting. To make the conservation of the paintings possible, first we had to make the structure safe ... and these two things were extremely difficult to achieve largely because the wall paintings were done straight onto the mud of the wattle and daub walls. This meant that to save the paintings we had to remove the entire wall with the paintings on it - in order to construct a false wall behind to take the weight of the roof. Needless to say we had to employ experts both to advise us and to do the work.

Lower Cockhill Farm in the 1920s, showing the original, lower, section to the right, with the jettied room covered in render. The portion to the extreme left is a seventeenth or eighteenth century addition.
A.V.Pearse collection.

The interior of the Hall, now open to the roof as originally constructed, showing smoke blackened jointed crucks and wind-braces, dating back to 1435.
P.Peppin.

The detail of how this was done is not for this account. All we need to say is that we now have two almost complete walls of paintings dating from around 1480. My husband Will Vaughan has been researching why a farmhouse like ours should have such a very unusual addition and while he has found some interesting information we do not yet have the complete story.

The farmhouse when it was built in the 15th. century was on an important road - a drovers' road along which the farmers would have brought their livestock to sell in the town (the market charter for Cary was granted in 1468) - it is well positioned having two water sources - the river Cary outside the front (Mrs. Boyer remembered there being a beach so that the cattle could drink - it has since been embanked) and a well at the back. The soil is also extremely good.

It seems that the old house was built in the 1430s by the Lord of the Manor of Cary who at that time was the Lord Zouche. It would have been an estate house built for a tenant farmer ... during the Wars of the Roses the Lord Zouche fought on the Yorkist side - which may account for the carved six-petalled rose (that was originally painted white) to be seen in the ceiling of the painted room. When the Yorkists were defeated at the battle of Bosworth the Lord Zouche - who fought in this battle and had his possessions confiscated - went to live in Stavordale Priory where, when he died a few years later, he asked in his will for a chapel to be built - dedicated to the Name of Jesus. Interestingly the painted room in the farmhouse seems to have a similar dedication as the main motif of the wall-paintings is the monogram IHC which stands for the Name of Jesus.

The conservation of the house has taken us many years and it will probably never be finished. It has been a long and exciting journey during which we have made many fascinating discoveries (such as the central hearth in the Hall; the wattle supporting the original thatch). We have tried to preserve every original feature even if it means living with worm eaten woodwork and crumbling plaster. Two years were spent in a caravan in the garden which brought adventures of its own such as the chemical toilet splitting one winter and Will's quartz watch freezing solid. Our children (the elder of whom once refused to get out of the car because of the smell of manure from the adjacent farmyard ...) have had strange experiences throughout their childhoods such as being bathed in a twin tub washing machine.

It was a great privilege to have known Mrs. Boyer who lived next door. She told us stories of the house in the more recent past - how they used to scrub the flagstones on their hands and knees every day, the endless brushing to get the mud off long skirts and coats, the making of tisty-tosties (balls of cowslips made by young women) in the spring - all told with humour and enthusiasm. At first she was worried because my husband and I sometimes used separate surnames - she didn't want any hanky-panky going on next door so hearing that we had been married for years came as a great relief to her!

A view of the jettied room, as restored, and with the cement render removed.
P.Peppin.

The interior of the painted room, showing the exposed and conserved wall paintings with their Christian iconography.
P.Peppin.

A Tale of Two Houses

**Notes on the history of two cottages in Castle Cary
by Chris Hicks**

Castle Cary has some unusual and striking buildings but much of the town consists of houses that are very typical of the simple cottages built in Somerset and elsewhere in the South West over the last few hundred years. Often the history of these houses is difficult to establish as many have been altered and extended. Original features have been hidden or removed and relatively few have surviving deeds or other documents. I have been fortunate to be able to piece together the linked history of two of these houses and some of the people who lived in them.

On the outskirts of Castle Cary is a small cluster of houses marked on some maps as 'Townsend.' Although some books apply this name just to the houses at the top of North Street, in others it also encompasses the houses running south alongside the main Wincanton to Shepton Mallet road. Built over a period of some two hundred years, two of the houses – The Cottage and Tor View - have a shared history as revealed by various documents, some in Castle Cary Museum and others with the current owners.

The two houses occupy a narrow strip of land on the eastern side of the road with the field known as Higgins' Close immediately behind. This strip appears to have been separate from the field for a considerable time; hedge dating techniques suggest approximately three hundred years. It probably owes its origin to the fact that in the days before proper metalled roads the tracks would become so muddy that they gradually widened across the adjoining fields. In time this often left pieces of land that were occupied by squatters and in time their rights became so established that houses could then be built with gardens

'The Cottage', built of Cary stone with coped gables and slated roof in the early nineteenth century. The extension and windows are modern.
C.L.Hicks.

running parallel to the road. In the 1673 manuscript map of Castle Cary the field is shown extending right to the road which would indicate that land was divided in the late seventeenth or early eighteenth century [The original map is in the British Library, with a facsimile copy in the Castle Cary Museum. On the map the field is spelt variously as Higens Close or Higings Close].

The land was originally split into two separate plots. Then for about a century the land was owned as a single entity before being split once again. The earliest written record dates from 1801 and indicates that the northern section had been owned by Stephen Small since around 1755 and here he had created what he calls a garden from some waste ground. In 1801 the southern section was purchased for the sum of 5 guineas from Job A'Court by Stephen's son John Small.

The Cottage

When Stephen died in 1808 his land passed to his wife Alice and then to his son John, thus joining the two pieces together. Sometime between then and 1830 he built the house now known as The Cottage or Cary Hill Cottage, taking out a mortgage from Priscilla Barker for £40. The document recording this suggests that the house had been built some years previously but does not give a precise date. The house is a very simple one, built not unnaturally from the local Cary stone. The mortgage was increased to £70 in 1837 and transferred to James Stockman.

John Small died in 1848 but it took five years for his will to be probated as there appears to have been some dispute about the validity of some of the wording. He bequeaths one feather bed to his daughter Sarah, and his 'best feather bed' to another daughter Maria. The house is left to his wife Hannah and on her death to his two sons Henry and George. In fact because probate was so long delayed, Hannah had died by the time the matter was resolved and the house passed directly to the sons.

Intriguingly in the will, John carefully states that the northern half of the house should go to Henry and the southern half to George. He further states that if there should be any dispute between them they are to build a party wall down the middle of the house. Quite what this says about the family relationship is not clear! In the event the two sons avoided any dispute, selling the house within months of the probate being granted to John Pond, one of the executors of the will, for around £110.

Following John Pond's death in 1864, the house was inherited by his two daughters and son-in law Hannah Pond and Zaccheus and Elizabeth Forse. Sold at auction for £162, it was bought by James White, one of the Cary horsehair manufacturers who in 1870 took over Matthews's old factory on Bailey Hill. Nine years later, in 1875, he sold the house to Charles Howell for £175.

The final sale that is relevant to this story takes place in 1904, when the cottage was bought by H. J. D. Barker for £250. At this point the land was once again divided so that in 1906 Mr. Barker could build the house now known as Tor View on the northern portion.

'Tor View', built of brick in 1906 and now rendered and painted, demonstrates the ascendancy of mass produced building materials facilitated by improved transport links, over vernacular traditions.
C.L.Hicks.

Tor View

The new house was again very simple. In the 1911 census it is described as having six rooms. This suggests that there were two rooms at the front on the ground floor, with two bedrooms above plus two further rooms, probably a kitchen and scullery on the ground floor at the rear. All trace of these two rooms has been lost with subsequent alterations. The first owner, in 1908, was Wallace Couzens who paid £200. To finance the purchase he took out a mortgage from a Mr. Weech. However Mr. Weech died within a year and the mortgage was transferred by his executors to Mrs. Mary Jones. A further transfer occurred in 1927 when the debt was assumed by Miss A. A. Naish. Mr. Couzens finally paid off the remaining debt in 1942. Mr. Couzens is still remembered in Castle Cary. One resident remembers visiting the house as child and recalls how nice the garden was.

Wallace Couzens was a railway worker for the Great Western Railway all his life. Following in the footsteps of his father Frederick, he began as a 'lad porter' and worked his way up to signalman working at various stations in the region but mainly at Castle Cary. The company records show that in 1910 he was reprimanded by the loss of bonus for 'causing the derailment of four trucks'; however in the following year he was 'commended' but no details are given. Mr. Couzens died in 1949 having lived in the house for some 41 years, and his son then sold Tor View, as the house was by then known, to Mrs. A. I. B. Butt who lived there from 1950 until 1963. The next owners, who paid £3,500, built a garage at the end of the garden. They also obtained a legal agreement that allowed them vehicle access to the road at a cost of £2 per year. Clearly prior to this only pedestrian access had been needed. In 1967 they also applied for permission to build another house in the garden. However this request was turned down by the planning authorities on the grounds that the plot is too narrow and that there is poor access to the road. At some stage, probably in the 1960s, the house was much enlarged with more bedrooms being added above the rear.

Between 1974 and 1986 the house changed hands no less than six times, involving, in one case, an exchange with another house in Castle Cary. Three of the sales all took place within a two year period with the price of the house climbing up to £52,000. The last of these owners stayed for some twenty years undertaking various improvements before finally selling the house in 2008.

Sources:
House deeds for both properties held in Castle Cary Museum and by the current owners.
Great Western Railway employment records

Some Early Memories

Some Early Memories by Valerie Nicholls

Ansford School Days

In 1950 at the age of 11, I went to Ansford Secondary Modern School. This seemed very large to me after the Junior school. We were placed in new class groups according to our abilities, by means of a written test. I went into 1A with a whole new group of boys and girls, mainly from surrounding villages. Most of us stayed together in our original groups throughout our schooling, which ended in form 4A at the age of 15.

Moving into different rooms for various studies was new to all of us. How well I remember the home-craft room at the top of the steps of the quadrangle. One of our first lessons there was shoe cleaning. The needle-craft room was on the opposite side of the quadrangle and here we made our cookery aprons and caps under the guidance of Miss Brown. I think the boys did gardening with Mr. Steer and woodwork with Mr. Smith while we had these lessons. Mr. Steer took the remains of the school dinners home with him in a dustbin tied to the boot of his car; he used this to feed his pigs.

We had assembly in the hall every morning and firstly had our hands and shoes inspected on the way to and from the playground. I enjoyed starting the days with prayers and hymns. All the school staff would be on the stage in front of us. We had respect for all our teachers and the prefects who also kept us in order. There was no running around the quadrangle and we walked in single file. Anyone in trouble in class was sent to stand outside the door, or worse, sent to the headmaster.

I sang in the school choir, which was under the direction of Mr. Collett. I remember singing the National Anthem unaccompanied when he auditioned me. We used to sing in all the school concerts and always ended by singing the school song; "Bless this House".

When we were thirteen, we had another opportunity to sit an entrance examination to grammar school, called the 13-plus examination. In those days there were far more pupils passing the written exam than places available (unless parents were prepared to pay), so if you were one of those successful in the written exams (as I was), you then had to go to Sunny Hill School, Bruton for an interview. I went with my mother by taxi as there was no other transport (pupils who passed, cycled to Sunny Hill or Sexey's schools). When we arrived at Sunny Hill we were all ushered in to a waiting room together and each girl was called, in turn, to be interviewed by the Headmistress and all the school governors, who were seated around a very large refectory table. I had to sit at one end and answer the various questions put to me. There were definitely not enough places for all of us. I was not accepted and at that time, thought little of it but looking back now, I realise just how unfair the system was, as we had all got there on the merits of written work.

I always came out well in most subjects at Ansford School. English composition and spelling were my best ones and we had a very good teacher in Mr. John Harrison. His wife Pat was my first P.E. teacher, her successor was Miss Sage. Mrs. Trickey taught us cookery and she was followed by Janet Vearncombe who later became Mrs. O'Hare. She was a very young and popular teacher with us girls. Her young man, as he was then, was in the R.A.F., and she iced her demonstration Christmas cake with blue icing and a white aeroplane. We were all very impressed. In the 4th year we took turns in pairs to spend a week in the school flat as part of our home craft. We had to cook a meal and invite friends to lunch and at the end of the week two members of staff were entertained. At the end of the 4th year, prior to leaving, I received the home craft prize from Mr. H. T. Gough, the Headmaster. It was a cookery book which I still refer to. I feel that the school stood us all in good stead for whatever life had in front of us, although I know from experience that you are never too old to learn

Valerie in her Ansford School uniform, aged 13 in 1952. V.Nicholls collection.

Ansford School teaching staff during the 1950s.

Henry T. Gough, Headmaster of Ansford Secondary Modern School 1940 – 1958.

Out of school activities were limited - I used to go to St. John Ambulance meetings, but transferred to the Junior Red Cross when I was about 12. These meetings were held in an upstairs room of the Angel Hotel which was owned by Mr. Biss. Mr. Biggs and Cyril Toop were our instructors. Princess Margaret came to Weston Super Mare to inspect us and many other cadets from the area. We all lined up on the beach and she was driven past standing in the back of a Land Rover. On Saturdays, I did shopping for my mother or went to Evercreech on the bus to see a school friend. I used to cycle to Hadspen to see another friend or she would come to Cary to see me. I also used to go shopping for our neighbour Mrs. Bush, when she had her son and daughter-in-law coming down from Bristol; I used to go to Mrs. Turtle in Vaux's bakery shop in the High Street and buy a box of 12 assorted fancy cakes for 2/6d (12 1/2p today).

The coaches from Bristol used to stop here on Saturdays on the way for a day trip to Weymouth. You had to go shopping early as the town quickly filled up. They also used to stop again on the way home in the evenings and the passengers used to queue up for Mr. and Mrs. Taylor's fish and chips. There were no car parks and the coaches used to line up on the side of the road by the Horse Pond, back as far as Fore Street, and on the other side of the road outside the Britannia Hotel.

When I was 14 I started to help Mrs. Chilcott at the Sunday School, which she ran with Miss Elizabeth Corp (Headmistress of the Junior School) and Miss Gladys Corp. Several other young people also helped and there were 60 children in attendance. The Rev. Molesworth was our vicar at that time, I took my first Communion from him on Easter Sunday 1954, having been confirmed in All Saints Church in March that year.

Employment

On leaving school in 1954 at the age of 15, I started work at Tom Trowbridge's drapery and outfitting shop in Fore Street. I still have my first wage packet which contained £1.10.3 (£1.51p) for a working week of 42 1/2 hours. The shop opened at 9 am and closed for an hour between 1 - 2 pm, closing time was 5.30 pm except Friday and Saturday, when it was 6 pm; early closing was on Thursday. The shop and house which belonged to it was three stories high and had a very large garden, which ran up to the bottom of Lodge Hill. Stock was kept on all three floors and we were kept very busy running up and down; there was not much that could not be supplied, from buttons to bed linen. The staff consisted of three young ladies and Frederick Neck who worked part time in the gents. department, though no longer a partner. He had originally been in partnership with Mr. Trowbridge and they had taken over from Joe Tullett.

A Sunday School outing to Weymouth in 1954 with, left to right;- Mrs. Chilcott and Margaret; Valerie (Higgins) with Glenys and Roma Billing; Mrs. Kathleen Ridout with Ann and David.
V.Nicholls collection.

Thomas Trowbridge in the 1950s.

Mr. and Mrs. Trowbridge, on the right, with the shop staff in the garden behind. Back row, from left;- Madeleine Baxter (nee Perrott); Brenda Brewin. Front row;- Ena Lee and Valerie.
V.Nicholls collection.

    As you entered the shop there were open fixtures to the left which held green stock boxes containing ladies underwear of all shapes and sizes. Other fixtures held Bear Brand and Ballito stockings (no tights in those days) and Fitu corsets with bones and laces. A polished wooden counter stood in front of this area. The opposite side housed fixtures and fittings for all the haberdashery; buttons, threads, darning wool and silks for stocking mending, lace of varying widths, some frilled, tape - black and white, bias bindings and ribbons. One small fixture consisted of many small drawers with brass handles. Clarks Anchor stranded embroidery threads were in a three tiered glass topped cantilever box. Knitting wool was sold in 1 oz. hanks which the customer had to wind; this was often done by placing it over two chairs put back to back.

    A door on the right went through to the living quarters and a little further down the shop was a large counter with a brass measure. This was for the curtain materials which were in big open fixtures on the wall behind. Only 36" and 48" widths were available - the 36" was mostly kitchen designs or check gingham in various colours, while the 48" was usually brocades in plain colours, floral patterns or regency stripes. Ladies often brought the measurements of their windows and we could work out how much they required and occasionally cut the length in two pieces so that a pair was ready to sew.

In later years Mr. Trowbridge made up curtains himself using an electric sewing machine in a spare room at the top of the house. We also sold dress materials made by Tootal; dress making was a very popular pastime and quite a few ladies attended Mrs. Win. Chilcotts sewing classes. Ladies knitwear by Donbros and Morley was stocked while another fixture holding towels and tea cloths, etc., was also behind that counter, with chairs placed in front for customers to sit a while.

Half way down the shop was the office, this was square with wooden panels at the base, glazed above with frosted panels at the top. In the front was a small sliding window; inside was a large roll top desk with drawers either side and above this a shelf which held all the ledgers. A large loose leaf ledger was used for all the accounts.

Mr. Trowbridge did a country round, four different journeys once a month, going as far as North and South Cadbury and Queen Camel on the largest one and Lovington area the shortest. Ditcheat area was covered on another week and Keinton Mandeville the next. This involved a lot of work - on Mondays and Tuesdays the orders were collected and booked out, packed up and delivered on Thursday afternoons; everything being discreetly boxed up or wrapped in brown paper and string. On Friday afternoons everything not required was collected and checked off back at the shop.

We also ran a Christmas Club and many people enjoyed coming and choosing their gifts from their yearly savings. Christmas did not start as early in those days and it was quite usual for gifts to be purchased on Christmas Eve, often simple things, like slippers, hankerchiefs, aprons, etc.

At the lower end of the shop open fixtures held ladies shoes. Many of these were made by 'Diana' and catered for the wider foot. There were also Pirelli slippers and gents' and childrens' shoes. Hob nail boots were on the shelves close to the ground and were often found to be growing blue mildew as the place was very damp, so we had to keep them well brushed. At the farthest end of the shop were gents' underwear, pyjamas, socks, ties, etc.

The floor was wooden with lino. through the middle. The first job on a Monday was to wash the floor, this fell to the most junior member of staff.

A paraffin heater at each end of the shop was our only source of heat. The paraffin was fetched from Jack Norris's garage next door. In later years the shop was refurbished, the floor replaced and tiled, and night storage heaters installed.

Turning left at the top of the stairs you came to an open gallery which ran around the area above the gents. department, which had a glass roof. Around the sides of the gallery was shelving which was covered with plain dark green curtains which ran on a brass track, the purpose of which was to keep the stock from fading. There were mens trousers, best and working ones, made from heavy grey flannel or derby tweed and various forms of work wear i.e., bib and brace overalls, boiler suits, overall coats and black oil skins. Wellington boots of varying weights and sizes for all the family were also stocked, in fact every kind of work wear imaginable; even the ladies had cotton flowered overalls, sleeveless and in three sizes and two different styles, either pulled over the head or crossed over in the front and both tied at the back.

At the top of the stairs on the right were cupboards and drawer fitments. One held sheets, pillow cases and feather proof pillow ticks, etc., while another held materials which came in folds, not on blocks i.e., woollen flannel, cheese cloth, butter muslin and calico. Two big drawers were full of ladies hats and these had to be stored carefully in order that they retained their shape. There was always great excitement when the hat company representative called as we had a good excuse to try them on. Alongside another cupboard was a clothes rail which held gents.' sports coats. Suits could be ordered made to measure.

Another room on this floor was the ladies' showroom which was full of rails of coats, suits, dresses, skirts, etc. Customers were escorted there and physically helped into the clothes, opinion passed, advice given, and if necessary hems pinned up ready for alteration by either Gwen Helps or Alice Chamberlain, both of them lived at West Park. Changing seasons and Christian holidays kept us very busy - Easter usually meant a new suit or spring weight coat and of course an Easter bonnet. No lady went to church without a hat or gloves and everyone kept an outfit for Sunday best. A ladies winter coat cost about £6.

On the top floor of the building was a room which held blankets, candlewick and folkweave bedspreads, eiderdowns, pillows, etc., and rugs. The display stands for the windows were also stored there, plus the boxes that goods were delivered in; those being re-used for parcels which Mr. Trowbridge took out on the rounds; all brown paper and string were re-cycled for the same purpose. I should mention that most goods delivered to the shop came by rail to Castle Cary station and brought early every morning in the canvas covered G.W.R. lorry driven by Alby Howard or Mr. Bate. The warehouse in Bristol which phoned for their order every Wednesday made their own deliveries on Thursdays.

Our tasks were many and varied, the outside journeys meant a great deal of preparation, while windows had to be dressed and stock kept tidy and shelves and counters, etc., dusted. The pavement was swept every morning and a schoolboy employed to clean the brass on the shop front.

There was a till in both the gents. and ladies department. These were wooden with a paper roll to write on, with the total added up at the end of each day. We had a tea break mornings and afternoons, which Mr. and Mrs. Trowbridge provided. We used to buy our buns from 'Jock' Lindsay's shop just down the road (now the Co-op); he had a café there with a juke box. If you had to wait to be served there was just time to put 6d in the juke box and hear Slim Whitman or Tommy Steele.

Once a year on a Thursday Mr. Trowbridge would close the shop and hire Jack Norris's taxi to take us all on an outing to Weymouth or Bournemouth and when Mr. and Mrs. Trowbridge took their annual holiday he employed the taxi and driver again; this time for Ena Adams and myself to do the country round. How amusing we must have looked going around the narrow lanes of North Leaze, North Barrow and Baltonsborough, etc., in a big black six seater taxi.

On Christmas Eve the radio was always brought into the shop to hear the carols from King's College chapel and we usually ended the day with a glass of sherry and hot mince pie made by Mrs. Trowbridge. We were always given a small Christmas box in the form of money in an envelope, extra to our wages. Postmen and dustmen were often the recipients of Christmas boxes as they did their rounds, and customers were offered a calendar.

Two days were usual for our Christmas holiday, three if we were lucky enough for it to have fallen on a weekend and we never had New Years Day off, it was not a recognised Bank Holiday then. The New Year saw us starting the stock taking; everything had to be counted, marked and written down, materials measured and rolled back onto the blocks, not always easy.

    At the end of stock taking we prepared for our annual grand sale; this was usually about mid-February. It was popular as there were genuine bargains to be had and customers formed a queue quite early. Once the sale was over everything was tidied up and the new spring stock began arriving ready to start another year. Every day had its own jobs and whatever else came along, we all worked happily together and shared many joys and sorrows with the customers - in fact it was a very happy place to work. The world seemed a happier place to be in, men whistled as they went about their work and I don't remember any talk of unemployment.

Mr. Trowbridge's shop and house in Fore Street, with Jack Norris's Garage adjoining.
LHG collection.

Mrs. Doris Trowbridge, Ena Adams and Valerie at Weymouth on a staff outing in 1956.
V.Nicholls collection.

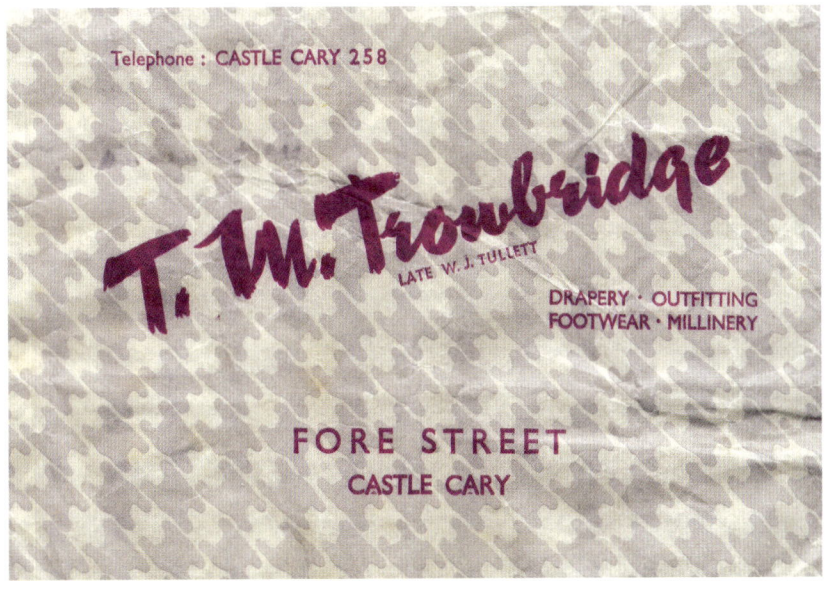

Detail from a Trowbridge's paper bag.
Kay Wilson collection.

A William Tullett advertising brush. Mrs. J.Cox collection.

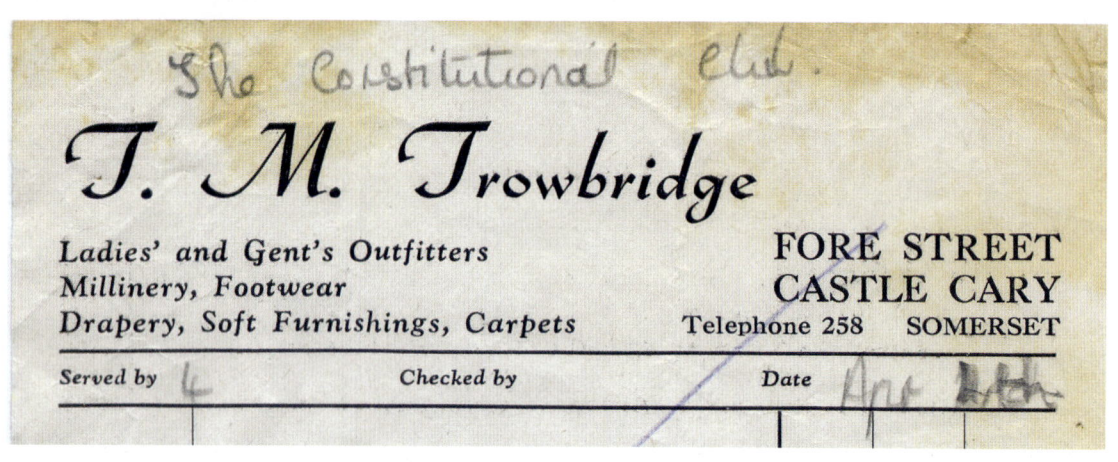

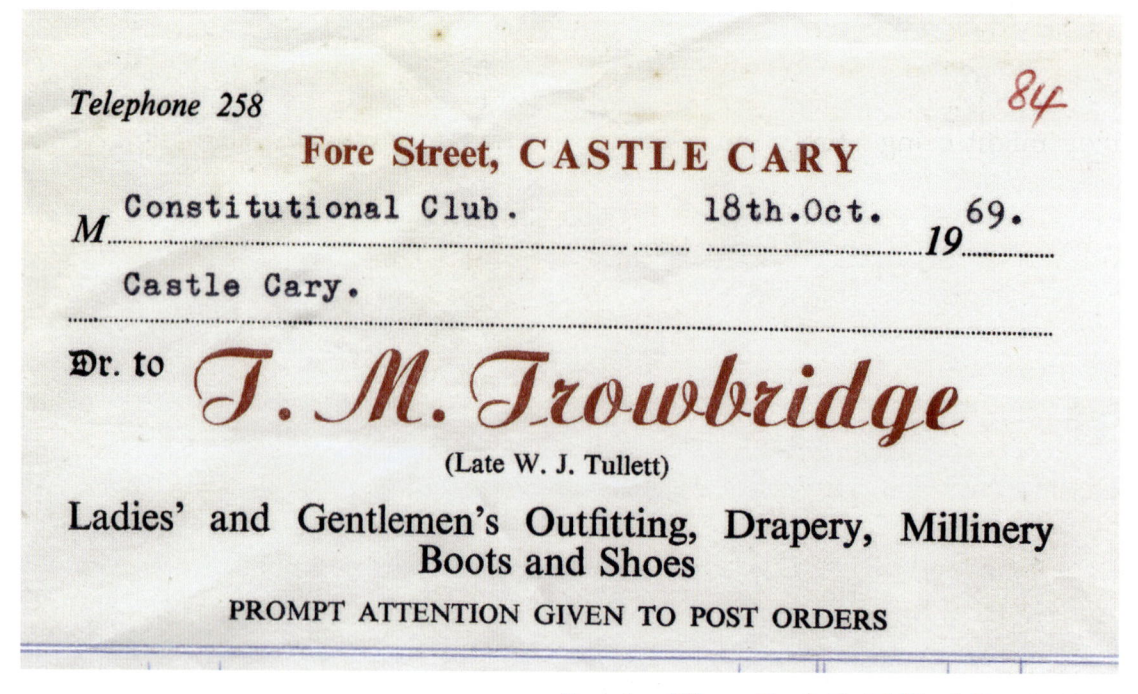

Examples of Thomas Trowbridge's billheads from the 1960s. LHG collection.

Childhood Memories of Castle Cary by Richard Burrows

Please mum, can I go back with uncle and auntie?"

As usual on a Sunday afternoon my mother and I were at grandmother's house. She lived in one of Plymouth's pleasant residential areas. Tom and Doris Trowbridge, my uncle and auntie, were about to return to Castle Cary and their drapery and outfitting shop in Fore Street after their customary week's holiday. It was 1951 and I was 6 years old.

What followed I am not too sure. Suffice to say that 30 minutes later my wish had been granted and, waving goodbye to a worried mother and bemused grandmother, I was on my way to the first of numerous summer holidays I was to spend in the little Somerset town I was to grow to love.

I had no idea where Castle Cary was or how long the journey would take. However, in those days a spin in a car was exciting in itself and the weather was glorious. By standing on the passenger seat I was just able to poke my head through the sunshine roof and in that manner, unburdened by today's traffic problems or our current paranoia with health and safety, travelled the 100 miles door to door. It is generally accepted that old memories are distorted by the mists of time. I am certain that this must be true of mine as well. Yet when I think of Castle Cary, a welcoming, friendly place populated by equally welcoming, friendly people, only good times register, spread over the following decade in a rich yet tangled tapestry.

As the Christmas and Easter school breaks were relatively short, I only ever visited during the summer holidays. However these seemed endless, always warm and sunny under an azure sky. As one looked down from Lodge Hill, near the site of the castle (it was at first disappointing to discover that little evidence of the castle remained), the town always appeared at peace with itself, the actual quietness and tranquility broken only by a modest flow of traffic through the main streets, the unobtrusive song and chatter of the birds, the reassuring quarter hourly chime of the church clock, the distant clatter of a train or the lazy drone of a light aircraft.

The church itself and the town hall rose proudly above other buildings which in turn clustered around the two landmarks, as if seeking the security they might bring. From the centre, roads radiated outwards like giant tentacles in three main directions, with old properties and newer developments clinging alongside. On the distant horizon Glastonbury Tor, shimmering in the haze, could usually be made out.

I remember the odd violent storm too - those rare occasions provided excellent sport. The rain hammered down, merrily bouncing off the street and pavements, as lightning flashed, illuminating a leaden sky and sudden, angry sounding claps of thunder reverberated between Spearman's opposite and the shop. There was an important job to be done though as, having raised any vulnerable stock above ground level, we battled with boards and brushes to prevent the torrents of water rushing down Fore Street from penetrating the entrance. Customers, trapped by the abrupt turn in the weather, would help too. It was 'all hands to the pump', almost literally, and pleasing to report that our efforts were always successful.

Ah, the shop itself - for a youngster untarnished by such modern day distractions as coloured TV, music systems, computers, video games and the internet, amusing oneself was the name of the game. The shop offered ample scope for this.

During early stays, with a modicum of imagination, the foot of the stairs, made the ideal location for my portrayal of the driver of the blue and white Yeovil to Shepton Mallet bus. Later, on a more practical plane, sorting out the drawers of brightly coloured reels of cotton, cleaning the brass below the display windows, dressing the windows themselves or helping uncle to count up, in pounds, shillings and pence, the day's takings remain vividly in mind. Notwithstanding, the highlight of each day was the morning teabreak and running down the road to buy the delicious buns and doughnuts, oozing with real west country cream, for the staff and myself. The term 'staff' however is a misnomer. Tullett & Sons, as it was then called, was a big happy family. I cannot recollect a single argument or cross word within the confines of the premises. Valerie, Brenda, Ena, Linda and Madelaine were big sisters. Even the somewhat gruff and seemingly ancient Mr. Neck treated me affably.

Obviously this unique atmosphere in the shop owed nil to employment legislation and everything to the way my relatives managed their business. My aunt's health was hardly robust, although a cigarette could often be seen hanging from the corner of her mouth together with a generous length of ash about to fall off, and her diabetes must have been debilitating for them both. Yet, two more kindly and even tempered people one couldn't wish to meet. I am sure uncle never attended a single management course in his life. He simply understood that if you treated people with consideration and respect they repaid you with hard work and loyalty. How different from the work place of today!

The shop formed part of a three storied home, spacious and full of character. A cricket pitch could have been laid in the space occupied by the kitchen and the lounge/diner. Next to the kitchen was a large cupboard converted into a larder. It was always stacked with bottled fruit, apples, pears and a variety of berries recently picked from the garden.

The kitchen itself housed an interesting piece of apparatus, namely an old fashioned washing machine. The machine resembled an upright and cumbersome metal trunk and was brought into service every Monday morning. It would take an age to fill, via a piece of rubber tubing connected to a tap, and chugged away for about an hour. Then with a pair of wooden tongs, I was allowed to extract each item of clothing from the steaming bubbly water below and feed it into the jaws of an even more ancient mangle, taking great satisfaction as the excess water gurgled into the adjacent sink.

The lounge/diner boasted a piano on which I would be encouraged to practice my limited repertoire. Uncle was a most accomplished musician and would play most evenings. 'The Teddy Bears' Picnic' was my early favourite, but his mastery of a range of music was extensive and eventually auntie and I had to sit alone at Sunday morning service as he became church organist.

Although uncle had little time and even less stomach for pop music, I was allowed to use the rather basic record player to listen to the singles of LPs I had borrowed from the girls in the shop. During the playing of one of Elvis' (I admit) rather repetitive ditties, despite my protestations, he insisted that the needle must be stuck. Jerry Lee Lewis, Little Richard and the less wild Ricky Nelson, Pat Boone, Brenda Lee and Connie Francis I also associate with Cary holidays. Without a television, uncle was totally anti 'the box' until late in life, the radio was the main focus of home entertainment. At one stage I almost became hooked on 'The Archers', but found '20 Questions' and 'Down your Way' of limited interest. For me it was the 'Lunchtime Cricket Scoreboard', comedies like 'Hancock's Half Hour' and the 'Paul Temple Mysteries'.

Richard mowing the lawn, in the garden behind the shop, in 1957. R.Burrows collection.

    The bench seat in the huge bay window of the master bedroom was my favourite place in the house. Here I would enjoy an early morning cup of tea and, watched over by a massively cuddly teddy bear, sit studying the traffic below or look inquisitively across at the billboard on the town hall, advertising the current cinema presentation. Despite a constant interest in what was being shown, I was never to venture inside.

    I indicated earlier how easy going both my uncle and aunt were. Yet each had their moments! The latter was a somewhat erratic driver, probably through lack of practice, and would become extremely irritated when, following trips to Street swimming pool, she would always stall the car on the incline at the T-junction next to the Constitutional Club. My younger cousin Kay, who spent two holidays in Cary with me, and I, knew when and where the incident would happen and were never disappointed. While we had fully appreciated the afternoon treat, we couldn't help guffawing long and loudly, which merely added to aunt's annoyance. I also clearly remember one instance when uncle's customary equilibrium cracked. Joker was a black spaniel, although his coat was liberally sprinkled with rather untidy smudges of white (or it could have been the other way around!). Sadly through lack of strict training, he was exceedingly boisterous to the point of hyperactivity and thus lived in a kennel in the outhouse. To both Kay and I he was wonderful company during the many hours we spent playing or working in the extensive garden. Anything thrown for him would be eagerly chased. One day, Kay broke a dining room window misdirecting an apple core.

The projectile landed on the table with Joker barking in frustration and puzzlement as he looked up at the window from outside. Returning indoors, we would often 'forget' to close the back door. Taking a seat, perhaps helping with the daily crossword, we would wait expectantly. Suddenly the peace would be broken as Joker charged into the house and slobbered over everyone in turn while his tail, wagging furiously, scattered the cats, rudely awaken from their slumbers, and sundry items of furniture. Having greeted everyone he would then roll on his back, legs kicking in the air like demented pistons, before being led outside in disgrace.

Such episodes we were never blamed for, but Joker's excursion to the station was a different matter. Joy and Tessa, distant cousins, had arrived for the day and the three of us decided to walk to the station with the dog. Taking Joker on the lead was always hazardous as he was immensely strong and liable to pull one over. Crossing the fields he was let off the leash and careered around in his usual frenzied manner. As we neared the station I managed to secure him again, but at this point he started to develop a limp. Arriving on the platform the problem appeared worse and, as the instigator of the expedition, I made a decisive executive decision. Uncle seemed far from pleased when I asked him, via the station telephone, to collect us in the car, but I suppose he felt he couldn't refuse the request. His mood had worsened by the time he drew up. As the door was opened to let us in, Joker, forgetting his limp, tugged out of Joy's grasp, barged past us all, and jumped in first. A few well aimed smacks barely contained his enthusiasm. For the duration of the mercifully short journey the dog jumped from lap to lap while all three of us in turn were severely chastised for dragging uncle away from work on such a busy morning. When home, the dog was banished to his kennel, to where he slunk still limp free, while we made ourselves scarce. As the years passed uncle and I often had a laugh about the incident. He steadfastly believed that we had concocted the story in order to secure a lift home, while I continued to maintain that the dog had been injured. Perhaps, living up to his name and not fancying the return walk, Joker had conned me and might still be chuckling over it in his doggy heaven!

Michael Hodges, a smallish, sun tanned youth with a perpetually cheerful countenance under a mop of black hair, became the best of many friends in Cary. Like all friendships it grew because of shared interests. One of those was trains. Many an hour was passed on the London bound platform of Castle Cary station. We could gaze across the tracks at the Friesians, busily munching the rich meadow grass or lying down in ruminant activity, as the August sun beat down on the slopes and reflected with great intensity off the tarmac and concrete of the station itself. We would talk about our sporting heroes, Colin Cowdrey, Peter May, Duncan Edwards, Danny Blanchflower, vaguely conscious of the tuneless humming of the station master as he went about his hardly arduous duties. There was much time for silent contemplation too. Trains did not pass by frequently. However the dull clank of the signal to our left announced the imminent arrival of a Penzance express. A mile or more away a whistle would sound to be followed by the panting of a furious engine and the rhythmic 'tickety-tock' of the coaches. Louder and louder became the noises until the steaming brute burst under the road bridge like a charging bull suddenly released from its pen. Swaying somewhat, yet powerful and proud like a schoolboy showing off, the engine would bear down on us and with a deafening cacophony race past, within seconds to disappear in the distance on its way to the busy metropolis. Sometimes a 'double-header', invariably both engines named after a famous monarch or castle, would lead the way! What magnificent beasts, how much more interesting than the bland and characterless diesels of today. Even then the Cornish Riviera was often pulled by this new machine. The excitement of such a 'cop' was due solely to its novelty value - and one that would soon dissipate.

Richard and the spaniel Joker in 1957.
R.Burrows collection.

A change in the signal to our right would then herald the eventual appearance of the more sedate passenger service to Weymouth. As it chugged alongside the far platform and halted with mighty expellation of steam, we would marvel at this massive feat of British engineering. A minute or so later, and having disgorged a few passengers, a pert 'peep' would announce its departure and with a big effort it would slowly pull away and resume its leisurely course to the coast. A journey to the railway sheds of Yeovil was sometimes undertaken but, combining two pleasures in one day, we would also travel on the 10.18 am. 'bucket', as it was called, to see county cricket at Taunton. The future England opener, a very young John Edrich, scored 96 in rapid time against the home side on one such visit. On another occasion Kay and I travelled in the opposite direction, via Westbury, to Bristol where another branch of the family greeted us at Temple Meads. I think they were somewhat disappointed to be greeted by 'can I go to football?'. Nonetheless I was driven to Ashton Gate, where I saw Rotherham beat the City 3-2, so much more enjoyable than an afternoon's shopping.

A lot of time was actually spent playing football at the recreation field. This was where I first met my Cary friends. 'Can I have a game please?' I rather shyly asked of a group of boys kicking a ball around. They looked at me rather dubiously, obviously weighing up whether I would be an asset to their game. A majority mumbled OK or something similar and I joined in, desperate to produce my best form. The fact that I could kick with both feet and head quite competently meant that I was immediately accepted into the gang. Sometimes we played with a real leather ball which to head, especially if you unluckily caught the lace, would feel like being hit by a heavy punch. At other times it would be a light, plastic 'frido' which, if you were playing against the wind, was difficult to kick out of your own half. We all assumed the roles of footballers of that era. I was Wilf Carter the Plymouth Argyle no. 8, for many years the Pilgrim's top goal scorer.

Some holidays coincided with the start of the Cary football team's season. I am not sure how good the players actually were, but Michael knew them all by name and would point out the stars. They would change in the outhouse of a building on the narrow road leading up to the recreation field. Perfect timing would ensure that, feeling good to be part of the scene, we could trail behind them as they trudged to and from the pitch. Michael lived in Cumnock Terrace. His parents possessed a TV, quite rare in those days, and were happy for both of us to spend a lot of hours watching the, albeit paltry coverage of the Test Matches (England often won in the 50s and 60s) and, during one year, the Tokyo Olympics. In between the viewing we would play cricket on the narrow footpath between the houses and raised front gardens. The path was barely 6 feet wide, but to us it was as good as playing at Lords. It was during one of these 'matches' that I first spied a neighbour of Michael's. She was about the same age as me and a really pretty girl. I saw her many times after this and longed to get to know her, yet never plucked up the courage to even speak to her.

A wealth of other non chronological memories come flooding back. As well as visits to Street, there were motor trips into the countryside and to the coast, not to mention the business visits with uncle, as he did his rounds collecting orders and later delivering the exciting looking parcels which I had helped to wrap. Evenings of tennis at Mr. Thomas' private court, with Wilfred, Margaret and many other grown ups, although Kay and I would sometimes also play there of an afternoon, contrasted with long hours of toil in the garden cutting grass, digging up potatoes or keeping the bonfire alight. Falling asleep upstairs while rehearsals for the forthcoming Gilbert and Sullivan production were held downstairs and listening to Radio Luxemburg in Madelaine's flat at the top of the house, when I should have been tucked up in bed, were also regular occurrences. I can also vaguely remember a big fete or business fair for which uncle, using all his undoubted flair and ingenuity, had devised an elaborate mechanical contraption to advertise his wares. I recall with perfect clarity watching Dennis Compton's winning shot at the Oval in 1953 when England regained the Ashes. I was one of a large number of people crowding around the shop window at Otton's!

Such was my attachment to the town that I chose Castle Cary as the topic for a talk I had to give in my early years at Secondary school. I was petrified about speaking in front of an audience in those days, but my knowledge and enthusiasm for the subject carried me through. I was bombarded with questions, especially about the Round House and the pond with its wildlife, afterwards.

*On Alf Baxter's motorbike in 1957 – Alf and Madeleine
lived in the flat above the shop.
R.Burrows collection.*

*Helping in the garden in 1960.
R.Burrows collection.*

So many happy memories! Yet as a 6 year old in Cary I experienced my first nightmare. The image of a man with an iron helmet on his head, similar to that worn by jousting knights in films like 'Ivanhoe', is still crystal clear to me today. At first like everyone else around the unfortunate soul I had laughed but then, suddenly frightened by the strange sight, started to cry. I awoke, trance like, to find auntie comforting me.

Returning home to Plymouth, whether from Cary station or the more distant Templecombe, was also never a happy time. After a few days back in my native Devon I was fine, yet leaving Cary, friends and uncle and auntie was invariably tearful. Moving from an almost idyllic to the real, more threatening world was certainly an underlying cause.

Holidays in Castle Cary were later replaced by calls en-route as I travelled between Plymouth, Sheffield and Reading Universities and, later, teaching appointments in Berkshire and Kent. When the Trowbridges retired, sold their business and moved further up Fore Street, things were never quite the same. Castle Cary had grown in size and population while I had matured and moved on. However, during these brief stops, I would still find time to walk down Fore Street, looking nostalgically at the shop, then of course selling books not clothes, wander up to the 'Rec' and sometimes even visit the station. The latter still reminded me of Nesbitt's famous story transferred into film 'The Railway Children'.

My last visit some years ago, was to attend the funeral of uncle, who had survived auntie by a few years. It was a doubly sad occasion for me. I was saying a final farewell to uncle and probably Castle Cary too.

Roger Otton

I would like to start with my family tree, which has been traced back to 1668 to a William Morton, a farmer in Broadclyst, Devon. I have several claims to fame in my family tree, one being that Lucy Pitt who married my great grandfather was a direct descendant of William Pitt the Prime Minister. This came out on an ITV programme in the Midlands about 30 years ago. Then there is the other we all like to have, which is a skeleton in the cupboard. My great, great, great grandfather's brother was sentenced to death for horse stealing, but the sentence was lifted and he was transported to Australia for hard labour, resulting in an Otton family branch in Australia. My great grandfather Frank Otton who was born in Baltonsborough was a master carpenter by trade and also a lay preacher in rather a big way, so I was told by my grandfather, and he actually preached in Keinton Mandeville on a regular basis in the old chapel, which is now the residence of my youngest daughter.

Ralph Otton's house in Station Road, in 1905, before the shop was built. R.Otton collection.

Ralph Otton outside the shop he built himself of timber and galvanized iron in Station Road in 1907. It was subsequently used by B. Hockey, and demolished in 2009. R.Otton collection.

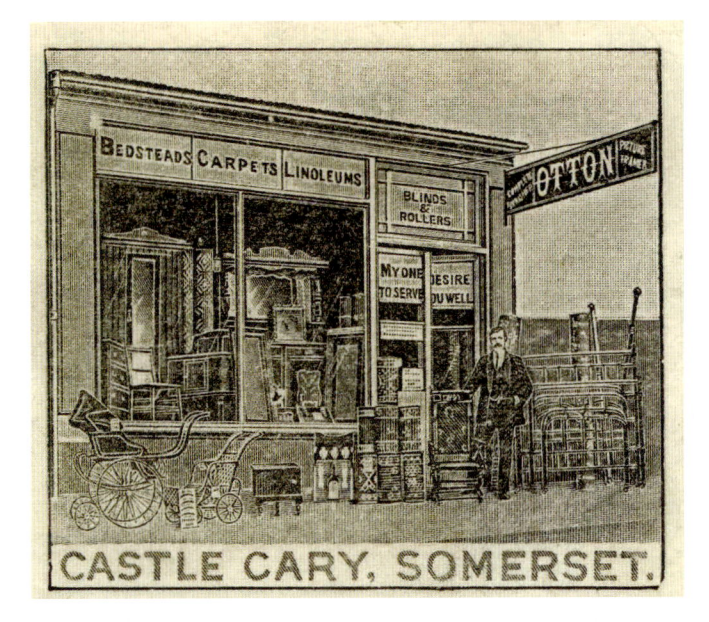

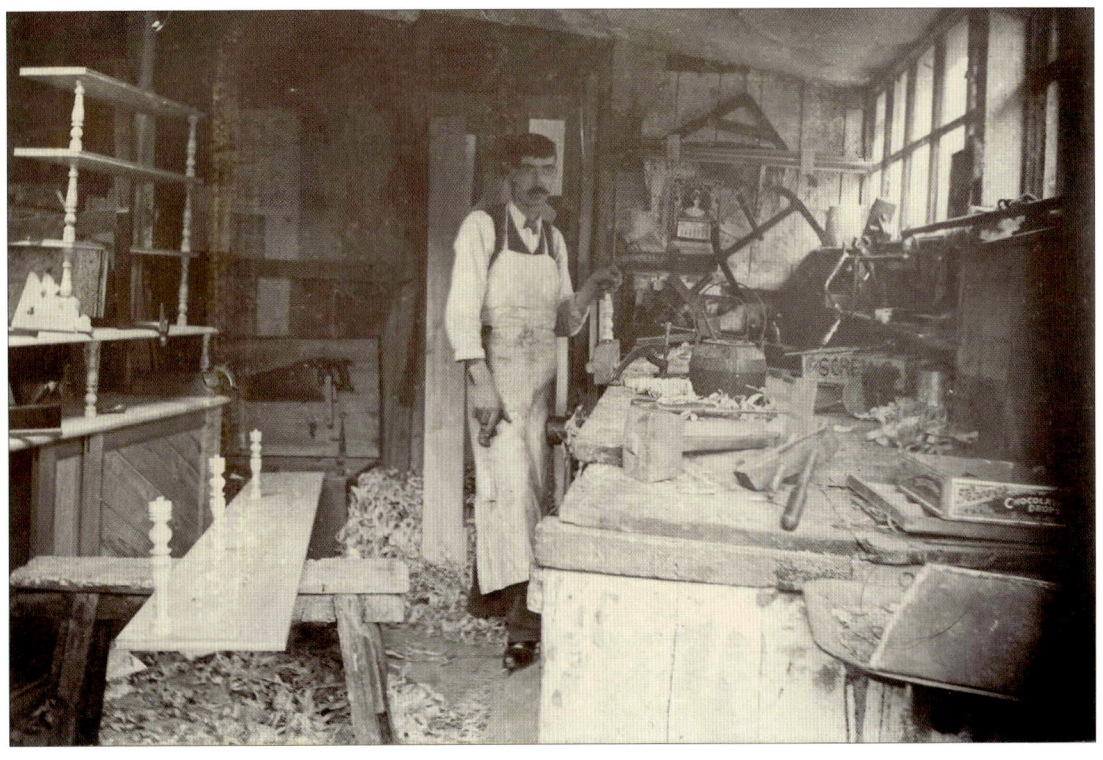

Ralph Otton in his workshop in 1908. R.Otton collection.

Ralph Otton's catalogue.
R. Otton collection.

A picture framing label.

My grandfather Ralph came to Castle Cary in approximately 1903 and worked for Pither and Son the furniture people. Later he started on his own in a property in Station Road and built himself a shop which has only recently been dismantled. He was selling picture frames and furniture in general. He was making furniture probably in 1920 when crystal sets came into being and he started selling those. He and my father moved to Fore Street by the Horse Pond in 1946 and carried on radio, television and electrical work. My father was also a Parish Councillor for 25 years, a District Councillor, and engaged in many other activities.

I was born on April 9th 1942 and moved with my father and grandparents to Radio House in Fore Street. I attended primary school until I was 10, then went to a private school, Wells Cathedral School, where I was a chorister for 6 months. On leaving school I was sent to Bristol on a radio and TV wholesaler course, where I attended college to learn basic radio and TV. After that I came back and worked for my parents. I met Molly and we got married and had three children. I was also a Town Councillor for 17 years. I was president of the Conservative Club, of which my grandfather was a founder member, and in those days the members bought a brick to help build the Conservative Club, which is now at the bottom of Station Road. Grandfather was snooker mad, he was a staunch member and was a member of the committee, as also was my father.

While on the Town Council, Gordon Stockman and I thought we should start a Carnival and a Museum. In both cases we formed a committee. I chaired the first carnival committee meeting and Gordon chaired the first museum committee meeting and as we now know, I became very involved with the museum and Gordon with the carnival. The museum started in John Crossley's shop in the High Street and he was very good letting us have a large room which was originally Asher's cafe. I remember working many hours on end until early in the mornings preparing this and the first item we had was a poleaxe, which he had used as a child, and now we all know it is installed in the Market House.

My grandmother was a Sunday School teacher at Hadspen. My mother was a Sparkford girl though born in Malta. When she met my father he had an egg packing station in Torbay during the war. My mother had a hairdressing business and was a founder member of the Castle Cary Choir, and also enjoyed dancing very much and attended Victor Sylvester dances at Mendip Hospital. She was also very busy organizing fire brigade dances with many helpers and these were a great success. Mother was also a bellringer in All Saints Church in Castle Cary. Molly and I have just celebrated our Golden Wedding Anniversary.

From left;- Jack Otton, Bob Biddle (brother-in-law), and Ralph Otton.
R.Otton collection.

Three generations – Roger, Ralph and Jack Otton.
R.Otton collection.

Roger Otton in a Morris van in 1947. R.Otton collection.

Ottons Radio and Electrical store in Fore Street in 1951. R.Otton collection.

From left;- Jack Otton, Roger Otton, and Bob Sansom in the shop. R.Otton collection.

House fire in Winter

House fire in Winter by Tony Price

Just after 8.00 am on Friday January 11th 1963 our fire brigade was called to a fire in a thatched roof of a house belonging to Captain Milligan at Pitman's Orchard, Woolston. We were having the worst snow and ice since 1947. I was working at John Boyd's factory in Torbay Road and when I heard the siren I ran from the factory to the Fire Station - I was one of the first six who had responded to the call out.

Castle Cary Fire Service personnel – a group photograph from the 1960s. LHG collection.

Most of the road to Woolston was single file except for a couple of passing places. As we were going down hill into Three Ashes the fire engine was forced off the road by an army lorry coming in the opposite direction. The fire engine embedded itself in a deep snow drift, the windscreen was smashed and Leading Fireman Les Powell, who was in the front passenger seat, was engulfed in snow up to his helmet. After checking everyone else was alright we set about digging him from his seat. Apart from a few scratches he was OK. Walt Meadon, who was riding in the back of the tender, said that his pipe had been jolted out of his mouth. We had a quick search and found it in the snow at the side of the fire engine. Station Officer George Stockley arrived with the Brigade Land Rover. He said he would try to pull the tender out of the snowdrift by putting it into four wheel drive. A rope was attached, but after a lot of skidding of the wheels the rope snapped and George shot across the road into another snowdrift. The six of us managed to get him out and he then continued on his way to Woolston. We, in the fire engine, managed to get a wire rope and were eventually pulled clear by another lorry.

When we at last arrived at Woolston we found the house completely destroyed but firemen from Wincanton, Yeovil and Somerton, with help from neighbours had saved most of the furniture and other belongings. Cary firemen had to stand by until Saturday morning. It was very cold that night - someone said minus 15 degrees C. At about 2 am., Ken Pennell said he would make a cup of tea but then found there was no milk. He asked if butter would do instead - which tasted so awful that we couldn't drink it. Ed Fussell, who was a farm worker, said if we could find a clean bucket he would find a nearby farm where the cows should be in the yard because of the weather and he would milk one. After about a quarter of an hour we heard a shout from Ed saying he had found a cow and he had got some milk. He asked if someone would take the bucket from him if he handed it over the fence. As he passed the bucket over, his foot slipped on the ice and he dropped the bucket. That was the end of our cups of tea!

Sadly, of the men serving in Castle Cary Fire Brigade at that time, there are only two of us still alive, Ken Pennell and myself.

*Tony Price and Percy White's
cattle transporter in the snow in the memorable winter of 1963.
LHG collection.*

Ansford Parsonage

In the 1940s, '50s and early '60s, The Old Parsonage at Ansford was owned by the Fullers, two brothers and two sisters. A brother and a sister died and the remaining two had a bungalow built in the garden of The Old Parsonage where Mr. T. Berry lives today.

In 1964 Mr. and Mrs. Mewes from Epsom Downs bought the old house which needed major work, for which the contract was awarded to Rossiter Bros., builders of Ansford. They needed to renew the whole roof: trusses were made to match by the late Brian Woolway; purlins and rafters were cut in, as were new ridge and wall plates. Double battens were nailed on every third rafter to give the roof a wavy look. The ridge tiles were also bedded up and down to make them appear old.

A few years previously Ralph and Arthur Rossiter had acquired an old cottage and orchard at the bottom of Coombe Common from Mr. D. Mullins. As the tiles on the cottage matched those on The Old Parsonage roof, they removed them from the cottage and used them to replace cracked and shelled tiles on the house. Both lots of tiles had been well weathered and were a good match. A garden room was built for Mr. Mewes with the best of the Cary stone from the old cottage.

An old mansion was being dismantled and some of the window shutters and some panelling were carefully removed and brought back to Ansford and fitted in the drawing room.

Coombe Bottom Orchard

The orchard at the bottom of Coombe Bottom had several sorts of apples including Bramleys, Morgan Sweets and a lovely small Russett.

One year Ralph and Arthur Rossiter brought some sacks and one Friday we went to pick the apples. Robin Easterbrook, who lived at Lodge View Farm agreed to go down to the orchard and to bring the apples back in his Land Rover. He asked me to give a hand and we loaded most of them and covered them over. I got in the back and he then set off - not down the track but straight up the steepest part of the hill. It was so steep that all I could see was blue sky. I was sure the Land Rover was going to tip backwards and down the hill. I was so glad when we reached the top! We unloaded the apples and then Robin said we would pick up the other sacks that afternoon. I quickly made the excuse that I had to go out - no more trips like that!

The Old Parsonage at Ansford – the materials from Coombe Bottom cottage were used to repair and extend the building.

The Coombe Bottom cottage stood in a garden and orchard now completely overgrown, as seen here in 2011. The views to the north are spectacular.

Janet Hutchfield

I was born in 1930 at Blackworthy, Castle Cary, and was six months old when my father Reginald Lush took over the butcher's shop in the High Street, as his older brother had died and the latter's son was unable to cope with the business. My grandfather on my mother's side of the family - grandad Asher, a local baker - bought the property and helped to set my father up in business, as it was very run down at that time.

Lush Butchers, in the High Street, established here in 1894 and still run by the family. J.Hutchfield collection.

Janet at the 50 Years Anniversary celebrations at Ansford School in 1990.

A particular childhood memory is that my cousin Graham Asher had a tricycle, and my brother Ted had made for him, by my father, a wooden ride-on train. Graham and I were about 4 or 5 years old when we tied the train to the back of the tricycle, and went off down the street along the pavement to the Horse Pond where we arrived at high speed and went straight in. I must say our mothers were not very happy at the time, but we've had many a laugh about it since.

I went to the local Primary School, and then on to Ansford Secondary School at the age of 11 years, leaving school aged 14 in 1944, to work with my father in the shop, as my brothers had to serve in the forces. At that time there were very few opportunities and I received 12 shillings a week and my keep. My ambition was to join the Police Force, but it never came to fruition. We had a basic education, which fortunately got us through life, and I am most grateful for it.

It was a very difficult time for everyone during the war, particularly with food and clothes rationing. Many children were evacuated to Cary, and also their teachers. At the beginning of the war the Grenadier Guards were stationed here, followed by the Green Howards and the American Army. Quite a number of Green Howards attended our Methodist church evening service, afterwards ending up in our lounge, to enjoy one another's company and sing around the piano.

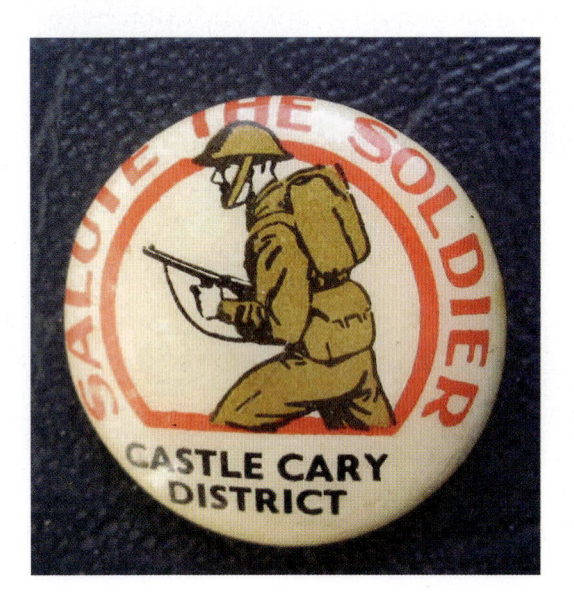

Badges were given to contributors to the fund raising drives for the forces during the War.

Petrol rationing was a big problem for us with regards to delivering the meat. For those unable to come to the shop we did a lot of the delivery with a carrier bike - on one occasion I used the front brakes coming down South Street and shot over the carrier - ending up bruised but with no broken bones. Fortunately the meat had been delivered! Several mornings when my father opened up the shop he discovered a two gallon can of petrol on the doorstep - I must say he panicked, picked it up quickly and hid it - a gift from the Green Howards.

The day that Cary station was bombed, in September 1942, I had misbehaved, probably by answering my mother back, and was sent upstairs to my bedroom, which I shared with my sister Ruth. I was looking out and up and down the street by hanging out of the window, when a German 'plane flew over Cary right above the High Street, very low. When we heard gun firing Leslie Webb, who was working in Pither's shop opposite, shouted at me to get back in and close the window. The next thing we heard was a tremendous explosion when a bomb fell on the station. The Railway Inn was almost completely destroyed, and Roy Turtle and Miss Ann King, who were both working in the station office, were fortunate to get out alive, but very shaken by the experience.

My family, and in particular my mother, were very musical - she was a pianist and organist; playing for the Youth Club dancing classes, and as organist at the Methodist Church. At the age of 15 I started piano lessons with Miss Grosvenor, my mother's old teacher, and soon decided I would like singing lessons, and with my father's approval took up singing with a tutor at Yeovil, Doris Waller, and so gave up the piano. I used to travel to Yeovil every Monday afternoon, my afternoon off, either by 'bus if wet, or sometimes with my father in the van, but more often than not I would cycle there and back, having had a one hour lesson costing 7/6d. I did this for many years.

Janet and Brian Lush with the butcher's barrow at Cary's Old English Market.
J.Hutchfield collection.

My singing career as a professional never really took off; I sang as an amateur receiving the odd 10s.0d. here and there - most weeks I was performing in churches and halls in and around Somerset and Dorset, or with the Castle Cary Choir, of which I was one of the founder members.

In 1946 a number of us went to South Wales for a week, supposedly a holiday, to what was then called "lend a hand on the land", picking up potatoes. My cousin Jean Barnes (née Asher) and I made friends with two other girls, and we promised to keep in touch. The following year we all met up again and booked a holiday at the Strand Palace Hotel in the Strand in London, travelling by train from Cary to Paddington. Before we left my grandfather Asher gave me a large white £5 note, which at that time paid for my accommodation at the hotel. What a venture it was, having never been to London before.

I was also a sports fanatic, and took part in athletics with the very active Youth Club here in Cary. I have played tennis, cricket, netball, rounders, hockey, football, table tennis, skittles, and more recently bowls. We have a most active Bowls Club in Cary, and I was a founder member - and in retirement I continue to enjoy a game.

Janet's home in Knight's Yard.
J.Hutchfield collection

Janet (standing) with Myrtle Parsons and Ruth Trott on the bowling green.
J.Hutchfield collection.

Memories of Jean Barnes

I was born in South Cary and we moved down into town when I was aged about three. My grandfather had bought Knight's Yard, 5 cottages and also the butcher's shop (Lush's). He came from Poole, married an Ilchester girl and set up shop – a bakers, just before WWI, was in business a year and then had to close down and join the army. He was put into a Scottish regiment, the Seaforth Highlanders, and came home wearing a kilt! After the war he started the business again. We lived in the cottage on the High Street - now the Green Shop.

In 1932 I remember my first day at school, also joining the Brownies. Phyllis Meaden and Joyce Crees were leaders. There were many happy evenings cooking our supper on a fire in a field, sausages and dampers.

In 1937 when I was 9 years old I was put on a train at Cary station and travelled to London (in care of the guard) and met at Paddington, so that I could go to the Coronation of King George VI and Queen Elizabeth. I still remember the day. I stood in Regent Street and watched the gold coach, etc., go by.

The school moved up to the new school at Ansford in 1939. Builders were still working there but the army wanted the old school, so we had to move. I remember taking old zinc baths up, for what reason I know not! It was a brilliant school, everything new, a kitchen to learn cooking, also a flat, art room, sewing room and gym. I enjoyed my time there.

Evacuees came from West Ham, a boy and girl stayed with us for a short time and then went back. We had two girls - sisters from Southampton who came in 1940. Various regiments of soldiers came, they marched through the town singing on their way to training in various fields in the vicinity. Hampshires, Irish Guards, Grenadier, Welsh. One time the Irish Guards marched down the High Street in their saffron kilts. After Dunkirk we had soldiers recuperating in various gardens that townfolk had opened to them.

Jean Asher, second from right, taking part in Castle Cary Carnival in 1948. LHG collection.

Next came the American soldiers, they gave fantastic parties with food we hadn't seen for some time, dancing and jitterbugging.

From school I went into the family business, bakers and confectioners, taking over a van, driving at sixteen. I took Cecil Farrant's job after he enlisted into the army and his wife also worked at the bakery and she taught me to drive.

I remember walking home for lunch from the junior school and seeing an elephant being scrubbed down in the horse pond. A circus had come to town.

I remember Bunny Biggin walking miles with large baskets on each arm, full of buns, selling them, and also Wuggy Perrot selling and shouting 'fresh mackerel', and watercress.

Jean, front row, fourth from left, in a production of the Dick Whittington pantomime in 1953.
LHG collection.

I remember pantomimes and being a part of them from an early age, as a dancer and later in speaking parts. They were first performed in the Town Hall (now called the Market House), the dressing rooms were where the museum is now. The Town Hall was also a cinema, with one film on Monday, Tuesday and Wednesday and another on Thursday, Friday and Saturday. Front seats were 6d, middle 1/6d. A lovely open fire was burning halfway down the hall, almost too hot to sit near. Dances were on most Saturday nights, either at the Drill Hall or the Constitutional Club, sometimes they were at the George Hotel which had a lovely ballroom. The Sparkford Inn and hunt balls were special, long evening dresses and men in dinner suits.

The Youth Club provided something to do most days of the week, including drama, and ballroom dancing was taught on Friday nights. There were keep fit and knitting evenings, and mechanics, car maintenance - Jack Norris taught this. I remember the gas lights and Mr. Thomas lighting them.

Jean, third from left, at Ansford School's Fiftieth Anniversary celebrations in 1990.

Hazel Merrifield

Hazel Merrifield

I was born in Clacton-on-Sea. Dad worked for a grocery chain and in 1935 he was offered the managership of World Stores, which was a large grocery shop in Yeovil. It was a big change but I moved to Yeovil with my parents and two brothers. We lived in a house in Goldcroft and a bungalow in Wraxall Road until the widow of the previous shop manager moved out, and then we lived over the shop in Middle Street, opposite where Boots is now. It was a large double fronted shop.

A Castle Cary bell-ringers group pictured in the late 1940s, and including the town's first lady ringers. Hazel is in the centre of the middle row.
LHG collection.

I passed a scholarship to the High School in 1939, and on my eleventh birthday war was declared and ten days later, I started school. This was also the first year when the school year changed from April to September as the county took over the education system from Yeovil Borough. My dad had joined the Observer Corps but he kept his job at World Stores until the beginning of the war. His war work was to warn the factories, especially Westlands, of potential air raids, which meant that he had to leave the grocery shop. When the war ended, his war-time work ended and he had to find another job so he decided to set up again as a grocer, and we moved to Castle Cary.

Thus my earliest memories of Castle Cary are in 1945, at the end of the war. I had just finished school and my father bought a business in Castle Cary. The shop had been closed for a long time but in those days you could not just go out and build what you wanted because there were great shortages of materials. However, there was an allowance of about £100 to buy timber, so it was all modernised and lined with recycled wood and other materials. The shop was on Bailey Hill and is now a private house (the front shop windows have been removed). Originally, there had been three cottages connected to the property and three staircases still remained when we moved in. We installed a cold room for bacon etc., in one room; and the entrance to the shop was at the front. There was a sitting room behind the shop, a kitchen, three bedrooms at the front, one over the shop and one that was over the old cottages. Outside there was a yard and a large back garden which overlooked the butcher's abattoir. The butcher was Mr. Newport and my brother used to watch the animals in the abattoir! Mr. and Mrs. Wade lived in the cottage next door.

Ellen Jesse Lees in the doorway of the family grocery shop at London House on Bailey Hill, c.1936. Established by her parents, Thomas and Louisa Lees, it was eventually taken over by Hazel's parents in 1945. The frontage has since been considerably altered.
LHG collection.

A Lees family group by the shop in the 1930s.
LHG collection.

Dad did all the refurbishing work himself and the shop opened selling bacon, sugar, tea, general groceries and provisions. Soon after the shop opened someone asked if we had any potatoes for sale. Dad said that he had a bag which had been bought for the family and could sell him some of those. This is what happened and so led to the shop starting to sell green grocery as there was not another greengrocers' in town. Mum was a 'pupil teacher' before she married and carried on working as a supply teacher at Ansford School and other primary schools in the district, now as Mrs. Stokes.

Soon after we moved to Castle Cary, my brother John started to attend Sexeys' School at Bruton, my brother Leslie went to the Primary School and I went to work with my parents in the shop and stayed there until I got married, when I went to live in Shepton Mallet for three years. George, my husband, was originally from Ditcheat but had served in the Malayan prison service after leaving the British Army. That is how it was in those days! I had my 21st birthday party at the Sparkford Inn, with mostly family friends attending but there was a youth club in Pither's old building on Bailey Hill, which is now new housing.

Hazel in an Ansford Youth Club production. Left to right, back row;- Ruth Bulley; Betty Yeabsley; Daphne Parker; Hazel Stokes; John Hart; Vera Creed; Dick Hutchfield; Jean Asher; Henry Gough; front row;- Pat Etherington; Michael Hutchfield; Eddie Carpenter; Stan Veryard; - Barber; Les Cleal; Vera Brown.
LHG collection.

Martin's had two grocery shops in town; one in its current position and another one in South Cary, which was managed by Mr. Hutchfield. Other shopkeepers included Miss Phillips, who was originally next to the primary school but subsequently moved to the property currently occupied by McColls, and Churchouse, bespoke tailors. The premises which are now Bishop's electrical store, was a grocer's shop, and next door was Mead's newsagents. There was also a cheese factory in South Street, which is now a private house and where Centaur Services started. Where Denela's is now was a small chemist shop owned by Mr. Foulis.

One day, dad took Les, my younger brother, to our bacon suppliers. The butcher gave Les a runt piglet so he brought it home and dad rigged up a pen in the yard. However, the pig soon became the family pet and had the free run of the downstairs rooms. It used to sit on our knees and was almost house-trained. Generally, the pig was well behaved but on one occasion he really disgraced himself. Following the hardship of the war years, products were gradually becoming available so we bought some beautiful black grapes. Unfortunately, the pig found them and started to eat them. He also ate some bars of washing soap, which was in extremely short supply. On another occasion, the pig escaped into the shop and somewhat startled the customers! Eventually, we did eat the pig but it was with us a long time!

The vet, Paul Greenough who lived in Florida Street, knew we had a pig and used to check it over for us. Later on, dad helped Paul with his Landrace piglets, one of the first specialist breeds of pigs developed after the war. He had six piglets, which had to be bottle-fed and as he could not manage them all, we looked after and bottle-fed three of them.

During the period 1945 - 1950, we were the first shop in Castle Cary to sell sliced bread. Fresh bread was delivered three days per week from Southampton and was very popular. We were also the first shop in the town to sell frozen food. An ice cream conservator was used to store the frozen products. Small quantities of peas, fruits, vegetables and meat were available but I do not remember selling ice cream. Ice cream conservators were the forerunners of present day chest freezers. The products were bought from a supplier who had a long list of products available including frozen swan!

We installed a 'cold room' in the shop for bacon, ham and sausages, etc., but we did not sell fresh meat as the butcher sold that. All this was before the days of self-service. The customer used to ask for an item and we collected it off the shelf for them. I really cannot remember if people were excited about the arrival of self-service when it happened. There were very few 'fridges' when I got married.

In 1954 I moved back from Shepton Mallet to Castle Cary, into the house where I still live today. George and I bought a shop for my brother Les to run on his return from National Service. This was a greengrocer's shop and is where Denela's bakery is now. I used to work in this shop with Les. After a few years, Les married and bought the fish and chip shop in the town. The greengrocery was rented out and then sold to Mrs. Wheaden, who ran the local plant nursery. Les ran the fish and chip shop, where Golden Plaice is today, until he subsequently moved away from Castle Cary.

The delivery van driven by Hazel outside the greengrocery shop in Fore Street in the 1950s.

I was taught to drive by Stan Veryard, our next door neighbour, so that I could make deliveries to local villages at night. I reached as far as Lovington and a Mr. and Mrs. Saunders, in Alford. In those days, the stream still ran down Fore Street in Castle Cary.

Sunday was a busy day! Each Sunday I drove to collect between fifty and seventy rabbits from the local trappers. I would put them on rods the same width as the van and dad or I would then take them to Mac-Fisheries in Bristol. We sold some in our shop and they were always skinned before selling. We would also send some to Bournemouth each week to be sold for half a crown each.

Dad died in 1957. Mum kept the shop going for about three years after he died and George and I bought three cottages in Woodcock Street from Charlton Brewery for her to live in. Mum continued to teach but lived with me until the work on the brewery cottages was complete. George worked for the brewery which was later bought-out by Courage.

When we owned the two shops, I would work between them. At other times I helped out at a café where the electrical shop now is. Many years ago, Castle Cary was the 'break' stop for coaches travelling between Bristol and Weymouth. The toilets were a particular draw! Coaches would line up through the town and on one occasion, there were more than fifty coaches parked on the same evening. Dad and I used to drive to Cheddar, fill the car with strawberries, drive back and sell the strawberries to the coach passengers. This was before car ownership was common! Many people travelled to Castle Cary on the frequent buses.

In 1978, I became a bus driver for Wakes and continued driving for them for nineteen years, principally with school children.

With my daughter Joanne, I co-founded the majorettes. One day in 1988, I was selling flowers in order to raise funds for the majorettes, when Les suggested that we sold flowers from his shop on the yard outside my house. We tried this and it was a great success, but I was soon told by the Council that I had to stop, so I then bought the public toilet block and converted it into a shop. John Fletcher did the conversion work and I continued the business for thirteen years and during that time, I put two assistants through Cannington College. When I sold the shop, it was briefly taken over by another florist but then became Studio 13.

Over the years I have seen many changes to Castle Cary, including the arrival of new people, new houses and new businesses, but I am still very much a part of the town and have lived in my current home for fifty seven years.

Kenneth Clothier

Kenneth Clothier - Oct.1st - 1922 - Oct. 1st – 2010 ; 88 Not Out!

I was born at Galhampton on October 1st. 1922. I shan't forget the day that I was born. It was on a grey and very frosty morn. The Doctor said l was a jolly chap, and laid me on the Nurse's lap. She washed me and she dried me all over, and after powder puffing me you see - she laid me in the cradle by the fender, in the little shirt my mother made for one. This of course is a lot of rubbish as far as I am concerned - but I am just trying to think of things to say and as l remember them. It was a long time ago.

Galhampton was a small village in Somerset, where everyone knew each other and probably their business as well. I had three elder sisters and one elder brother. The nearest school was North Cadbury to where they had to walk each morning and then home after class come rain or shine. There were a few lads of the village including my elder brother Charlie. Come week ends they led me a merry dance. I was under five and could not keep up, so they would sometimes cart me around in our own dairy trolley on iron wheels. One day we thought how about scrumping? Apples were plentiful and falling to the ground. One of the local farmers was rather grumpy and did not approve of giving away things that he wanted to get money for, he hoped. Upon spying the farmer approach, the lads all bolted and left me bawling in the old deep sided cart. He said he would report us to our parents and let that be a warning. My first black mark…. Just one of the pranks leaving me holding the baby so to speak. We also got caught in the village hall. I was lifted in through the high windows and we were having a wonderful bit of fun skittling, but this reached the ears of the nearby caretaker and the lads saw her coming and were out through the high windows, leaving dopey caught again; I was let off with a caution.

I remember being sent up to Mrs. Andrew's shop around the corner with a urgent order for a pint of pigeons' milk. The kindly old lady shop owner guessed the lads had been at it again and with a smile said she was out of stock on that particular day. Mostly we had harmless fun, and did not have need of a policeman in Galhampton.

Our father was very clever, as they had to learn fast in those days and twelve was the normal time to be leaving school and getting on to work full time. Father was amongst other things a skilful hay-rake maker, with training from his father and perhaps generations before that. He was also a contractor to other farmers for cutting grass and haymaking, being a specialist at building the hay rick so that it finished up looking the genuine thing. There was plenty of bread and cheese and cider. Dad kept cart horses for the work, and we had stables and also an orchard where we grew apples for making the cider. I remember amongst the cider apples was the famous Yarlington Mill. Not the best for eating - but great when fermented into best farm house cider, taking care not to leave the apple pulp unguarded - as if the pigs had a taster they would get drunk and race around the field like mad things. On Sunday mornings, a few of the locals, including the gypsies who parked their wagons in the nearby lane, joined in the ritual of cider drinking and banter just like you get in the pubs. I took notice that father had on blocks, several large wooden hogsheads filled with mature cider. One of the gypsies had plenty, say a drop too much. He asked father to supply him with some to take home. Father disliked greed - so he took off the gypos hat and filled it with cider, and no doubt it had filtered through to the ground before reaching the home caravan. It was necessary to use wooden taps as metal would corrode on contact with the cider, don't think too much on what it did to your guts. Regarding the drippings from the taps, father used to hang half a coconut under them, and there was usually a drop in the hanging half nut, so when there was no one around we used to try a drop - but don't tell anyone, as under five drinking was not strictly legal.

When contracting to local farmers for hay making, etc., I remember being invited into the house of a lovely old farmer's wife. She had plenty of cream and home made cakes. It was there that I heard of a new invention called the wireless. If you had this wireless contraption, you could hear voices and noises from many miles away, all without connections or wires; - they said it was the 'cat's whisker' - but I saw no cat.

I lived in Galhampton from 1922 to 1927 and became five years old and soon had to attend school. Father wanted to find new premises, so made enquiries regarding a small holding in the New Forest. Oh the excitement when father hired the local taxi owned by Mr. Hutchfield at the local garage. He had a beautiful yellow open top car, and to get a ride in a car was something special. We wanted to see the deer in the forest and lots of other things including the keeper's cottage. The cottage looked rather primitive against our Galhampton home - to say nothing of the isolation. Mother turned the proposition down flat and that was the end of the matter. That is how our lives all rest on decisions we are asked to make throughout our lives.

My aunt Alice who lived in Galhampton had friends in Warmley, near Bristol. She had made arrangements to go to Warmley for a week or so, which meant getting a train from Castle Cary station; 'would I like to go for a ride to the station?' What a silly question, of course I would. However, after arriving at the station, things took a turn and it was suggested that I also should get on the train and join in the holiday. The taxi driver was given a message for my mother and off we went, and arriving in Warmley, met uncle Sam and aunty Polly and they were a jolly couple. They grew lots of rhubarb and made plenty of rhubarb wine, which at the right time can be quite potent and I watched with amusement how the atmosphere became rather lively after they had supped a few glassfuls. I prefer cider myself.

It was a good holiday for me as we went to Bristol and had rides on the trams. They ran on metal rails embedded in the roads, but are not there now. I was still under five, and was getting quite a few "firsts" for a young-un. At home and away there was horse riding, car rides, train rides, etc., to say nothing of my early rides in the old creamery cart with the iron wheels.

At home, for special events such as going to North Cadbury church for weddings, funerals, harvest festival and the like - my father would hire the local horse and carriage service from Mr. Hunt. My mother used to say she had rather a posh wedding - getting to the church by a carriage and a pair of "greys". She liked to tell that story, but as I was not there at the time, I would not wish to argue. Unlike often now in modern times, children in those days did not attend the weddings of their parents.

I was soon coming to the end of phase one of my life – viz. 1922 - 1927. We were getting near the time when we were due to move to Wyke Road in Ansford, and I was not looking forward to this move at all. Why would I want to leave the lovely village of Galhampton, with all the friendly people, the local lads and it would also be goodbye to my girlfriend? Well - so this is 1927 and we have landed at Wyke Road, the cottage is not so modern as the one at Galhampton - but it had diamond window panes and a very old day oven where in previous days they used to bake their bread.

I remember my first day at Cary infants school. The teacher was Miss Naish, a dear old lady really but I took one look at her and bolted off-down the road. This did not work as my mother caught me and escorted me back to the school and informed me that this is where I would spend quite a lot of my future time, boohoo! I soon made a lot of friends, and l had curly hair which seemed to appeal to some of the girls who chased me around the playground. I don't know what I would have done - even if they caught me, but you have to start somewhere. Some of the boys looked upon me as a challenge to their gang leadership and I was forced into a wrestling match by the opposition leader. We were both tough and it ended in a fair draw. From then on that boy was a great friend of mine to the end of his life which ended in the 1939 - 1945 war, as recorded on the War Memorial in the Horse Pond.

Near the school was a small shop owned by the Hoskins brothers, where we bought broken biscuits for tuppence a bag. Mr. Lewis Hoskins owned a boat which he would sail across Park Pond to the island where the swans would nest and bring up their cygnets and to train them to go to and fro to the Horse Pond. They were real swans and a great attraction to visitors; l think their names were Joe and Mary and a very happy couple they were. When they wanted a rest from swimming, they would stand out on the pavement, and if you had the cheek to walk too closely by, then they might try to give you a friendly peck, just to show you who was boss.

At Cary school I had lots of friends, and some of them in their spare time would join me at Wyke Road, where we played football or cricket. The local pub was the Waggon & Horses where lived my great friend Frank. We played lots of cricket on the concrete slab roof over the bar area; Frank owned the bat which lasted a long time and was treated between seasons with the proper linseed oil. The bat was very narrow and this was good for training as you had to be sure to hit the ball in the middle of the bat. No edges allowed or your bat would soon split and be gone. Frank's mother obtained the bat by sending in lots of Oxo coupons; - I do not think you would get that now - even on special offer. I remember quite a lot of Waggon landlords over the years; they had to do various jobs to supplement their income. There was a carpenter using one of the basement rooms for his workshop, and another was a London family who started up a wholesale chicken pick and preparing food for the London market. You should hear the noises as the chickens came to their demise and were swiftly crated and off to London in the van - feathers flying everywhere.

Entry to the Waggon games room was by outside steps - now demolished. We played billiards, boxing and anything going. At one time this room was rented by a television engineer, and he built the first television set in the district. I knew him well and he gave me a demonstration. The picture was small and of course in black and white. I bought a set which lasted for years and gave years of pleasure to my family and friends. On Saturday evenings, the Waggon was a splendid centre for music around the piano; Gladys was our star singer, the repertoire mostly a little high class with lvor Novello the favourite. Sadly all things come to an end and I bought the piano to amuse myself. The pub is closed at the present time. Some described it as where "East Meets West" We hope one day it can be re-established.

In the late nineteen thirties, I was growing up - neither child nor man. I lost the benefits of cheap fares and tickets, etc., and could not go to pubs or do the things grown ups do or what we think they do. We had to make the best of available facilities, such as going down to the Town Hall Cinema or perhaps occasionally enjoying plays put on by the travelling repertory company, all at the Town Hall. I remember some of the popular ones, including "Jack White's Gibbet." The room would be in semi darkness and took on an eerie atmosphere, which was meant to frighten us and it succeeded. The Town Hall clock would on the hour strike out with a solemn death bell gong – gong, and from the stage would come a ghoulish howl. This would be the brother's cry of anguish when he found out that the man he had just murdered was his brother. Some still get the creeps when travelling along Gibbet Lane. I remember getting lost there one night when in dense fog with a motor car. I was collecting a young lady from Templecombe station who wanted to go to Hall School at Galhampton, but we landed in the fellow Bratton school, which she also knew and she then helped to guide me back to the beloved old Galhampton. I could have said that I had run out of petrol - but that is old hat and does not fool the ladies anymore. I was then of course old enough to drive and help out in a taxi service. I had a lot of friends in Hadspen; they had built the new village hall and it was open to all on payment of a small fee. We played darts - table tennis - billiards and the normal club games, and had our own band - being piano, drums and saxophone by the local virtuoso. We had dances and plays and all without having to find any more cash.

The Hindenburg airship over Castle Cary in 1937.

On a Sunday evening in early 1937 - the lads joined up to go for their usual stroll and this time it was up Nettlecombe hill. Out of the blue came a low buzzing noise. We saw a strange flying object heading towards France - it was a German airship named Hindenburg. It was said to be taking photos of the landscape in preparation for the looming 1939 War. The airship came to a very sorry end crashing in flames somewhere in USA... pity old Hitler was not on board. I have not seen or heard of any airships since.

I had friends in and around Cary, and we had to make our own fun and amusement. At weekends we might decide to go up Paddock Drain and on to the old Castle Site, where we would "Fly the Birds". You may have all sorts of thoughts and interpretations as to what this might be, but you would probably be wrong. It was the French game boules or the English version called pitch-and-toss. As with Rudyard Kipling's "If" I can't say it "It made a man of us" as we did not win or lose very much. We played with pennies and we did not have a lot of cash anyway. I suppose strictly speaking, gambling in public was illegal. This probably did not occur to us at the time. In any case, we only had two coppers in Cary / Ansford - and we could run fast. I had to be careful as I had a previous caution for "scrumping" before I was five. The police sergeant used to live at Wyke Road and was a friend of me and the neighbours, while the police constable had living quarters in the Town Hall. He was rather a pain in the backside and was looking for early promotion. Any gathering of young men having a chat on the corners such as by the Angel Hotel would result in him telling them to move on or a threat of prosecution.

We were young lads making our way as we saw it, mostly pretty good - but sometimes a bit like the boyfriend in Sally's Garden, "young and foolish". We thought it was BIG to buy a packet of Woodbines at 5 for 2 old pence and then hand them round one apiece. After a few coughs, that would be enough for ever, but others became addicted, and it is well known how hard it is to give up for good. So we could (hopefully) live and learn that fags are not a good habit. Being young pimply youths - we were not particularly attractive to the young girls. They mature earlier than boys and quickly learn the art of seduction, what with mini skirts, powder, lipstick and what have you. They were looking for older young men, and so us lads spent more time looking for other things like trying to get into the local football team, etc. I was into games from an early age, having to play mainly against men. I played for Evercreech as they only had ten men available that day. We went to Henstridge and played against a very hostile team and crowd, and won the game from a penalty that I was awarded when having been tripped when going for a certain goal. One of our players had rather long hair for that period and he was chased around the field by a rather fierce old lady brandishing an umbrella and shouting "Get your hair cut." I played for the Cary team YMBC, which was the only team in Cary in the pre-war time. To qualify, as Mr. John Pither owned the field - you were expected to attend his Sunday class at the Congregational Chapel in South Street. Mr. Pither was a good speaker and we enjoyed his talks, - he even predicted that before many years, we would be able to sit back in our own homes and watch Arsenal playing against say Manchester United or your own favourite sport and events. We thought this was a lot of tosh - but Johnny was proved to be right.

In September 1939 came the war against Germany. Terrible things had been going on and although not long before we were promised "Peace in our Time" that was not to be. A lot of our local lads had joined the Territorials; minimum age was supposed to be 18, but few even added a year to their real age in order to get in. When the war was imminent, the lads were soon posted off to Somerset Light Infantry HQ. Those who survived over the next six years or so lived through what Winston Churchill called "Our Finest Hour", but at what a price, what with Dunkirk and the bombs falling on London and the UK. We have a lot to thank the services and all the brave citizens for saving our way of life. Who did Gerry think they were kidding as they say?

There was no National Health Service in the thirties. We had one doctor and one nurse to cover the whole area and they were both very kind and did not make expensive charges so l don't know how they could make a good living, as when parents had large families, I am not sure if they were charged at all. Perhaps the doctor made a profit on his magic potion at half a crown per bottle. This was guaranteed to kill or cure so he had a good each way bet. It all came from the same jar but must have contained the secret elixir on which he should have taken out a patent and could then have been a good income for life. Patients rarely came back for a second bottle. Perhaps it was the half crown, or the taste or the effect! When I was seven, my younger sister and I were taken down with an epidemic of measles and whooping cough, which kept us in bed for around six weeks, missing all the time and lessons being taught at school. Sadly at next term time when most scholars went on to the next higher class, I was told that I would be held back to catch up. They were probably right, but I did not see it that way as I wanted to remain with the friends that I had made. It made me determined to learn well and to get on even better than those in the higher class. This I did and I then started to leap frog ahead of my so called class as laid down. I did well each year and I was proposed for and received the prize book paid for by the Francis Moore, Esq. fund. I still have and treasure these books with my name inscribed on the inside cover.

We had great respect for our teachers, even though all kept in the lockers their special 'wacker' canes with which they would administer several strokes, mainly across the palm of the hand. If you were quick and withdrew your hand before the strike, that would cause laughter amongst the class, but only ended in extra strokes, so you took your choice. We always called our male teachers "Sir" - even after we had left school, as in fact we knew they had given us a good education. There were no school leavers in our class who could not reasonably deal with the "three 'r's".

I think the headmaster knew that behind his back he was nicknamed "THE WIZARD" - but it was mainly only in fun. The head was also a good musician and singer, and composed the school signature tune. It ran something like this –

Our school is in Cary Town –
and we be the scholars you zee.
From villages near we do come in be dozens,
some brothers and sisters
and some of us cousins –
jolly vine scholars we bee
and jolly vine scholars we be.

This would be sung gleefully on the Friday afternoon singing session along with the other traditional songs that most of us know. Some boys were growing up and could no longer reach the high notes. They would then be discarded from the class and be told that they would have to go up to Catherine's Close for football or cricket. Was I glad when I could no longer sing "Oh, for the Wings of a Dove" or reach the high notes, - you bet I was!

We also enjoyed our outside school activities. They were all funded on a shoe string, as in the thirties the country was in dire straits, paying off the huge debts from the first war; - so much for the modern day credit crunch.

The headmaster was in charge of the nearby garden where the older boys were placed two by two to each plot. Plenty of moisture from the stream and nearby Park Pond was good for quick growing, and it could produce plenty of top but not so good underground crops. Tools were kept in the shed and were good as new after years of wear, always being cleaned and oiled after use; another lesson in the way to look after things. The Wizard kept his wheelbarrow in the cloak room and it would be used for many purposes, including a rough ambulance - but see later. Along the garden stream side, we had several apple trees, from which we were allowed the fallers. This was not good enough for a few of the lads, as just like Eve - they thought forbidden fruit might taste the sweetest and they would walk under the trees with their rakes on their shoulder and "accidentally" connect to some of the prime apples and so turn them in to fallers. The Wizard was not silly and we could hear his voice bellow a loud rebuke such as "no more apples for you my friend". My pal Tom and I were allocated a plot each, and our assistants were willing but not too bright; mine had very big boots, so was good for treading in the soil firmly when planting peas or beans, etc.; everyone had some talents. We felt rather proud when we were allowed to take home some of the garden produce such as potatoes and beans, etc., and show our dad. He might have said that now you know how to help me on our home garden, but we could be rather lazy in that respect; which is rather sad when we look back at it.

Woodworking was another outside class activity. We went up to the nearby Drill Hall once per fortnight, and my friend Tom and I were made partners. And as we were rookies we had to start by making a mahogany tray each. The woodwork teacher came from a nearby village and was a nasty piece of work and nobody liked him. He had a vile temper and was very fond of clipping you around the ear without warning, and you were not allowed to hit back. I made a mess of sticking on the base veneer, so had to strip it and then finish-off with French polish, which looked quite good and lasted for years. One lunch time we were playing football as usual on the small grass area between the school and the Drill Hall. Tom and another boy went up together and clashed heads. This is not an uncommon injury in football and resulted in Tom getting severe concussion which did not go away. We were afraid to report it as we thought it might end in our losing our football. Aha! - someone had a brilliant idea, - get him down to the cloakroom and lay him in the Wizard's wheelbarrow, where he could rest until coming round. We then went back to woodwork and the teacher naturally enquired as to Tom's whereabouts. When we explained that he was not well and that we had put him in the said wheelbarrow, the woodwork teacher exploded and demanded that we immediately reported the matter to his normal school teacher to get a doctor. Tom was pretty tough like most boys, came round eventually and came back to woodwork; good old wheelbarrow!

School sports were held on Friday afternoons, the lucky ones at that level, went up to Catherines Close for football or cricket according to season. At football I would be told to pick 10 others to make up my team. Likewise another boy would pick his 10 at alternative choices to make up the two teams to play against each other. You of course both tried to pick a balance of players according to position. No good having 10 goalkeepers or 10 say left wingers. I always played as centre forward and scored lots of goals. There was plenty of talent with other boys just as good as me. In addition to normal duties, our sports master was Mr. Steer - called Sammy by us; he was our favourite overall. He once bet me a tanner (sixpence in old money) - that I would not score a hat trick that afternoon. I did not intend to lose a week's pocket money and so duly obliged and made a gentle reminder before he paid up. The headmaster's son was older than us and went on to college and would visit us to help when University was closed. He was an outstanding player of football and cricket, and once played for Somerset County Cricket Club and also played a few times as centre forward for West Bromwich Albion. No duds allowed, but if your parents were rich and qualified as "Gentlemen" - then you may well get into Somerset CCC as Captain or something like that. It was the professionals in the main who did most of the work. We were proud of Somerset although those days they often finished bottom of the League. I remember watching the likes of big hitter Arthur Wellard, Bill Andrews (he would say shake hands with the hand that bowled Don Bradman - but only after he had hit about 270 runs) star batsman Harold Gimblet, Bertie Buse with his off cutters, Horace Hazell, slow left hander and brothers Jack and Frank Lee, opening bats and Wally Luckes, they said at the time to be best wicket keeper not to play for England. There were plenty of snobs about at the MCC and they would glorify in the Gentlemen v. Players match. They had to use separate bats when coming out from the pavilion (Pardon Me Sir). Len Hutton from Yorkshire would be our first pro. captain. No more of Jardine and Larwood or there would be serious consequences (now it's only a game old boy). At the end of the season at school, Tom and self were asked to work out the cricket averages. Sam said it was a fiddle because I came top best at bowling and Tom best at batting and second at bowling, with me just second at batting. We did not get awarded any caps or things like that, but just a few dirty looks from some of the wannabees. That was our story and we are sticking to it!

We were growing up at 13 years old. Exams were soon over and we were looking forward to going out into the big bad world of work and new activities. Cary School had already adopted mixed classes. We were not allowed to decide who sat next to us in class for obvious reasons. Competition was keen with the class divided into four sections. I was leader of Yellow group, and this label of Yellow Leader remained with me by some of the girls for years after school and I would sometimes be greeted in the street with a nice smile and "Hello Yellow Leader." At school we began to take more notice of the girls and they had become very attractive. They had no need of make up as they had an inbuilt beauty. There was plenty of choice and enough to go round, although we all had our favorites. All shapes and sizes, with blondes, brunettes and one or two with the special auburn or ginger if you preferred. In the main we had enjoyed our school life, but the time was coming to say goodbye to some of the boys and girls. They came from some of the outer villages and had lives of their own, although some remained friends for life.

In retrospect I have various memories set in no particular time scale. From the age of five onwards, as stated, I was living at Wyke Road, where we had good neighbours and plenty of friends who came up from town and the various surrounds. They joined in with our activities of which there were plenty. There was no television and the like to distract us. We lived mainly out of doors with sport, etc., to keep us on the move and no time to get bored. We had fields to play football and cricket in, or if wet we would play out in the road - not much traffic about and we had plenty of time to get out of the way when horses or cows came along. We also had a good yard to play in which was attached to our three houses. One disadvantage was that the yard was next to the road with an entrance for the tradesmen to call with their wares - all brought to your door and no housewives had to lug heavy bags of groceries and all the other necessary things to their home. The rare passing of the yard by motor cars led me into a sense of false security and I ran out recklessly into the road to fetch a ball and got bowled over and into the side of the roadside bank. The driver was so relieved when he found he had not killed me, that he gave me half a crown to settle the matter, just like the owner of the zoo when his lion ate Albert. We kept goats, rabbits, ferrets, hens and ducks. Father had a sow and when she had a litter of piglets, he would pick one out and ask the local butcher man to slaughter and prepare it for the table. Plenty of goodies were made by mother such as faggots, all sorts of joints and plenty of chitterlings.

Father had a few cows and I helped with the milking, before and after school. The cows and myself had no need of a watch when each morning I would be calling in the cows at five minutes to seven. We knew the time because of the hooter calling in the workers at Evercreech Brickworks - there was a repeat hooter at seven o'clock when workers should be ready for work or lose pay. We had a young heifer who did not like me at all. She would sometimes kick the bucket over and to spill some of the milk, just for spite. I sometimes had to defend myself with a long handle pitch fork when the beast came charging at me.

Castle Cary Association Football Club, 1946 – 47, assembled for the first game after World War II, against Yeovil Baptists, 31st. August 1946. Ken is in the front row, extreme left.
LHG collection.

We were mad on sport, particularly football and cricket. We would walk across the adjoining fields in a short cut to Maggs Lane and the Ansford Rovers football field passing through Solomon's Lane, which we called Joey's Lane, I suppose because of the old man who lived in the cottage near the lane junction. The cottage has since been demolished. One wonders about the history of this famous lane. They say it was on the main route from the West to London. They could stable horses at the old Ansford Inn, rest overnight and set off with the splendid horses and carriages, through Solomon's, on to Knapp Hollow, through to Hadspen, on to Nettlecombe and away. The old Ansford Inn had a history of its own. It is also said that the Landlord at one time was a Mr. Tucker, and that later he came to a sticky end, having moved to the lane now known as Tuckers Lane. He must have done away with his wife and was hanged on the gallows. Parson Woodforde would have known all the latest history on this area and round about.

When we were young boys and lads, we were keen on cycling. This took us on many trips of a sort I especially remember one in August 1939. War was looming, although we did not realize it as far as UK. was concerned. Mr. Chamberlain was Prime Minister and he had been to see Hitler who was putting Europe under threat. Neville came home and gave a speech promising "peace in our time" and he waved the piece of paper signed by Hitler to prove it. Winston was one of the few in power not to believe or put much trust in the situation. This brings me on to my point of cycling and cricket. On Bank Holiday August 1939 - Gloucester was at Home to Somerset. I was sixteen and my friend at the Waggon & Horses was about thirteen and had just learned to ride a bicycle. l asked him if he wanted to go out on our bikes for a nice ride and he did not hesitate to say "Yes." I had Bristol and cricket in mind but of course did not breath a word as the answer would have been different. We had got as far as to Ston Easton and were sitting down for a little rest when he suggested it was time to turn back - I then said Bristol was the target and that he would have to follow me. When we reached the Centre at Bristol we made enquiries as to the location of the Gloucester cricket field, and were slightly put back by being informed that it was up Nevil Road and still quite a long way to go. It must have been the second day and Gloucester was batting. Somerset was quite pleased to have got some of Glos. top batters out, including the world famous Wally Hammond. We were sat amongst a hostile crowd, egged on by my friend, who kept telling them that George Emmett would not get his century. l can still picture the scene when Emmett had got to 96 and went with a left hander's hook to square leg, only to be caught by the safe hands of Frank Lee. Soon after we decided to start our long journey home. The rest is history as they say. We lost the match and finished bottom of the league as usual.

I had to look for full time work upon leaving school at 14. My first job was at the twine and webbing factory of T. S. Donne & Sons Ltd. The pay was for a full week of 48 hours at twopence half penny per hour (in old money at 240 pence per pound). Work was hard to find in those days, and I remember meeting some of the young lads and others, over from a depressed area of South Wales, and who mainly worked on the twine walk which was quite a hard and dirty job involving constantly being shouted at and urged on by the walk foreman. I had a pleasant job working in the mill and helping to produce the webbing and winding the same into neat rolls. I also helped with maintenance of the looms. One day whilst working under strands of material going into the weavers threaders, one of the heavy iron weights keeping the strands taut, suddenly came down and hit me in the middle of my unguarded head. I was knocked out for a while and then sent

Ken, third from right, in the 'Squatters Removal Band' entry in Castle Cary Carnival in 1946, the first held after the War.
LHG collection.

home. I remember being in the Scouts, and we were looking forward to trip to London on the following day and as I did not wish to miss that, insisted that I had made a full recovery. l went to London for the first time and came back safe and sound. We had tea on the roof of Selfridges. That was in 1937.

The war started in September 1939, and by 1940 we were in a very bad position we had to try and catch up with our defences. I went to work at Yeovilton, where we were building the runways for the RNAS airplanes to come soon. I was working near to the first hanger when a lone German bomber came over the site and dropped three bombs, but did little important damage. That was 70 years ago and myself and a friend who was also on site that day, were invited to help with the press pre-view. The station Royal Marine Brigadier spoke to us and then the BBC and the local press reporters made their notes. The Brigadier and myself did speak for a short time on the later news programme and there was a good report in the papers.

After our contract with Reed & Mallick came to an end, l had to find another job and this time it was local. The contract was with Warings of Portsmouth and named I think Alford I.A.D. - this being intermediate ammunition depot, better known today as Dimmer Dump. I was number one as in my official works pass, being the first with one other on the contract. We erected the office first and I built a crazy paving surround to help access to the office with as little mud as possible. Warings brought their general foreman, together with an office manager and surveyor, and I was instructed to assist the surveyor as chain man, etc. There was nothing there except for green fields; we did all the roads and drainage, etc. The army laid the new rail track to form the siding from Alford to the ammunition huts, which were built by Waites of London. I was seconded to the

The Waggon and Horses at Castle Cary – Ken lives in the house to the left.
LHG collection.

Castle Cary Football Club, 1952 -53, Festival Cup winners. Ken is in the front row, extreme left.
LHG collection.

MOD to help the garrison engineer when he needed to do some surveying, and I also had to carry out general duties for the MOD once and did some important work in copying some drawings for the site works. This was quite tricky and depended on the strength of the sun as to how long you exposed them before developing in the appropriate box. As Warings sacked their wages clerk for drinking off the job I was then asked if I could do figure work and take on this job. This I did and also continued with the following Street contract - this time being in charge of the clerical staff office being several senior men. On pay day, I would walk around the streets to the various work places and pay out the men; I carried the wage packets openly in a tray basket, without fear of being mugged. –I don't think I would do that or likewise these days.

Looking back so many of my friends have gone before me and I am thankful for my present good health. I survived a couple of dangerous operations, and in recording these memories bring to mind the poem of Omar Khayyam who said –

"The moving finger writes; and having writ, moves on.
Nor all your Piety nor Wit, shall lure it back to cancel half a line.
Nor all your Tears wash out a word of it".

Thoughts on Cary by Maurice Adams

I was born in Wyke, Somerset, to Kathleen and Leonard Adams in August 1938, the fifth of eleven children. My first school was in Lamyatt, which as I remember it was a single classroom with a large stove in the middle in to which the teachers had to keep shovelling coal. We moved to Cary in 1945 when my father got a job at Manor Farm; Guy Churchouse was the manager. We lived in the house behind the Horse Pond on the right hand side. I went to Castle Cary infant school and then on to the junior school. These were the days of rationing, but we used to buy 2d. of broken biscuits from Hoskins' store on the way to school as these were not rationed, a great luxury in those days. Teachers I remember are Miss Corp and Miss Hill. I had a Saturday morning job working for Miss Warren cleaning the car and breaking up dog biscuits for her corgis. She was also our Cub and Scout Leader. I was in the Woodpeckers patrol. I moved on to Ansford Secondary School, but was not an academic child; in our last exam at the junior school I came second to bottom. I was in the "C" stream at Ansford, moving to becoming 2nd in the "B" stream when I left. I was hopeless at English and spelling, and only recently discovered the reason for this. Mr. Gough was headmaster; teachers I remember are Mrs. Stokes, my first teacher, Miss Barns, Mr. and Mrs. Harrison, and Mr. Steer.

Maurice with his brothers and sisters just after the family moved to Castle Cary. Left to right, back row:- Ruth; Doreen; Douglas; front row:- Marion; Jean; Jeffery; Margaret; Maurice; and Vera. R.Lodge collection.

I left school in 1953 when I was 15. While at Ansford School I used to go to work before and after school, plus weekends, for a small farmer, Frank James, whose farm was off North Street. He only had a cart horse with which I used many implements, the hardest being ploughing. All milking was done by hand. My wages for a forty seven and half hour week was 47 shillings and 6 pence or £2-37p per week.

Manor Farm decided to make cheese, and because the house we lived in was required to house the cheesemaker, my father had to find another job. He found another farming job at Chewton Mendip on Chewton Farms, Lord Waldegrave's estate, so I moved with my family to Chewton. My first job was working for a butcher, not a good job as I was ordered about and the boss took his problems out on me, and then I worked for a small farmer, Mervin Speed, where I was very happy. While working for Mervin I got my "call-up papers" for National Service, and decided to go and joined the RAF as an armament mechanic - "bombs", a move which changed my life in that I became very interested in mechanical devices. Unfortunately I caught rheumatic fever and was registered disabled so could not return to my job and went on a trade training course as an instrument maker. Employment at Marconi in Chelmsford followed, and I married in 1961. Subsequent employment included Leo Computers, which produced the first bar code reader, Pyrene Chubb, and Vokes Filtration; before creating Langman's Property Services installing office and other facilities in and around London.

Maurice in his National Service RAF uniform in 1955.
M.Adams collection.

Except for the occasional brief visit I did not return to Cary until 2006, when I organized a three day stay including a reunion of old school friends, which gave us time to look around, visit old haunts and talk to some of the inhabitants.

I set off to Cary on a cold overcast day with some excitement, not quite knowing what to expect. Had you returned to my home town of Woking after only 20 years you would not have recognized it. So what had happened to Cary?

I came along the A303 turning off at Wincanton, and memories started to flood back. On the winding road from Wincanton to Cary I had one of most frightening experiences of my life. I owned a 125cc. B.S.A. Bantam motor cycle which had broken down in Wincanton; a friend who had a much larger Triumph 500 motorbike offered me a tow back to Cary and I accepted, - how I got to Cary obtaining speeds my motorbike had never reached before, and certainly not at the end of a tow rope. My brakes seemed ineffective against the more powerful machine and there was no communication between us. Somehow we got back to Cary in one piece - I still do not know how I managed to stay on my motorcycle.

I was coming into Cary from the north down Cary Hill past fields I had worked in when I was a teenager. In those days I went to work after school and at weekends and left school at 15 starting full time work on a local farm. Turning left at the Wagon and Horses, now a Chinese restaurant, which seemed strange to me as in my last stay in Cary you would have been lucky to have any type of restaurant let alone another nationality; and then it would be only for the better off. Driving down North Street and into Market Square, except for cars cluttering the streets and a few changes to the shops I felt I had returned to the Cary I once knew. I booked into the George Hotel and found my friend Carroll Baker, at the bar already chatting to the local people, and we had a couple of drinks before going for a walk around the town.

Castle Cary is a delightful town which could equal the Cotswolds' towns. We found the people very welcoming; nothing was too much trouble. The Living History Group spent several hours with me and lent us several volumes of photographs of Cary through the ages.

We were shown around the Rural Museum by a couple we met looking at the church, and we were personally shown the Scout premises by the Scout Leader. We also met with many other inhabitants who kindly offered to help and other acts of kindness.

Starting our walk from the George Hotel, along Fore Street the first shop I can vividly remember was Whites - I can still smell the paraffin and oil when it was a hardware shop. I understand it has only recently changed. Although the shops have changed the street was generally as I remember it but there was something missing; it took a while for me to realize that the small stream that ran along it was gone. As a child this stream fascinated me and it was a unique feature of Cary. Why was it removed? Continuing along Fore Street we walked into the White Hart - it seemed familiar and Carroll was pleased when he saw a photograph on the wall of his grandfather with horse and cart outside his butcher's shop. My excitement stopped when we came to the Triangle; no it was not that my favourite sweet shop was now a kebab take away or the fact that Ottons where I bought my first radio was no more; it was the area behind the Horse Pond. When in Cary I lived in the house on the right hand side behind the pond - on the left hand side was a bicycle shop owned by a Mr. Pike, and behind these buildings was Manor Farm. The front of my house had a front door with porch and wood windows. What modernising has done is to leave what looks like a flat wall with four plastic windows, however what really shocked me was the area where the shop had been and the farm behind. The shop was not anything special and as I remember did not fit in with the other buildings. In the centre of the farm behind was a beautiful timber framed barn which had two sets of double split doors that you could drive vehicles loaded with hay, straw or other goods through. At the age of 15 I looked at this building with awe and admiration, - how could they pull this down? You talk about vandals - this was vandalism by the planners or whoever allowed it to be demolished. The row of terraced houses directly behind the pond is not in keeping with the town and it looks as if the houses are packed in for maximum profit with no consideration for the aesthetics of the area. What an opportunity has been missed as this area could have been the focal point of Cary, but instead I believe it has degraded the town. I could go on but I think the opportunity has now been missed.

Maurice in his garden in Surrey in 2009.
M.Adams collection.

Moving towards Park Street the Petrol Station car park area and Fire Station surrounds look a little tired. This area was a deserted army camp when I lived in Cary. I assume the petrol station was allowed because a small garage used to be adjacent. I am sure it would not be allowed so close to the centre of Cary if planning was applied for now. Maybe it would if the same planners are still employed. This area would not be difficult to smarten up. A little further up Park Street is Park Place - this street did not exist when I lived in Cary. Some of the terraced houses must have been pulled down to gain entrance. What a pity as these are some of the worst designed houses I have seen anywhere and are already deteriorating. Along the street and on the left are my old schools, from the outside they are as I remember them but I am sure the teaching methods have changed. Turning down the footpath along the side of the school used to lead to one of our favourite play areas with its ponds, trees, uneven terrain and our best hide-out, a large hollow old oak tree. I see that the grounds of the school have been extended and an interesting play area built. The tree is gone - I understand it caught on fire and had to be cut down.

    Opposite the school is the Church which although generally as I remembered, looked smaller and the galleries and font have been removed. We were sorry to see the grave stones heaped up against the walls and the grave yard not in very good condition. Walking on up through South Cary I wanted to see South Cary House where I had a Saturday job and the Cubs and Scouts meetings were held, again not a lot had changed. I now understand that South Cary House is a home for the elderly. If it is as I remember with its large garden it should be a pleasant place to live. Opposite there is a small development of new houses, these are a much better design than others I had in seen the town.

The Parsons brothers, Cary blacksmiths, with their mobile shoeing forge in the 1970s.

We walked back into the town through Lower Woodcock Street where Carroll's grandfather had his butcher's shop and my family, of at that time seven, lived in a two up two down house for six months while our other house was being modernised. Along this street was the blacksmith's shop, - I must have spent hours watching him work from shoeing horses, putting hoops on wheels, to making and repairing all sorts of machines and tools. I see the split doors are still there. What a magical place it would be if I was to open the top door and it was all still there, I can still dream! I was delighted to see the old public toilets were still there with the Ladies and Gentlemen signs still in place, and now an Art shop. There is still imagination with a sense of humour around. Moving a little further up the street tucked back from the road there are some more houses that do not fit in.

At the top of Lower Woodcock Street there is a very drab grey building which looks like it is made from concrete blocks - someone said it once belonged to the Ambulance service; otherwise the area looks similar to 50 years ago. Squibbs' Garage, where my brother bought the first car ever owned in the family, is now a housing estate. Woodcock Street has not changed a lot. I thought Woodcock Mews, a recent development, was tastily done except for the plastic meter boxes outside each house. Bailey Hill and the area of the Round House are exactly how I remember it, even the Post Office where I took out my first savings account 57 years ago has not changed.

I carried on to the playing fields. Bungalows that have been built on the lower parts where the swings used to be were not very inspiring. A new play area has been constructed which looks fun but I see the vandals have been at work. The toilets look like a miniature top security prison. I understand that the youth of the town with the help of others have raised a considerable sum of money to build a skateboard park but it has not been undertaken. Returning to the George and inquiring about the building works I could see going on behind the shop that was Whites, I was told by a local councillor that four houses and two flats were being built. Part of an old (over two metre high) stone wall had been demolished and it was thought the stones were to be used to face the house. I pointed out that as the builders had only 75mm space to the face of the wall they could not use the stone and the house would have to be rendered, not blending in with the shop, hotel or the adjacent wall. Are the vandals still at work? I also asked where were the new owners going to get access for a possible 12 vehicles, as there seems to be no access. The vehicles will be parked in the street which is already over parked. I understand that since raising my concerns the builders, not the planners, have agreed to face the wall to match the adjacent stone.

One of the nice surprises coming from Surrey is that there are no parking charges, but you still have the problem of all towns, off street parking. There is a large car park off the Triangle that could be utilized more, however in my experience most motorists will not walk more than they have to. I was very surprised to hear that there was not a full Town Council and equally important in my eyes, no Chamber of Commerce, no wonder the District Council overrule the local people's decisions.

A family group taken in 1984 at Wincanton Racecourse, left to right:- Kathleen; Margaret; Ruth; Douglas; Jean; Maurice; Marion; Vera; Doreen; Jeffery; Brenda; and Christine.
M.Adams collection.

From press reports and talking to local people, houses are being bought by "outsiders" some even travelling to London to work. How the area has changed. I assume they chose Castle Cary because they liked the area and town therefore will be interested in the welfare of the town. If I still lived in Cary I would welcome these people and get them involved in trying to make Cary a place to be proud of. I know some people are taking an interest in the town such as The Living History Group; I understand there is a Carnival each year, and there are the Wives Group, the Women's Institute, the Museum Committee and others. But some aspects of the structure and future of the town seem badly neglected. I hope the people who read my account of my brief visit will not think I am interfering; they are what I found and felt. I am a Caryite as I fell in the Horse Pond twice! A lot of damage has already been carried out. If you do not organize now more will be done. The vandals may have done some damage around the town but I think the planners have carried out a lot more. More Cary inhabitants need to start taking an interest in their town before more damage is done. It is everyone's responsibility not just the councillors'.

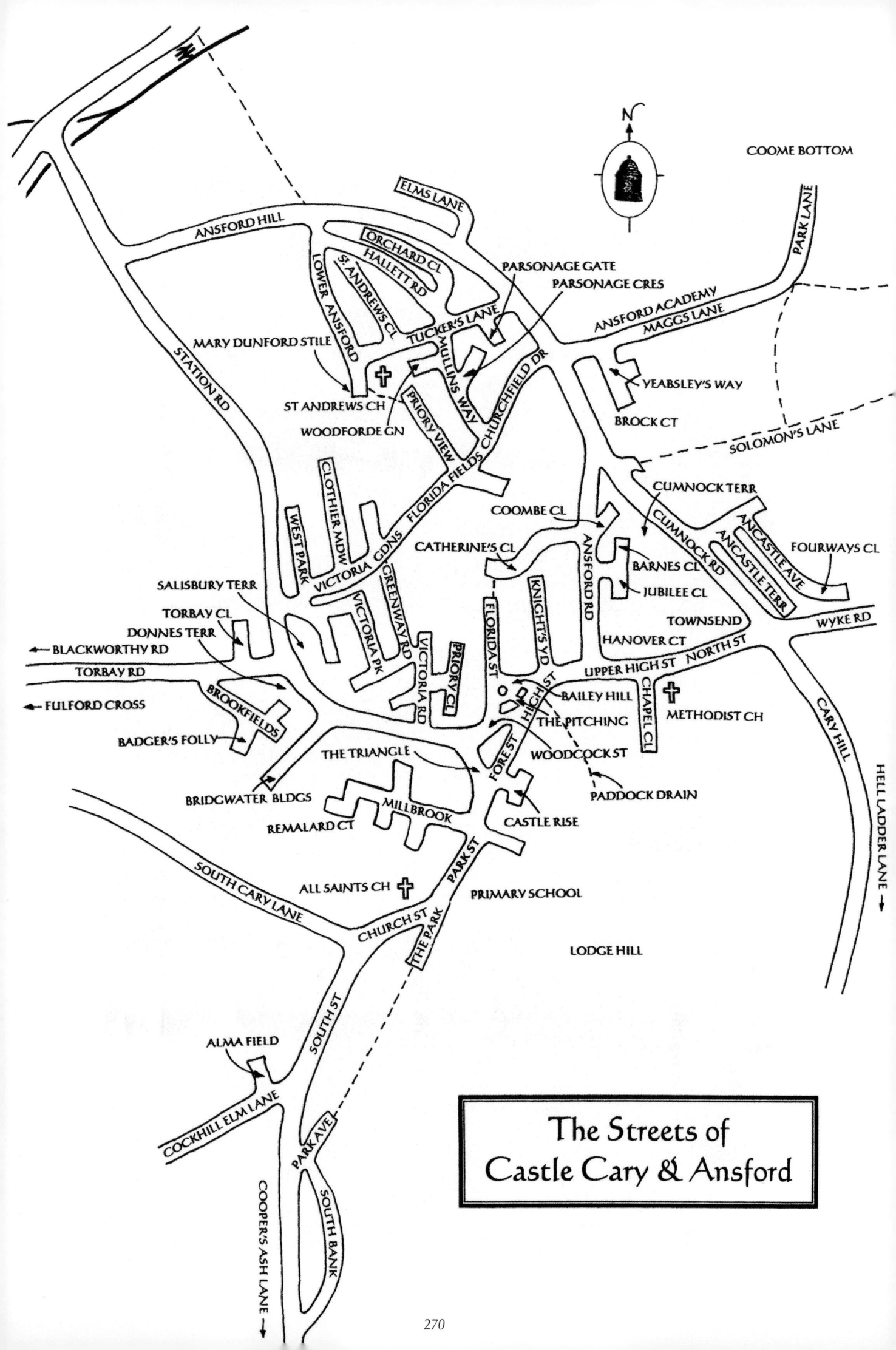

The Streets of Castle Cary & Ansford

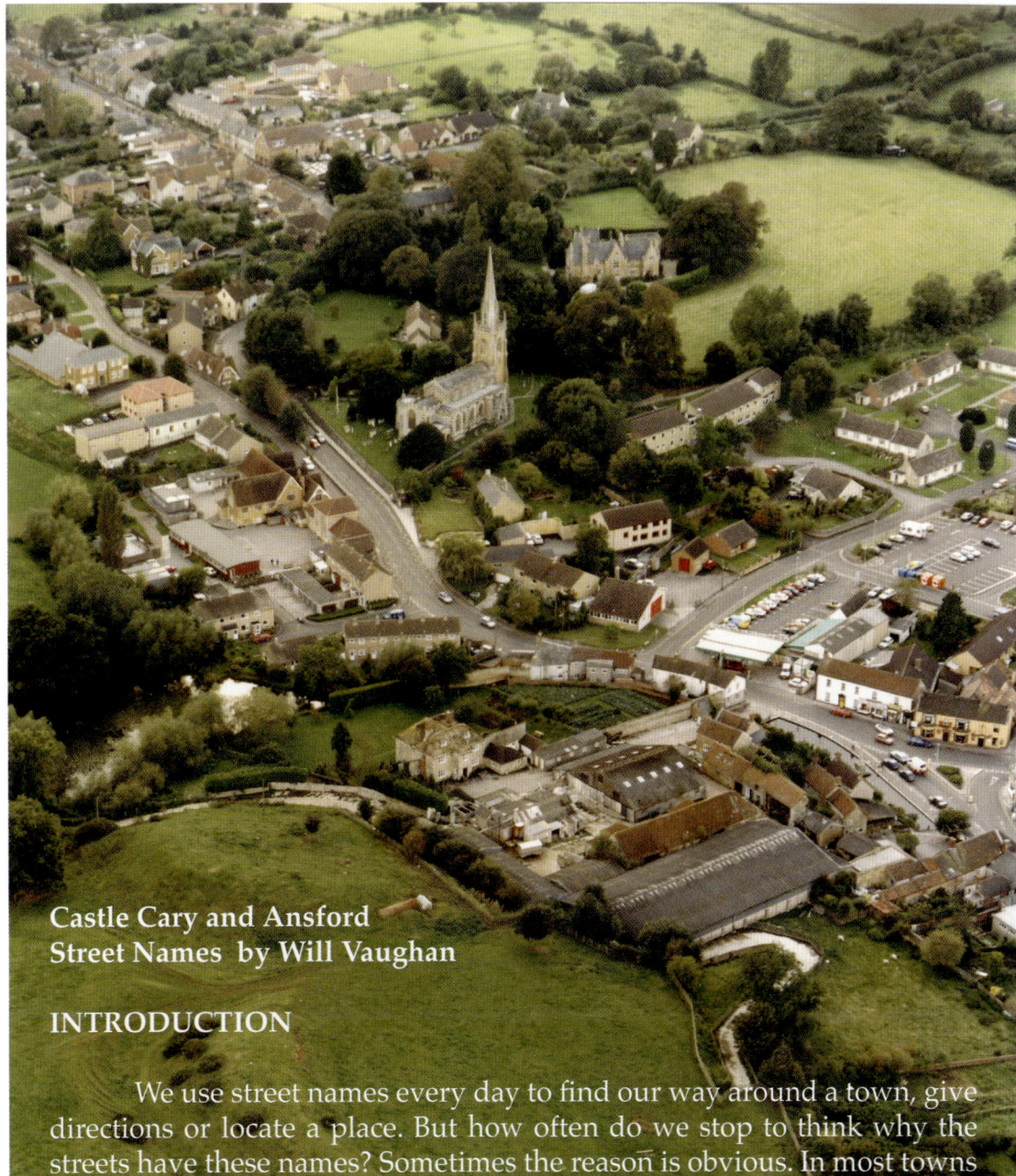

Castle Cary and Ansford Street Names

Castle Cary and Ansford Street Names by Will Vaughan

INTRODUCTION

We use street names every day to find our way around a town, give directions or locate a place. But how often do we stop to think why the streets have these names? Sometimes the reason is obvious. In most towns the main street is called the 'high' street, and names like 'church street' or 'north street' are usually fairly clear. But others are more of a puzzle. Why is one of the main streets in Cary, for example, called after a water fowl? Why are some of the others named after a part of America, a town in Scotland, or a battle in the Crimea War? How did 'Hell Ladder Lane' get its name? These streets, roads and lanes were all given names for some reason, and usually they tell us something of the history of the town and the people who lived in it. Mostly these reasons are soon forgotten. However, with some digging, many can be recovered, and in the street names of Cary and Ansford there are glimpses of the town and its inhabitants from medieval times to the present day. While all the names cannot be explained – or even have the correct explanation – it is at least a start. Hopefully it may stimulate further research and explanations. The examination has been arranged as a journey around the town, commenting on the street names as they occur.

STREET NAMES BY AREA

Central Cary; from Fore Street to Florida

An enamel street sign, dating from the 1920s, and part of a large collection of Cary signs now preserved in the town's Museum.
Museum collection.

Cary is shaped by an invisible presence - the Castle from which it derives its name. The castle, levelled in 1147, was situated on the lower slopes of Lodge Hill and mounds marking its remains can still be seen. But it extended further into the town, and its outer limit is marked by **Fore Street**, which curves along the base of this hill, following a wall that is no longer there. Presumably the name means that it was the street in front of, or before the Castle. In recent years new housing has been built in the area originally occupied by the outer reaches of the castle, which is recorded in the name **Castle Rise**.

A view of Fore Street in 1961, from the Horse Pond, which was created from part of the moat around the former manorial complex, now occupied by the Castle Rise development.
A.V.Pearse collection.

Lower Fore Street in the 1920s – before the current one-way system in the opposite direction was established. The barn, used as stables, on the right, has since been demolished.
A.V.Pearse collection.

The upper section of Fore Street decorated for Queen Victoria's Diamond Jubilee in 1897.
A.V.Pearse collection.

MARKET PLACE *Museum collection.*

Fore Street runs into the **Market Place**, the heart of the town. Markets were already held in Cary in the thirteenth century, though possibly not on a regular basis. The first surviving charter for a regular market comes from 1468. The market has fallen into abeyance at times since then, but in modified form is still active today. Rising behind the market is **Bailey Hill**, now best known for the Lock-up that was erected there c.1779; it seems that this was originally the site of the residence of the Bailiff, who would have had charge of managing Cary for the Lord of the Manor. 'Bailey' derives from the middle English word 'baili' which means – unsurprisingly – bailiff. It is perhaps significant from this point of view that the town was the focal point of local secular and ecclesiastical administration already by 1215 and that the manorial court met regularly in Cary throughout the middle ages. The name **Pie Corner**, preserved in the house on the north side of Bailey Hill, is believed to relate to a Piepowder Court that was held before the bailiff in Cary to regulate the conduct of the fair.

CASTLE CARY,
SOMERSET.

MR. HARROLD
WILL SELL BY AUCTION,

On Monday, September 28th,
AT THE GEORGE HOTEL, CASTLE CARY,

At Four for Five o'clock in the Afternoon, subject to such conditions as will then be produced,

The Undermentioned

WELL SITUATED & DESIRABLE FREEHOLD

DWELLING HOUSE
WITH

SPACIOUS SHOP,
WAREHOUSE, & PREMISES,
COMPRISING

A Lofty and Well-built Freehold Dwelling House containing five good Bedrooms, Landings, W.C., a pleasant Drawing Room, Dining Room, Pantry, Kitchen, Back Ditto, Coal Cellar, Court, a spacious Shop with Double Plate Glass Front, and Warehouse with 3 Rooms. The Property is unusually well situated, having frontages to Fore Street, Woodcock Street and the Market Place. It is part of No. 76 on the Tithe Map of the said parish, was for many years in the occupation of the late Mr. Thomas Coles, Chemist, and is now occupied by Mr. William Longman, Grocer, whose tenancy will expire at Michaelmas.

The above Property is situated in the centre of the Town, and commands the very best position for business; it is substantially and well built, in good condition, and offers a rare opportunity to those seeking good roomy premises for any kind of trade.

To view apply to the Tenant, and for further particulars to the Auctioneer; or to

Mr. J. H. Ralph Smythe,
Solicitor, Castle Cary.

Dated Auction and Estate Offices, Castle Cary, September 8th, 1885.] [MOORE, PRINTER, CASTLE CARY.

An auction poster for the premises now occupied by Barclays Bank.
LHG collection.

The Market Place, normally bustling with activity, on a quiet day in 1906.
A.V.Pearse collection.

BAILEY HILL

Bailey Hill contains Cary's most iconic building, the Round House, and the fine eighteenth century house that now contains the Post Office.
Museum collection.

The steep walkway that leads from Bailey Hill down to Market Place is called **The Pitchings**, a name relating to the pitching stones with which it is paved. Cobbling a steep slope with specially laid pitching stones was a common practice in earlier times. There are similar 'pitchings' surviving in some other towns – for example The Pitchings at Matlock Bath in Derbyshire.

WOODCOCK STREET

Museum collection.

It is harder to explain the name of the third central street in Cary that shapes the group known as 'the triangle', called **Woodcock Street**. The earliest record of the name comes from 1768, and an explanation of the name was offered by F.W. Harrold in the Castle Cary Visitor in 1897; "I have heard an old resident say that this street obtained its name from the fact that it was formerly a marsh frequented by woodcocks and other birds." This may not be altogether impossible as the river Cary rises on Lodge Hill and flows west at this point. Before it was properly channelled (as it is now) the level area beyond the Horse Pond was marshy and could have attracted water fowl. A less colourful explanation would be that it was named after some former owner or resident called Woodcock, but there is no record of this. It is possible, too, that the street was originally named Woodville Street; the house at the corner of Woodcock street and Bailey Hill being called Woodville House.

A view of Lower Woodcock Street in the 1920s.
The cottages on the right have since been demolished.
A.V.Pearse collection.

The 'Triangle' in the 1950s.
A.V.Pearse collection.

By order of the Mortgagees.

CASTLE CARY,
SOMERSET.

Mr. F. W. HARROLD
WILL SELL BY AUCTION, AT THE

GEORGE HOTEL, CASTLE CARY,

ON TUESDAY, APRIL 25TH, 1899,
at 4 o'clock in the afternoon,

subject to such conditions as shall then and there be produced, the undermentioned valuable

FREEHOLD PROPERTY

VIZ:—

All those Four Messuages, or

DWELLING-HOUSES AND SHOPS,

situate in Fore Street and Woodcock Street, Castle Cary, now in the respective occupations of Mr. T. Thorne, Mr. H. Porter, Mr. Herbert Noble, and Mrs. Francis.

The Buildings are in a good and tenantable state of repair, three being newly erected, and let to responsible tenants at the total annual rental of

£42 10s. 0d.

The property is well and centrally situated, and offers an excellent opportunity for Investment.

To view apply to the respective Tenants; further particulars can be obtained of the Auctioneer, Castle Cary, or of

Mr. J. O. CASH,
SOLICITOR, CASTLE CARY & WINCANTON

Dated Auction and Estate Offices, Castle Cary, 6/4/99.   J. H. ROBERTS, Printer, Stationer, Bookbinder, etc., Market Place, Castle Cary.

LHG collection.

CASTLE CARY,

February 29 1912

M*r* Stockman

Dr. to S. HERMAN,
FAMILY BUTCHER.

BRITANNIA COMMERCIAL HOTEL,
CASTLE CARY,

_____ 190

M*r* Frank Barrington

Dr. to S. HERMAN.

Dominating the 'Triangle' was the Britannia Hotel, in 1912 occupied by Samuel Herman and his family, who emigrated to the United States on board RMS Titanic. Samuel, together with George Sweet who lived with the family, perished, while his wife and two daughters survived.

FLORIDA STREET

Florida Street leads from Bailey Hill to Florida House and the new developments that now surround it.
Museum collection.

The area of high land running northwest of Bailey Hill is in known by the name of **Florida**. Its origin is something of a mystery, - the most popular explanation being that it is named after an ill-fated expedition to Florida, America in the seventeenth century. The other explanation is that it is named after Strata Florida in Wales, as it is thought that the original owners of the large house known as **Florida Place** that once occupied this area came from Strata Florida. The house was approached from Bailey Hill via **Florida Street**. In 1877 the industrialist John Donne built a mansion beyond this, which he called Florida House, the former house being demolished, though parts may be incorporated in the stable block.

An aerial view of Florida House, grounds and outbuildings, taken during the 1940s.
A.V.Pearse collection.

Florida House is nowadays referred to as **The Priory**, because it was renamed St. John's Priory by an order of nuns, The Sisters of Jesus Crucified, who occupied the premises between 1959 and 1996. Since then the house and grounds have been redeveloped as a private residential estate (at the time of writing the house itself is virtually derelict). A footpath leading to it has been renamed **Priory Path**, and a new residential complex close by has been called **Priory Close**.

The brick-built houses and flats in Victoria Park were erected by C. Thomas & Son in the years around 1950.
V.Nicholls collection.

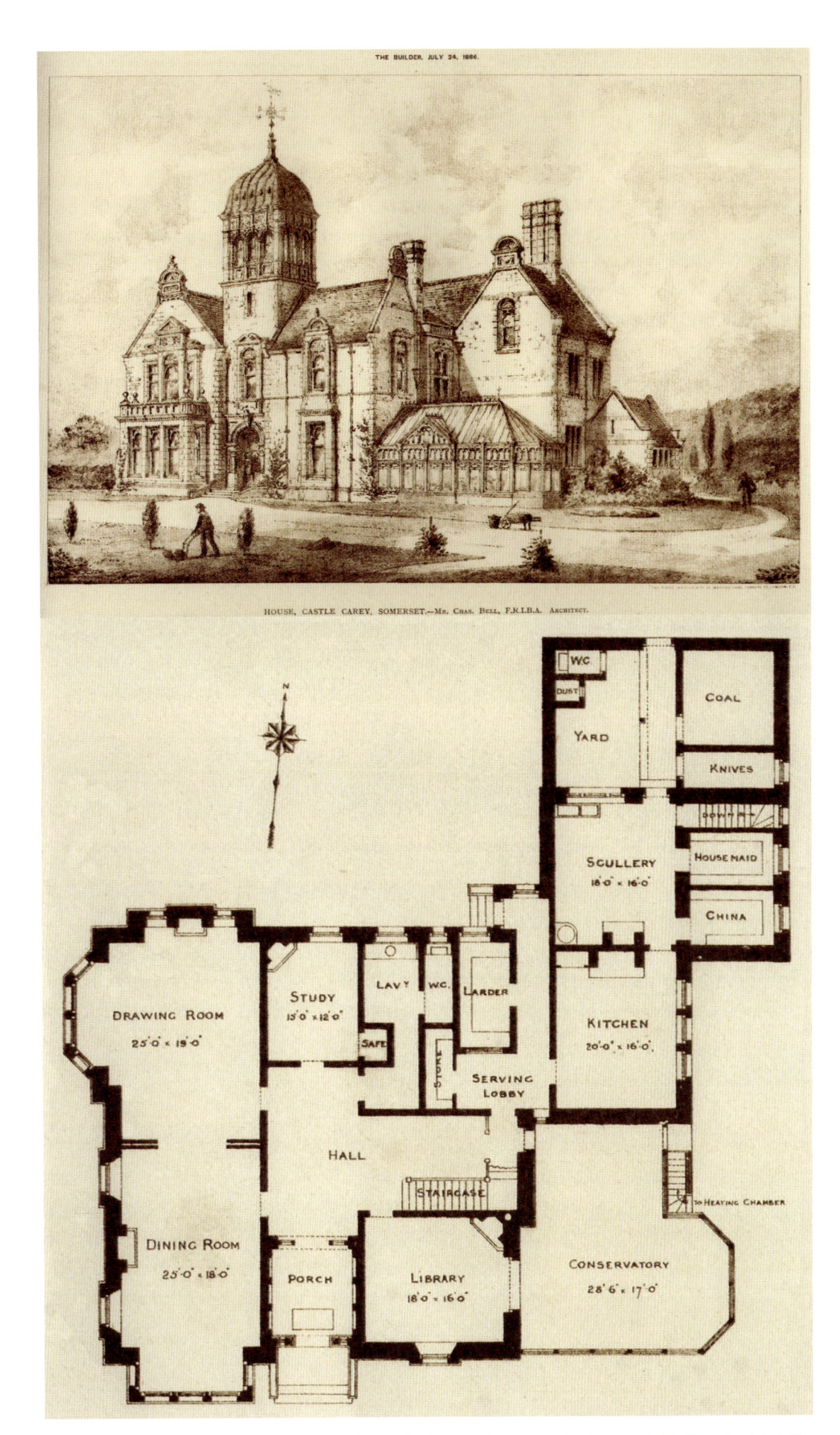

The architect Charles Bell's design for Florida House as published in The Builder for July 24th. 1886. It was built by Cary builder, E. O. Francis & Son, the following year, but is now in a derelict condition facing an uncertain future.
A.V.Pearse collection.

Further west along Woodcock Street, a road leads up to the Priory, now called **Victoria Road** and also leads to the estate known as **Victoria Park**, built by the district council in the twentieth century. Previously it was known as **Blind Lane** (as seen on a map of Cary of 1839), presumably because it was at that time a cul-de-sac. In 1854 the Castle Cary Gas Light and Coke Company was formed and established a gas works on the corner of this street and Woodcock Street. After that it was known as **Gas House Lane**, before becoming **Victoria Road** in the early twentieth century. This road is a section of a very early route running directly across the area north – south from the bridge over the Brue by the Railway station, through Ansford and south to South Street.

Going West; from Millbrook to Fulford's Cross

The area west of central Cary – whether marshy or not – became the site of mills that were built to harness the resources of the river Cary. A mill is still recalled in the name **Millbrook** which has been used for the estate developed here in the later twentieth century. **Badgers Court** records another former occupant of the area, and **Remalard Court**, in Millbrook Gardens, is named after Rémalard, the town in Normandy that is twinned with Castle Cary and Ansford.

The 'lodge' house to the Higher Flax Mills complex has attractive detailing.
A.Brittain collection.

CASTLE CARY,

SOMERSET.

IMPORTANT SALE OF VALUABLE

FREEHOLD BUILDING SITES

situate close to the town, and abutting upon the principal approach from the Railway Station and surrounding neighbourhood.

Mr. F. W. HARROLD

has received instructions to SELL BY AUCTION, at the

GEORGE HOTEL, CASTLE CARY,

On THURSDAY, the 12th day of APRIL, 1900,

At 5 for 6 o'clock in the afternoon.

Subject to such conditions as shall then be produced, ALL THAT the lower or Western portion of the

PIECE OF GROUND

known as the Brickyard, situate on the North side of Mill Lane, in the parish of Castle Cary, together with

THE WORKMAN'S COTTAGE,

Brick Kiln, Shedding, & other Building Material standing on same.

This Sale affords an opportunity seldom met with in Castle Cary of acquiring Freehold Land suitable for the erection of Artizan's dwellings (for which there is a good demand), or other residences with a Southern aspect and pleasant view in a main thoroughfare of the town.

The Property will be offered in the following or such other Lots as may be determined upon, and possession of the whole will be given on completion of the purchases.

A Plan of the Property may be seen at the place of sale, or on application to the Auctioneer, Castle Cary, or to

Mr. RANDOLPH WOODFORDE,

SOLICITOR, CASTLE CARY.

A row of terraced houses was built over part of the brickworks site; Squibb's garage occupied the remainder until replaced by Victoria Court.
LHG collection.

CASTLE CARY
SOMERSET.

MR. F. W. HARROLD

has received instructions from the Executors of the Will of the late Mr. Richard Corner, to Sell by Auction, at the

GEORGE HOTEL, CASTLE CARY,

ON THURSDAY, MAY 28TH, 1903,

at 4 for 5 o'clock in the afternoon, subject to conditions to be then produced,

LOT 1. All that

FREEHOLD COTTAGE

containing 5 rooms, together with the Garden and Outhouses pleasantly situated in Mill Street, now let to Mr. Arthur Apsey at the yearly rent of £12

LOT 2. Three fully-paid £12 10s. 0d.

SHARES IN THE CASTLE CARY MARKET HOUSE Co.

Nos. 110, 111, 112,

LOT 3. Two £20 5 per cent.

Debentures in the Bruton Girls' School Co., Ltd.,

and also two £5 shares in the same.

Further particulars may be obtained of the Auctioneer, Castle Cary, or of

Mr. J. O. CASH, Solicitor, Castle Cary.

Dated Auction and Estate Offices, Castle Cary, 1/5/1903.   ROBERTS, PRINTER, CASTLE CARY.

LHG collection.

SOMERSETSHIRE.

IN THE PARISH OF CASTLE CARY.

Particulars of Sale of a Small Valuable

Freehold Residential & Agricultural Estate,

situated in and near the Market Town of Castle Cary, comprising:—

DESIRABLE CLOSES OF RICH PASTURE LAND,

RESIDENCE AND GROUNDS,

known as "TORBAY,"

Convenient House, Cottages, Gardens, Orchards, Eligible Building Sites, Valuable Accommodation Lands, and Old Mill with Water Power,

THE WHOLE IN EXTENT

20a. 1r. 11p.,

or thereabouts.

MESSRS.

WAINWRIGHTS & HEARD

have received instructions to Offer for SALE by AUCTION, at the "BRITANNIA HOTEL," CASTLE CARY,

On THURSDAY, 17th AUGUST, 1899,

at 2 for 3 o'clock precisely in the Afternoon, the above Valuable PROPERTY, in Lots, and subject to such Conditions of Sale as shall be then produced.

To view, apply to the respective Tenants.

Particulars may be obtained, and a Plan of the Property seen, at the place of Sale, of Messrs. MACKAY & SON, Solicitors, Shepton Mallet; or of

Messrs. WAINWRIGHTS & HEARD, Surveyors & Land Agents, Shepton Mallet.

A. BYRT & SON, PRINTERS, SHEPTON MALLET & WELLS.

LHG collection.

Torbay Road – currently a mix of old and recent developments, industrial and residential.
A.Brittain collection.

There were several mills that used the power of the river Cary as it descended the hill; in the Domesday Book there are already three mills mentioned in Cary, and they were probably all in this area. The name **Torbay** has been associated with the area for a long time, but its origins are unknown, though the substantial house erected in the lower part of the area in the early nineteenth century was named Torbay House, while **Torbay Road**, which skirts the area, only received its current name in the twentieth century. In the nineteenth century it was known as **Mill Lane**, a reference to the mills that were sited beside it. However before that it was known as **Market Way**, a name that it already had in 1610, when there was a complaint that the market way was in a bad state of repair between Cockhill and Cary Mills. In those days the market way was the main route into Cary along the river Cary from the levels, and it was also a drovers' road.

At the bottom of Torbay Road there is a crossroads known as **Fulford's Cross**, or sometimes simply as **Fulford Cross**. 'Cross' might seem to refer simply to the fact that it is a cross road. However there was an actual stone cross here, recorded in Pooley's Somerset Crosses. It was quite common to have crosses in the middle ages at major crossroads and its presence here is a reminder that this was an important thoroughfare in foregone times. The name Fulford might seem to refer to some person, but it might equally well refer to the ford that was recorded here in the seventeenth century, as the river Cary crosses the road at this point, which might explain the term 'full ford', for the river would have been likely to be particularly vigorous here, being forced to slow down by meeting level ground after having sped down the hill. Nowadays the river is sent through a tunnel under the road; nevertheless, it often overflows.

Blackworthy Road heads towards Clanville. To the right is the large Crown Pet Food factory, a recent addition to Cary's industrial development.
A.Brittain collection.

The road to the right is **Blackworthy Road**, referring to Blackworthy farm, which is beside it. 'Worthy' was an old name for very good land, and was often used for well-favoured farms. The road formed part of the main route into Cary from the Somerton and Langport turnpike (established 1778), and there was a tollhouse here.

The Crown Pet Food Factory, constructed in 2007 east of Blackworthy Road.

STATION ROAD

Station Road was built as part of the re-organisation of the road network occasioned by the construction of the railway station which opened in 1856.
Museum collection.

Built as social housing in the 1920s, West Park borders Station Road, and has superb views across the central Somerset lowlands.
A.V.Pearse collection.

The upper end of Torbay Road runs into **Station Road**, built in 1853-4 to connect the town with the recently built railway station. Originally it was known as **New Road**, gaining its current name in the early twentieth century, by which time it was no longer new. The change of name appears to have occurred at the time when there was considerable housing development along it, including, **Salisbury Terrace**, **Victoria Park**, and **Greenway Road**. Salisbury Terrace is named after the industrialist T.Salisbury Donne, who donated the buildings.

WEST PARK *Museum collection.*

Salisbury Terrace was built in 1913, with Moore Villas just beyond.
LHG collection.

288

SALISBURY TERRACE *Museum collection.* **MOORE VILLAS** *Museum collection.*

Greenway Road contained Airey houses built after World War II and designed by Sir Edwin Airey as part of the Ministry of Works Emergency Factory Made housing programme. The construction features prefabricated concrete columns, reinforced with steel recycled from military vehicles, and clad in shiplap style concrete panels.
LHG collection.

'South Cary'; from South Street to Cooper's Ash Lane

Going south from the centre of Cary we come to **Park Street**. The Park referred to in this name is the ancient Park of Cary that lay on the slopes of Lodge Hill, running south from the Castle to the southern edge of the town. Already mentioned in the Domesday Book, the park was for the use of the Lord of the Manor. In the middle ages it was a deer park, but later became farming land, as it is today. Several roads around the ancient park contain the name park, such as **The Park** and **Park Avenue**. **Lodge Hill** itself appears to have acquired its name because there was a lodge sited on it, at a time when the Park was tended by a keeper.

PARK AVENUE *Museum collection.*

Park Street runs into **Church Street**, which leads past All Saints, the Parish Church of Cary. It is believed that there was originally also a road that ran to the west of the church and directly through the Millbrook area to Ansford, which has, however, long since vanished.

CASTLE CARY,
SOMERSET.

HARROLD, SON, & PITHER

will Sell by Auction, at

THE ANGEL HOTEL, CASTLE CARY,

ON MONDAY, SEPTEMBER 16TH,

at 3 o'clock in the afternoon,

subject to such conditions as shall then and there be produced, the undermentioned

FREEHOLD

DWELLING HOUSE

containing 4 Bedrooms, 3 Sitting Rooms, Kitchen, Pantry, Cellar, Outhouse, 2 w.c.'s, Pig Stye, Stable with Loft over, a good Well of Water, large Paint Shop, Yard and Garden, with entrance to the Park,

TOGETHER WITH A FIVE-ROOM

COTTAGE

adjoining, in the respective occupation of Mrs. CULLIFORD and Mr. BROWN.

The Property is well and centrally situated with an extensive frontage to the street, and with a little outlay may be much improved. It offers advantages for occupation or investment.

To view the same apply to the Tenants, and for further particulars to the Auctioneers, Castle Cary,

OR TO

MESSRS. BARTLETT & SONS,
Solicitors, Sherborne.

Dated Auction and Estate Offices, Castle Cary, 14/8/1907.

ROBERTS, PRINTER, CASTLE CARY

LHG collection.

CASTLE CARY
SOMERSET.

TO BE SOLD BY AUCTION,
BY
Mr. T. O. BENNETT, Junr.
AT THE "GEORGE HOTEL," CASTLE CARY,
On Thursday, the 2nd of May, 1878,
AT FOUR O'CLOCK IN THE AFTERNOON,

Subject to Conditions, to be then produced, and in the following or such other Lots as may be determined on at the time of Sale, the undermentioned

DESIRABLE PROPERTY

LOT 1, (FREEHOLD)
A DWELLING HOUSE and Premises, with Coach-house, Stable, Yard, Lawn, and Garden, situate at South Cary, known as

"PARK COTTAGE,"

In the occupation of Mr. Thomas Gifford as yearly Tenant, and being part of number 111 in the Tithe Commutation Map.

LOT 2, (FREEHOLD)
SIX COTTAGES with GARDENS

In South Cary adjoining the above, in the respective occupations of Thomas Mogg, Thomas Colley, Charles Noble, Mary Burfitt, Alfred Bond, and William Perrott, at rentals amounting together to £33 16s. per annum or thereabout, and being the remaining part of number 111 in the Tithe Commutation Map.

LOT 3, (FREEHOLD)
Comprises the Messuage or Dwelling House formerly known as "the Bank," but now used as the

"TEMPERANCE HOTEL"

Situate at Bailey Hill, in the Town of Castle Cary, and in the occupation of Mr. Foden Lawrence or his under tenant, together with the DWELLING HOUSE and SHOP adjoining and also the Yard at the back thereof now occupied by Mr. Edwin Spears.

LOT 4, (LEASEHOLD)
A Messuage or Dwelling House

In two Tenements, with the Yard at the back, also situate at Bailey Hill aforesaid, now in the several occupations of George Northam and Ann Barnard, as quarterly Tenants, at rentals amounting together to £7 16s. per annum.

This Lot is held on Lease for a term of years determinable on the life of a person aged 45.

The Dwelling House at South Cary, known as "Park Cottage," is an attractive and comfortable detached residence, stone built and slated, most pleasantly situated facing the Park, in a good state of repair, replete with every convenience, and well supplied with water. The Dwelling House lately used as "the Bank" and the adjoining premises at Bailey Hill are situate in the centre of the Town of Castle Cary, with an extensive frontage towards the Market.

Possession of Lot 1 may be obtained if desired on the 25th day of March, 1879; of the Temperance Hotel, part of Lot 3, on the 25th day of December, 1879; the other part of Lot 3 at Michaelmas next; and of the remaining Lots on settlement of the purchase.

Lot 1 may be viewed on application to Mr. Thomas Gifford, Lot 2 on application to Mr. Henry Gosling of Ansford, and Lots 3 and 4 on application to Mr. Silas Hoskins.

Particulars may be obtained of Messrs. T. O. BENNETT and SON, Land Agents, Bruton, Mr. C. RUSS, Solicitor, Castle Cary, or of

Mr. William Bennett, Solicitor, Bruton.

[MOORE, PRINTER, CASTLE CARY.]

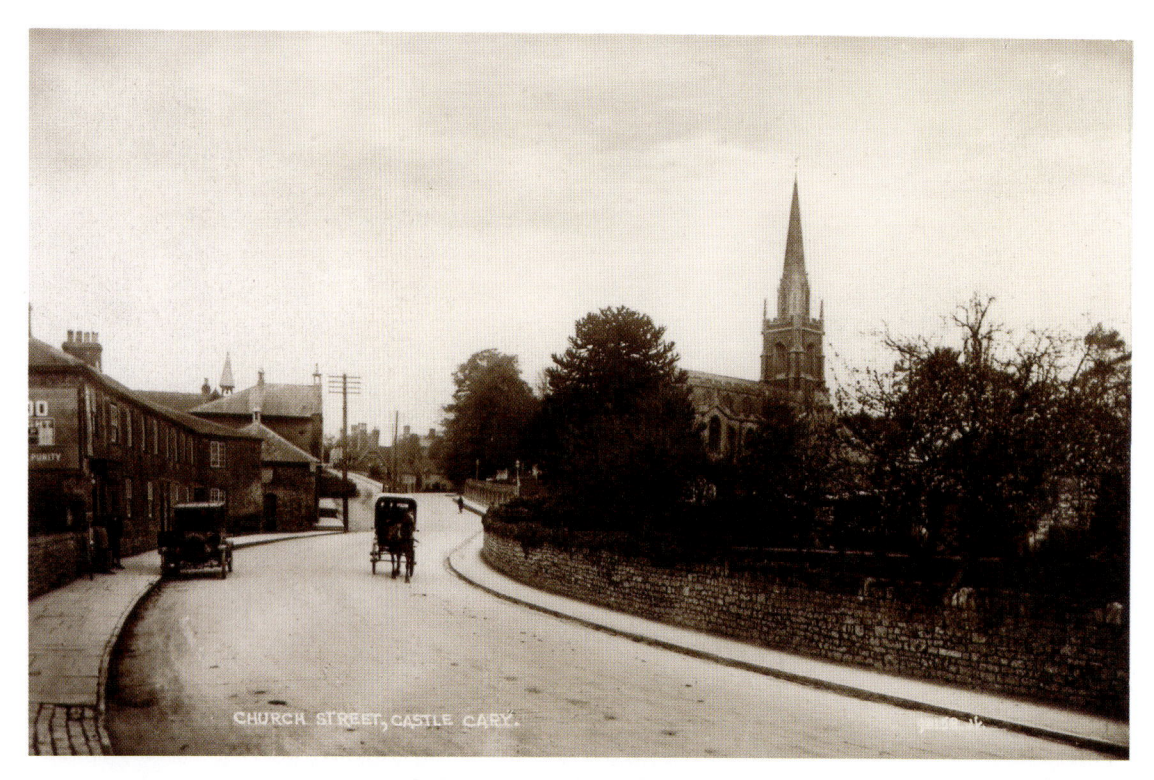

Church Street in the 1920s; the Monkey Puzzle trees and the orchard on the right belonged to Church Villa.
A.V.Pearse collection.

'Sandbanks' accurately describes the crumbling sandy stone that forms the bank to the left in this view from c.1905.
A.V.Pearse collection.

South Street, c. 1905. Note the raised pavements in this part of the town.
A.V.Pearse collection.

South Cary Lane runs west out of Church Street down the hill to Fulford Cross. Originally South Cary was a separate settlement, known as 'South Town'. The road that runs through it is now called **South Street**. Further along South Street, to the left (east) is **Chapel Yard**, named after the Zion Congregational Chapel that was once here, now a private house.

The Zion Congregational Chapel in Chapel Yard was built in 1815 and closed in 1979. It has been converted to residential use.

CASTLE CARY,
SOMERSET.

TO BE SOLD BY AUCTION,
BY
MR. HARROLD,
AT THE "GEORGE HOTEL," CASTLE CARY,

On TUESDAY, the 16th of MARCH, 1875,

At SIX o'clock in the Evening, (subject to such Conditions as will be then produced)

THE UNDERMENTIONED VERY DESIRABLE

FREEHOLD
DWELLING HOUSES
AND
COTTAGES.

LOT 1. All that Comfortable and Commodious DWELLING HOUSE comprising a good Entrance Hall, Parlour, Kitchen, Back Kitchen, 3 roomy and healthy Bedrooms, large Attic, and a good, dry, airy underground Cellar, with that part of the GARDEN abutting on the Park, late in the occupation of Mr. STEWART.

And all that Comfortable COTTAGE adjoining thereto and the GARDEN occupied therewith now let to JOHN STACEY.

The above Premises are situated in the Chapel Yard, South Cary.

LOT 2. All those SIX DWELLING HOUSES or COTTAGES with the Wash-houses, Outbuildings, and Pieces of GARDEN GROUND belonging and adjoining thereto in the respective occupations of SAMUEL KYNASTON, GEORGE BOND, TOM BAKER, JOHN GULLIFORD, LUCY PARSONS, and RICHARD GIBBS, situated near the Church, three of such Cottages facing the Park and the remainder facing the Street.

To view Lot 1 apply to John Stacey, and Lot 2 to the respective Tenants.

For further particulars apply to the AUCTIONEER, or to

Mr. RUSS, Solicitor, CASTLE CARY.

Dated Castle Cary, 27th February, 1875.   [MOORE, PRINTER, CASTLE CARY.]

LHG collection.

To the west is **Cockhill Elm Lane**, a cul-de-sac that causes some confusion, as its name suggests that it leads towards the hamlet of **Cockhill**, at the base of the hill. There is indeed a footpath that leads there, and that is now part of the **Macmillan Way**. Probably this was a more important route in earlier times and this is how the name got attached to it. In the nineteenth century it was known simply as **Cockhill Lane**. It probably began to be called Cockhill Elm Lane after houses were built along it. There was a line of elm trees at the end of the lane, which fell victim to Dutch Elm Disease during the 1970s.

Alma Close leads off Cockhill Elm Lane, the name being a reference to an Inn that used to lie between it and South Street, which in more recent years was known as The Countryman and then The Bay Tree. Originally the Inn was called The Alma, and was in business by 1859, being run by Richard Andrews, a former soldier. The name refers to the Battle of Alma, one of the decisive victories of the Crimean War in 1854. The victory by British and French troops against the Russians was widely celebrated at the time and the name The Alma was used frequently for inns and pubs. established then throughout the country. It was also the beginning of the use of Alma as a girl's name.

Museum collection.

Parallel to the southern end of South Street is **South Bank**, so named in the early twentieth century when a row of houses was erected here.

Just beyond the limits of the town is the road leading down to Cockhill, which has the intriguing name of **Cooper's Ash Lane**. Ash was one of the woods used traditionally by coopers for making barrels. There were several coopers active in Cary – as there were in all towns prior to the twentieth century. Possibly one of the Cary Coopers had some property along the lane with ash trees – or else had the possibility of getting wood from them, and there are still some fine ash trees along the lane.

Museum collection.

Going north from Market Place, the **High Street** has two cul-de-sacs running off it with names recording recent local figures. To the north is **Knight's Yard**, named after William Albert Knight, the first Head Master of Sexey's School, Bruton (known to some as 'Wacker' Knight) who once lived here. To the south is **Pither's Yard**, formerly the site where the furniture and cabinet makers Pither and Son operated; a large employer in the town. After the turning **Ansford Road**, the High Street becomes **Upper High Street**, and in turn becomes **North Street**, which ends at **Cary Hill. Chapel Close**, which runs off Upper High Street, refers to the Methodist Church that lies beside it. North Street was known in the middle ages as **Townsend**, the earliest record of this name is from a tax roll of 1327, when a "William atte Towneshende" is recorded in Cary. The name Townsend is still used for the very end of North Street, at the point where it joins Cary Hill.

Sometimes called Bull Street, as bulls were tethered to rings in the walls bordering Ansford Road.
Museum collection.

CASTLE CARY.
SOMERSET.

Mr. F. W. HARROLD

Has received instructions to offer for SALE BY PUBLIC AUCTION, at the

GEORGE HOTEL, CASTLE CARY,

On MONDAY, MAY 5th, 1890,

Punctually at 6 o'clock in the afternoon, subject to Conditions to be then produced, the undermentioned

FIRST CLASS FREEHOLD
PROPERTY

In One Lot, viz:- All those

VALUABLE BUSINESS PREMISES

Now and for many years past occupied by Stuckey's Banking Company as their

BANK HOUSE IN THE HIGH STREET,

containing Offices, Dining Room, Drawing Room, Bedrooms, Kitchen, Scullery and commodious Cellar with the Stable with Loft over, Coach-houses, Flower Garden, and productive Kitchen Garden thereto belonging, and Roadway approaching the same;

And all that Orchard stocked with Apple and Pear Trees, at one end adjoining the last mentioned premises, and at the other abutting on Catherine's Close; and also all that

COMMODIOUS DWELLING-HOUSE AND SHOP

adjoining the Bank House, formerly occupied by Mr. Rose and lately by Mr. W. Bentley, containing Lofty and Capacious Sitting Rooms, numerous Bedrooms, Storerooms, spacious Kitchen, Scullery, and Court, and Printing Office, with the large Walled Garden, well stocked with Fruit Trees in the rear of the same.

The Residences have a commanding aspect and face South.

The whole Premises contain 1a. 1r. 27p., more or less, and are numbered 36 on the Tithe Commutation Map.

The Bank House and Premises have been held by Stuckey's Banking Company for many years on a lease expiring next Lady-day at a rental of £60 a year, and a very considerable outlay has been made by them on the Property. The Shop Premises which have been for some time past let at a rental of £40 a year being now in hand offer to a purchaser a favorable opportunity for occupation or investment.

A Portion of the purchase money can, if desired, remain on Mortgage.

To view apply to the Auctioneer, and for further particulars to

MR. J. O. CASH,
SOLICITOR, CASTLE CARY.

Dated Castle Cary, April 18th, 1890.

MOORE, PRINTER, CASTLE CARY.

Stuckeys Bank was refronted in 1891, and the premises are now occupied by the National Westminster Bank.
LHG collection.

A shop in the High Street decorated for the Coronation in 1953.
LHG collection

A view of North Cary from the south c. 1905, showing Beechfield House and the Methodist Chapel.
A.V.Pearse collection.

The use of these premises as a bakery continued until recent decades.
LHG collection.

Ansford Road, as the name suggests, leads towards Ansford. It was, however, known as **Castle Cary Lane** before the twentieth century. To the west is **Catherine's Close**, a new development of sheltered housing named after Councillor Catherine Hobhouse. On the other side of Ansford Road there have been further housing developments. **Barnes Close** is a reminder of John Iles Barnes, who left land here to house poor people, and **Jubilee Close** relates to cottages (now demolished) built by John Boyd at the time of Queen Victoria's jubilee, while **Hanover Court** is a block of flats built by the Hanover Housing Association on part of the land endowed by John Boyd.

CASTLE CARY.

Mr. HARROLD

WILL SELL BY AUCTION,

At the GEORGE HOTEL, Castle Cary,

ON

THURSDAY, June 11th,

AT 6.30 P.M. PRECISELY,

Subject to conditions to be then produced, THE UNDERMENTIONED VALUABLE

FREEHOLD PREMISES,

viz:- A

COTTAGE

In HIGH STREET, with the PLEASANTLY SITUATED

GARDEN

In the rear of the same, adjoining on the North and East the House and Nursery Garden of Mr. Walter Bergman, and on the South and West the property of Mr. T. C. Parsons.

The Cottage is let in Two Tenements, to Mr. G. Naish, and Mrs. Newport, at a total rental of **£12 7s.**

The above Property contains in the whole

14½ perches,

(more or less,) and affords a valuable opportunity for Investment.

To view apply on the premises, and for further particulars to the Auctioneer, or to **Mr. J. O. CASH, Solicitor,**

CASTLE CARY.

Dated Castle Cary, May 21st, 1891.   ROBERTS, PRINTER, CASTLE CARY.

LHG collection.

A view looking down North Street, very little changed since this view from the 1920s.
A.V.Pearse collection.

North Street itself was originally known as **Townend**, a name that is preserved at the very end of North Street as it joins **Cary Hill**, which leads up out of Cary towards Hadspen. At the top of the hill there is a bridlepath leading towards Pitcombe that has the colourful name of **Hell Ladder Lane**, presumably obtaining its name because of its steep decline into the depths. Less poetic souls claim it was originally called Hill Ladder Lane. However both names can be found elsewhere for vertiginous lanes. Although now only a bridlepath/footpath, Hell Ladder Lane marks the original road that went to Wincanton past the front of Hadspen House, and moved further away when the route from Wincanton to Shepton Mallet was turnpiked in the eighteenth century. In those days, it has been claimed, Hell Ladder Lane became a useful diversion that enabled drovers to drive their cattle or flocks across to the Bruton road without having pass the turnpike at Hadspen corner and be forced to pay a toll.

The clump of Scots Pines on Cary Hill.
A.V.Pearse collection.

The carved datestone on Cumnock Terrace commemorates John Boyd who built it in 1877-78.

A view of Cumnock Terrace from the north in 1906. A.V.Pearse collection.

Moving in the other direction, the main A371 road heads for Ansford along **Cumnock Road**, a name deriving from the houses in the adjacent Cumnock Terrace, built by the industrialist John Boyd in 1877 for some of his workers. Boyd was a Scot coming from Cumnock, Ayrshire (where his father was a merchant, while he migrated to England firstly as a travelling draper); the name celebrating his birthplace.

A much later development on the other side of the A371 is named **Ancastle**, a combination of Castle Cary and Ansford; the housing estate being built on the site of allotments.

Ansford; from Ansford Hill to Lower Ansford

The parish of Ansford is separate from Cary and until recently the two settlements, while close, were distinct from each other. In coaching days Ansford had a quite separate fame from the Ansford Inn, which was one of the best known coaching Inns in Somerset. It was situated on **Ansford Hill** that runs north from Cumnock Road, continuing the A371 towards the station and Shepton Mallet. **Ansford Road** leads back to Cary, and there is a building once serving as a toll house on the corner. Close by is **Solomon's Lane**, which was once the main road to Bruton. Proceeding along Ansford Road we come to new buildings on both sides. **Maggs Lane** leads up to Ansford Community School, and on to **Ansford Park**; originally laid out from woodland in the fourteenth century. **Coombe Bottom**, where there was once an isolated cottage, lies beyond. **Brock Court** marks the site of a former badger set, and on the right is **Yeabsley's Way**, named in memory of George Yeabsley, a forceful former chairman of Ansford Parish Council who, it is said, ' always got his way'.

Coombe Bottom, where survives the overgrown garden of the isolated cottage that stood there.
A.V.Pearse collection.

On the other side of the road is **Churchfield Drive** that connects back to **Florida Fields**, and so named as it is built on the field adjoining Ansford Church. In the last two decades, a network of new roads have sprung up here. The most extensive is Mullins Way, named after Donald Mullins, a local farmer who also left land for the benefit of Castle Cary Museum. Further along is **Priory View**, a road that allows a good view of the Priory, standing high on its ridge across the field. **Parsonage Crescent** and **Parsonage Gate** abut the grounds of the former Ansford Parsonage, where Parson Woodforde lived.

The 'Old Parsonage' – Parson James Woodforde's boyhood home.

A contemporary account of the Tucker trial.

Further along Ansford Road is the site of a tragic history, known as **Tucker's Lane**. Reginald Tucker, who lived in a house here, murdered his wife with a hammer on 8 June 1775 and was hanged at Wells later that year. Tucker's mother ran the Ansford Inn, and the family had been established in Cary for some time. It has been suggested that the name of the lane refers to the family in general rather than the murderer in particular.

The Tucker Murder

Tucker's Lane is said to be named after one of Cary and Ansford's most notorious inhabitants. This was Reginald Tucker, a former soldier, inn-keeper and bellows maker, who was hanged for murdering his wife in 1775. According to the Castle Cary Visitor of 1897, "old people tell that the murderer's house stood on the site of the present schoolhouse, but was pulled down at least 70 years ago." The schoolhouse itself is now a private dwelling, situated close to the old Ansford Parsonage in Tucker's Lane.

The murder allegedly took place after a perhaps not altogether unprecedented domestic incident – an argument over the quality of a meal! According to an account in the Bath Chronicle, Tucker and his wife "dined together on some stinking pork, when words arose, and he beat her in a cruel manner, and afterwards dashed her brains out with a sledge hammer". Elsewhere the weapon is described as a "a large hammer, such as [is] used to drive nails into wheels."

The Tucker family were neighbours of the celebrated diarist Parson Woodforde, who recorded the course of events as it unfolded over the summer of 1775. Woodforde had previously been in the habit of referring to Reginald as 'Riddle' Tucker, an intriguing name that suggests that he was something of an enigma. Tucker was, as will be seen later, a resourceful and ingenious character who had had a varied and somewhat adventurous life before this tragic event. At the time of the murder, Woodforde was resident in Oxford, where he was sub-warden at New College. Previously he had been curate at Cary and Ansford, and he was soon to take up the post of Parson in Weston Longville, Norfolk. He learned of the event from a 'letter from Ansford' published in an Oxford journal. His transcribed the account in his diary on June 17th;

" Thursday last, about six o'clock in the Evening the Inhabitants of this Parish were alarmed by a report that Mrs. Tucker, wife of Mr Reginald Tucker had dropt down dead in an apoplectic Fit. Several People immediately repaired to the house where a scene most shocking to human nature presented itself, one of the finest Women in these parts dead on the floor, weltering in her blood, with her Skull fractured, ... her face, breast, shoulders, arms, and one of her ears bruised in a barbarous manner. The Coroner was sent for and a Jury empanelled to sit on the body, before whom it was given in Evidence, that Mr Tucker left the house about half an Hour after twelve to go to Mr Petty's, at Hatspen, only about a Mile distant: that when he came there he was in such a Sweat as to be obliged to strip of his Shirt, put on one of Mr Perry's ... Mr Tucker was examined, but insisted on his Innocence: Blood however appearing on his Cloaths, and strong grounds of Suspicion arising against him, the Jury brought in their Verdict Wilful Murder, and he was taken into Custody. A second Jury were summoned the next Day, who gave the same Verdict."

Woodforde's thoughts were immediately for the unfortunate daughter of the couple – characteristically followed by a note about a bill for wine;
"May God preserve poor Miss Tucker in her great distress.
For Wine this afternoon in M.C.R. pd 0.0.6."

Tucker was incarcerated in Shepton Mallet prison to await trial. Woodforde, now back in Ansford, was sub-poenaed to act as a character witness for Tucker on 21st August. On 25th August Tucker was tried at Wells and convicted. Woodforde was present at the trial, but missed his chance to deliver his character witness as he was out of the court having a meal at the time he was called. He gave the following account of events in his diary;

"August 25th. ... At half past 8 this morning I went to the Assize Hall ... Tucker's trial was the first that came on. Tucker walked into the Hall very undaunted and behaved without any Concern for a long Time. The first thing he did was to object to the major Part of the Jury and others put & sworn in their Room. ... I went to the Goat & ate a bit of Dinner, ... the Judge was summing up the Evidence to the Jury which lasted a great while, and after that the Jury was a long Time in how to bring him in. At last however at about a quarter after six the Jury delivred in their Verdict and brought him in guilty. The Judge then immediately passed Sentence of Condemnation on him, and to be executed Monday next. The whole Hall seemed to rejoice at the Sentence, as it was the general Opinion that he was guilty. He persisted still in his Innocence at the very last. When Miss Tucker gave her Evidence most of the Ladies cried and greatly pitied her in her Situation. The Judge greatly condemned the Evidence given in by John Perry and his Wife of Hatspen, as they varied greatly from their first Examination. ... [The trial] lasted near ten hours. ..."

Woodforde also noted the execution;

"August 28th. Poor Tucker was hung this Aft. about 5 o'clock near Wells--& it is reported that he persisted in his Innocence to the very last--however I cannot think him innocent: if he is I doubt not but he will be amply rewarded, if he is not--Lord be merciful unto his Soul."

Tucker does indeed seem to have borne himself with dignity during the trial, as is recorded in the fulsome account of events given in the Bath Chronicle;

" His behaviour during his trial, which lasted near eleven hours, was in the highest degree astonishing to the whole Court; he never was observed to change colour, or in the least to be affected but once, which was, when the sledge hammer, with which he committed the horrid deed, and his bloody clothes, were produced in Court, when he was seen to drop a tear.

After his condemnation, he received the sacrament three times, yet to his last moments persisted in declaring his innocence, (Though he acknowledged he had been guilty of offenses that deserved death), and ascended the cart which carried him to the place of execution with the greatest alertness and seeming unconcern.

He was dressed in deep mourning, was accompanied by a clergyman, and carried a prayer book in his hand, which he read all the way from the prison to the gallows; and just before he was turned off, he threw away his cravat, opened his shirt collar, and put the halter round his neck.

A hearse in waiting conveyed his body to Langport, where it was delivered to a surgeon for dissection."

Tucker's protestations of innocence are striking and suggest that the whole story perhaps never came out. His calm bearing during the proceedings also imply a strength of character that does not fit with the general vilification of his name that the press indulged in, in true tabloid form, at the time.

The Bath Chronicle gave the following sketch of his life in their account of the trial;

"He was a native of Hewith, [Huish] near Langport, and being left young without a father, his mother apprenticed him to a bellows-maker at Wells, but turning out very wild, he absconded his master's service, enlisted in the army, and was at the Battle of Culloden, where he was wounded, and in consequence obtained a pension, and came to Ansford, where his mother lived, and kept the Ansford Inn. He there carried on his trade for some time, but being of a rakish and brutish disposition, was always engaged in riots and quarrels. In 1750 he was married to his late wife, Martha, and soon after went to London, where he followed different branches of business chiefly in the mechanical way, and obtained a premium for the invention of a ventilator. A fire happening in the neighbourhood where he lived, he was burnt out, but having insured very high, availed himself of that circumstance, and as a considerable sum of money belonging to some rich Jews who lodged at his house was also missing, he was suspected to have made free with it, as he soon became rich of a sudden, dropped his trade and retired to Ansford to live private on his fortune, where he purchased an estate of about 30 pounds a year, on which he commenced farming, but that not answering his expectations, he let his estate at a very advanced rent to a potato planter, and lived private with his wife and daughter, keeping no servant.

He was about 50 years of age, his wife 53; he had two children by her, the eldest daughter now living aged 23, the other a son born in London, whom he is said to have killed by an unlucky blow aimed at his wife, while she had the infant in her arms."

Miriam, the Tuckers' daughter, was cared by friends in Shepton Mallet. They were amongst the minority who remained convinced that Reginald Tucker had been innocent of the crime.

[Editor's note;- John Cannon touched upon early signs of Tucker's "vile" character, when he mentioned in 1736 fruitless efforts to obtain a second apprenticeship for him at the behest of Tucker's re-married mother.]

To the north of Tucker's lane there runs a network of recently built roads. **Hallett Road** is named after Walter Hallett, a member of Ansford Parish Council who worked at the local milk factory. **Orchard Close** marks the site of a former orchard, and **Elms Lane** records the site of former elm trees. **Mary Dunford Stile** commemorates Mary Dunford, a popular local resident, and daughter of George Dunford, foreman at the milk factory nearby. Tuckers Lane runs down hill to St. Andrews' Close, which records the name of Ansford Parish Church, and beyond it runs into Lower Ansford, which was once a separate settlement.

Ansford Junior School, built on the site of Tucker's residence.

Ansford Junior School converted to residential use.

ANSFORD.

NEAR CASTLE CARY, SOMERSET.

MR. HARROLD

has been instructed to SELL BY AUCTION, at the

George Hotel, Castle Cary,

On TUESDAY, the 21st day of JULY, 1896,

at SEVEN o'clock, p.m., subject to such conditions as shall be then and there produced,

ALL THAT

DWELLING HOUSE

with STABLE,

AND LARGE PRODUCTIVE GARDEN,

late in the occupation of Mr. THOMAS BURGE, deceased, at the yearly rental of £8.

This property affords an excellent opportunity for the erection of a Villa Residence, being within 5 minutes' walk of the G.W.R. Station, and near Ansford Church.

For further particulars apply to the Auctioneer, Castle Cary, or to

Mr. J. O. CASH,

SOLICITOR, CASTLE CARY and WINCANTON.

Dated Castle Cary, July 3rd, 1896.   ROBERTS, PRINTER, CASTLE CARY.

LHG collection.

Three Barrett sisters by the farm buildings in Lower Ansford c. 1930.
A.V.Pearse collection.

A stone at Lower Ansford marking the site of the death of Canon Longman.

The much battered milestone at the junction of Lower Ansford with Ansford Hill.

SOURCES

As well as information from Ray and Olive Boyer, and members of the Living History Group, the following publications have been utilised to investigate local nomenclature:-Aston, Michael and Roger Leach, *Historic Towns in Somerset – Archaeology and Planning*, 1977 (Craggs); Collinson, John, *History and Antiquities of the County of Somerset*, 3 Vols, 1791; Hershon, Cyril P., *The Castles of Cary*, 1990, Pavalas Press; Living History Group, *Memories of Castle Cary and Ansford*, 1998; Living History Group, *Time to Reflect*, 2002; McGarvie, Michael, *Castle Cary*, Avalon Industries, 1980; Phelps, William, *History and Antiquities of the County of Somerset*, 4 vols., 1836; Pooley, Charles, *Old Stone Crosses of Somerset*, 1877; Siraut, Mary (ed.), *A History of the County of Somerset. Volume X. Castle Cary and the Brue – Cary Watershed*, [Victoria County History], 2010, Boydell and Brewer; *The Castle Cary Visitor*, Castle Cary, monthly periodical 1896 -1915.

The Domesday Book entry for Castle Cary and Ansford 1086.

Index

A'Court, Job 206
Adams, Bert 149
Adams, David 143, 144, 150
Adams, Ena 215, 217
Adams, Jean 150
Adams, Maurice 263-269
Adams, Mrs 154
Adams, Tony 154
AEC Matadors, vehicles 176
Alford 15
Alford I A D 259
Alford, Rev. 23
All Saints' Church 33, 35
Allen 150
Allen, John 144
Allen, Ronald 159
Alma 29
Alma Close 295
Altrop, John 15
Alvan Blanch drying plant 141, 144
American Army 236
Ames, Miss 135
Ancastle 301
Andrews, Bill 256
Andrews, Mr 29
Andrews, Mrs 249
Angel Inn 15, 29, 211
Ansford & Ditcheat Friendly Society 38
Ansford Factory 166
Ansford Farm 56, 155
Ansford Hill 302
Ansford Inn 258
Ansford Lane 23
Ansford Old Scholars 164
Ansford Park 302
Ansford Primary School 236, 306
Ansford Road 295, 299, 302
Ansford School 81, 123, 135, 172, 209, 236, 239, 241, 263
Ansford School Teaching Staff 210
Ansford Youth Club 246
Ashdown, Paddy 145
Asher family 29, 185

Asher, Graham 192, 236
Atwell, Mr 154
Auchinleck, Ayrshire 49
Avalon Components 146
Avalon Leatherboard Co Ltd 181
Babcary 15
Badgers Court 282
Baghurst, Jean 144
Bailey Hill 23, 24, 243, 268, 273
Baker, Carroll 265
Baker, George 26, 28
Baker, Mr 122
Baker, T 29
Baltonsborough 39, 227
Barber 29
Barber, Elias 32, 33
Barber, Hetty 169
Barker, H J D 206
Barker, Priscilla 206
Barnes Close 299
Barnes, Jean, née Asher 185, 237, 239-241
Barns, Miss 263
Barrett sisters 308
Barrett, Elizabeth, née Bettey 49, 52, 56
Barrett, Jack 81, 155, 162
Barrett, Wosson 49, 56
Barrett's Farm 121
Barretts Field 139
Bartholomew, Mr 26
Bartlett 26
Bartlett, Alan 136
Bartlett, Mrs 116
Bartlett, Robin 107
Bartlett, Trevor 107, 135
Bate, Mr 215
Baxter, Alf 225
Baxter, Madeleine 213
Bazell, Basil 56
Beechfield House (The Villa) 34, 37, 116, 297
Berry, T 232
Bibbys 144
Biddiscombe, Alan 170
Biddiscombe, Barbara 170
Biddle, Bob 229

Biggin 26, 29
Biggin, Bunny 240
Biggs, Mr 211
Billing, Glenys 212
Billing, Roma 212
Bird, Obadiah 26
Biss, Dick 136
Biss, Mr 154, 211
Blackmore, Miss 135, 168
Blackworthy Farm 155
Blackworthy Road 287
Blind Lane 282
Bliss, Herbert 53, 54, 57
Bliss, Rev. Alan 53-58
BMI 146
BOCM Pauls 144
Bond, J O 110
Bond, Reg 154
Bond's Chemist 110
Bowles, Benny 23
Bowles, Patty 26
Boyd, John 24, 30, 301
Boyd, John, & Co Ltd 91-95, 97-102, 146
Boyer, David 138, 148
Boyer, Olive 150, 151, 195-198
Boyer, Percival 135, 150, 151, 189
Boyer, Philip 139, 148
Boyer, Ray 135-148, 149-162, 150, 151, 189-192, 195
Boyer, Rosa 135, 150, 151, 199
Brake, Mr 29
Brake, Roy 155
Bratton 17
Bray, Isobel 110
Brewin, Brenda 213
Bridge Farm, Alhampton 52
Britannia Inn 29, 193, 211, 279
British Army of the Rhine (BAOR) 177
Brock Court 302
Bronzeoake 189
Brown, Miss 209
Brown, Philip 110
Brummel, Joan 83
Bryant, Albert 83
Bull Street 23, 295

Bulley, John 84
Buncombe, Henry, & Son 25, 26
Buncombe, Misses 29
Burrows, Richard 219-226
Burton Bradstock 187
Buse, Bertie 256
Bush, Mr & Mrs 154, 155, 168, 211
Butt, C 26
Butt, Mrs A I B 207
Butwell Cottage 53, 54, 56
Butwell Villa 56
Cadman, Ethel 83
Cannon, John 13-22, 52, 305
Cant, Norman 200
Carnival 58, 228, 259
Carpenter, Mr 154
Carr, Mr & Mrs R 56
Cary Comedians Carnival Club 147, 150
Cary Fitzpain 15
Cary Fruit & Greens 139
Cary Hill 295, 300
Cary Hill Cottage 205-206
Cary Team YMBC 253
Cary, Cliff 136
Castle Cary Bell Ringers 243
Castle Cary Bull Show 160-161
Castle Cary Carnival 58, 228, 259
Castle Cary Choir 229
Castle Cary Fire Brigade 231
Castle Cary Football Club 83, 257, 260
Castle Cary Friendly Society 38
Castle Cary Gas and Coke Company 24
Castle Cary Lane 299
Castle Cary Majorettes 248
Castle Cary Museum 228, 265
Castle Cary Parish Council 146
Castle Cary Primary School 135, 148, 185
Castle Cary Station 103, 104, 123-128, 136, 236
Castle Rise 155, 272
Catherine's Close 255, 299
Centaur Services 110, 144, 246
Central Garage 115, 116
Chalmers, Allis 145
Chamberlain, Alice 215

Chamberlain, Jack 82
Chancellor, Fred 148
Chapel Close 295
Chapel Yard 293
Chapman, Annie, née Lowe 43, 44
Chapman, Ethel 44
Chapman, Frank 44
Chapman, Gertrude 44
Chapman, Gladys 44
Chapman, Joseph 43-46
Chapman, Lily 44
Chapman, Nora 44
Charlton, Mr 168
Charlton, Tommy 135, 172
Charolais cattle 139, 140, 142, 145
Chewton Farms 264
Chilcott, Charlie 83
Chilcott, Mr 168
Chilcott, Mrs 211, 212
Chilcott, Win 214
Church Street 289, 292
Church Villa 29
Churchfield Drive 302
Churchouse Mr 29, 196, 246
Churchouse, Guy 155, 263
Churchouse, Joseph 26, 27
Clanville 56, 87, 89, 111
Clanville Manor 155
Clarke, Mr 26, 154
Clarks Factory 150, 181-184
Clarks International 181
Cleal, Charles 165
Cleal, Mrs 165
Close, Freda 131
Close, H & Son 26
Close, John 25
Close, Joyce 169
Close, Len 83, 131
Clothier family 56
Clothier, Chas H 182
Clothier, Edwin 169
Clothier, George 131
Clothier, Jim 136
Clothier, Kenneth 249-261
Clothier, Mr 155

Clothier, Stella 167-170
Clothier, Tom 139, 155
Cockhill 135, 189, 193, 295
Cockhill Cottage 151
Cockhill Elm Lane 295
Colberts 150
Cole's field 131
Coleman, Mr 29
Coles, Tom 26
Collard, Rita 144
Collett, Mr 209
Collick, Don 111, 113
Collings, Ray 185
Compton, Bernard 15
Congregational Church 45
Coombe Bottom Farm 234, 302
Coombe Bottom Orchard 233
Coombes, George 137
Coombs, Dr. Carey 29, 31, 116
Cooper's Ash Lane 295
Corner, Richard 29
Cornick, Vic 144
Corp brothers 155
Corp, Elizabeth 211
Corp, Gladys 211
Corp, Miss 263
Cotton, Rev 23, 30
Couzens, Wallace 207
Coward, Charles 135, 151, 155
Coward, Mr & Mrs 155, 193
Cox, Jennifer 168
Crane, Keith 119-120
Creed, Ernest 154
Creed, Harold 154
Creed, Len 136
Creed, Nicky 113
Crees, Joyce 239
Crendon Building 182
Crossley, John 228
Crown Pet Food Factory 146, 287
Cruse & Gass Sawmill 87-90, 155
Cruse, Jonathan 87, 89, 105, 155
Cumnock Road 301
Cumnock Terrace 33, 45, 301
Curtis, Mr 151

Curtis, Mrs 151
Cutler, Miss 135
Daniell, Thomas 26
Dare, Mr 196
Dauncey, Sally 170
Dauncey, Timothy 170
Day and Masters map 21
Day Bros 26
Day, Son & Hewett 144
Delaware House 108, 109
Delaware Veterinary Group 107-113
Denela's 246, 247
Derrett, Mr & Mrs 168
Derrett, William 155
Dill, Barbara 131
Dill, Ernie 131
Dill, Joan 131
Dill, John 131
Dill, Nell 117
Dill, Norman 131
Dilling, Mr 154
Dimmer Farm 154, 189
Dimmer Hobby 154
Dimmer Munitions Dump 154, 189-192, 259
Ditcheat 56
Doble, Jim 136
Domesday Book 310
Donne family 165
Donne, Capt. William S 60
Donne, Charles 59
Donne, James 59
Donne, John 30
Donne, Nicholas 59
Donne, Stephen 30
Donne, T S, & Sons Ltd. 24, 59-79, 81, 126, 146, 181, 258
Donne, Thomas Salisbury 30, 60, 81
Dorset House Farm 155
Down, Mr 154
Dr Barnardos at Southborne 187
Drake, Mr & Mrs 154
Drew, Ernie 131, 163
Drewett 32
Drewett, John 169

Drewett, R B 169
Drewett, R J 169
Drill Hall 255
Dunford, Mr & Mrs 56
Dyke, Ernest 136
Eason, Robert 26, 27
Easterbrook, Robin 233
Eavis, Philip 146
Edwards, LAC Frank 177
Elliott, Sergeant 30
Ellis 26
Ellis, Martin 192
Elms Lane 306
Etrick, Madam 15
Evercreech 81
Evercreech Junction 23
Evison, Charles 145
Falkingham, Bob 141
Farming in Castle Cary 135-148, 149-162
Farrant, Cecil 240
Farwell, Nathaniel 17
Fennon, Len 147
Ferguson tractors 145
Ferrey, Benjamin 35
Fir Tree Cottages 121
Fire Station 267
Fletcher, John 248
Florida 24, 280
Florida Fields 302
Florida House (The Priory) 30, 33, 122, 280, 281
Florida Place 280
Florida Street 280
Flower, Martin 144, 151
Flower, Mrs 151
Foot, Charles 189
Foote family 153
Foote, George 154
Foote, Hilda 154
Foote, Sylvia 154
Fordson tractors 145
Fore Street 56, 272, 273
Forse, Elizabeth 206
Forse, Zaccheus 206
Fox & Hounds Inn 29

Fox, Mrs 168
Foxcombe Farm 149
Francis family 30
Francis, E O, & Sons 29, 53, 281
Francis, J H 30
Francis, Norman 131
Francis, Yvonne 129-134, 163
Franks Farm 154
Friesian cattle 140
Fry 154
Fulford House 112
Fulford's Cross 199, 286
Fullers 232
Fussell, Ed 232
Fussell, Frank 83, 121
Gas House Lane 282
Gass, David John 87, 89, 105, 155
George Hotel, The 16, 17, 20, 29, 33, 265
Gibbet Lane 252
Gibbs, John 15
Gibbs, Leonard 155
Gibbs, Manuel 149
Gibbs, Richard 38
Gibson, Miss 167
Gifford, Tom 29
Gilbert, John 17
Gillingham 39
Gilson, Jack 145
Gimblet, Harold 256
Glastonbury Tor 56
Golledge, Fred 155
Gomm, Arthur 135, 168
Gospel Hall 105, 106
Gough, Henry T 135, 168, 172, 263, 210, 211
Gould, Mr 149
Gower, George 81
Graham Paige car 116
Grange Farm, West Lydford 13
Gray, George 29
Green Howards 122, 236
Green, J M 26
Green, Joseph 26, 30
Green, Ted 179
Greenough, Paul 108, 110, 111, 246

Greenway Road 123, 193, 288, 289
Gregory, David 110, 111, 112
Grenadier Guards 236
Grosvenor, Miss 237
Grosvenor, Rev. James 32
Grove Farm 155
Groves, Gordon 121-128
Hadspen (Handspen) 14
Hadspen House 300
Half Moon Inn 53, 56, 105
Hall, John 110
Hallett Road 306
Hallett, Ada 117
Hallett, Mr & Mrs 53, 56
Hamblin, John 29
Hanover Court 299
Harrison, Bert 116
Harrison, Bill 108, 110, 111, 112
Harrison, John 81, 209
Harrison, Mr & Mrs 263
Harrison, Pat 209
Harrold, Arthur 29
Harrold, C & E M 29
Harrold, F W 275
Hastings, Rev. 105
Haywood, Mr 149
Hazell, Horace 256
Heal, Nick 145, 147
Heart & Compass 29
Hell Ladder Lane 300
Helps, Captain 29
Helps, Gwen 215
Helps, Len 121
Henderson's powerlooms 43
Herman, Maurice 145
Herman, Samuel 279
Higgins, Harold 83
Higgins, Mr 151
Higgins, Sister 135
Higgins' Close 205
High Street 24, 29, 295
Higher Dimmer Farm 153, 154
Higher Farm 149
Higher Flax Mills, Torbay Rd. 81, 84, 181
Hill House 56

Hill, Bill 179
Hill, Miss 263
Hill, Richard 113
Hillcroft Farm 53
Hillier, Henry 161
Hillside Farm 155
Hindenburg Airship 252
Hodge, George 48
Hodge, Hugh 49
Hodge, Stanley 48-52
Hodge, Susan 50
Hodges 29
Hodges, Michael 222
Holbrook House 17
Honeywick 14
Honor, Sandra 113
Hopkins, Bert 145
Horlicks 144
Horner 29
Horner's Yard 34
Horse Pond 2, 33, 56, 155, 211, 272
Horse Pond Inn 193
Horse Show & Gymkana 140
Hoskins brothers 251
Hoskins, Silas, & Sons 29, 32
House, Philip 144
Howard, Alby 215
Howard, Mr 167
Howe, Mr, of Somerton 17
Howell, Charles 206
Hudson and Martin 39
Hughes, Alan 110
Huish Episcopi 59
Hunters 29
Hutchfield, Janet, née Lush 235-238
Hutchfield, Mr 246, 250
Hutchings brothers 141
Hutchings family 154
Hutchings, Monica 73-74
Hutchings, Mr 136
Ilchester Gaol 18
Ilford, Essex 43
Ireland, Mr 154
Jack White's Gibbet 17-20, 33
James, Frank 263

James, Mr & Mrs 165
James, Mr 155
Jeffrey, Len 110
Jeffrey, Mrs 83
Jenkins, Owain 113
Jersey cattle 137, 138, 196
Jewel, Widow 18
Jolliffe, Miss 81
Jones, Flight Sgt. 178
Jones, Mary 207
Joyce, Mr & Mrs 56
Jubilee Close 299
Jubilee Cottages 30, 31, 38
Katharine Wheel Inn 15
Keinton Mandeville 227
Keniston House 171
Kerby, Mike 111, 112
Kightly, Allan 144
Kimble, Mr 151
King, Ann 237
King, Miss 135, 168, 172
Kingston, Cecil 144
Kirby, Norman 141
Knight, John 30
Knight's Yard 238, 295
Kynaston family 155
Lamyatt 263
Law, Colin 144
Laylocks 56
Le Rue, Francis 137, 196
Lee, Ena 213
Lee, Frank 256
Lee, Gilbert 149
Lee, Jack 256
Lees family 29, 245
Lees, Ellen Jesse 244
Lemon, Nathaniel & Son 26, 27, 29
Lewis, Roger 113
Leyland Hippos 176, 177
Lindsay, Jock 215
Little Cary 15
Llewellyn, Arthur 110, 111, 112
Lodge Hill 289
Lodge View Farm 233
London House 244

Longman Group 144, 149, 155
Longman, Canon 308
Longman, Richard 147
Longshaw, Miss 103-106
Lower Ansford 119, 120, 121, 308
Lower Ansford Farm 122
Lower Cockhill Farm 151, 195-198, 199-203
Lower Woodcock Street 268, 276
Lucas, Mr & Mrs 56
Luckes, Wally 256
Lumbard, John 47
Lupton, Reginald 135
Luscombe, Peter 111, 112
Lush, Edward 172
Lush, Eli 117, 155
Lush, Mrs 172
Lush, Nell 117
Lush, Reg 117, 235
Lush, Ted 236
Lush, Winifred 117
Lydford Agricultural Group 146
Lydford, Miss 135
Lydford, Reginald 107
Lytes Cary 15
Mackie, James 24, 33
Mackie, John 47-48
Mackie, Mary 167
Macmillan family 165
Macmillan Way 295
Macmillan, Gordon 115
Macmillan, William 30
Maddever, Miss K 136
Maggs Lane 155, 302
Manor Farm 47, 155, 263, 265
Manor House 29
Maperton 17
Market Place 58, 273
Market Way 286
Marsh, D. Hardware 116
Marsh, Ted 146, 147
Martin, Cornelius 23-42, 105
Martin, Cornelius Charles 39, 41
Martin, Richard William 39, 40
Martin, Walter 155, 167

Martins Stores 42, 122, 246
Mary Dunford Stile 306
Masters, J F 23
Matthews 206
May, Bill 131, 165
McNab, Ian 108, 110, 111, 112
Mead's Newsagents 246
Meade, Prebendary R J 23, 36
Meadon, John 165
Meadon, Mary 165
Meadon, Phyllis 239
Meadon, Walt 231
Merrifield, Hazel 243-248
Metford Jeanes 145
Methodist Church 23, 34, 37, 297
Mewes, Mr & Mrs 233
Mid Somerset Young Farmers Club 137
Middle Farm 150, 154
Mill Lane 286
Mill Lane Dairy 193
Millbrook 282
Milligan, Capt. 231
Ministry of Food Storage Depot 126
Mitre Inn 29
Mole Valley Farmers 144
Molesworth, Rev. 211
Molly, Mr 18
Montague House 108
Montgomery, John 145
Moore, F S 26
Moore, Francis Samuel 25, 254
Moores, Tom 116
Morley & Co 15
Mullett, Alan 139
Mullins Way 302
Mullins, D 233
Naish, A A 207
Naish, Miss 251
Nash, John 47
National Farmers Union 145
National Service 126, 175-180, 264
National Service Medal 180
Neck, Frederick 212
New Road 288
Newport, Alice Amelia 53, 54

Newport, Mr 29, 244
Newport, Reuben 53
Nicholls, Julien 175-180
Nicholls, Valerie, née Higgins 209-218
Noble, Edward 36
Norris, Ivy 117
Norris, Jack 115-118, 240
Norris, Robert John 115
Norris's Garage 214, 216
North Street 295
Nursery 164, 166
O'Hare, Janet, née Vearncombe 209
Oakdale Creameries 193
Oakes, Rachel 162
Oborne, Alison 110
Ochiltree House 181, 183
Ochiltree, Ayrshire 49
Old Cumnock 49
Old House, Lower Cockhill 199
Old Parsonage 105, 232, 234, 303
Orchard Close 306
Orchard Farm 135, 140, 146, 150, 196
Orchard Villa 56
Otton, Frank 227
Otton, Jack 115, 196, 229, 230
Otton, Ralph 227, 229
Otton, Roger 227-230
Padfield, Mr 121
Painted Room, Cockhill Farm 203
Palk, Mr 150
Palmer & Snell 169
Pantomime 240
Park Avenue 289
Park Farm 154, 155
Park Place 267
Park Pond 105, 106
Park Street 267, 289
Park, The 289
Parry, Jim 144
Parslow, Digs 168
Parslow, Miss 135
Parsonage Crescent 302
Parsonage Gate 302
Parsonage, The Old 105, 232, 234, 303

Parsons Brothers Dairy 145, 155, 186, 267
Parsons family 154
Parsons, Arthur J 193
Parsons, Mrs 135
Parsons, Myrtle 238
Patenall, Dr. 165
Pattle, Eileen 193
Paul, Douglas 185
Paull 32
Pearce, Mr 29
Peaty, Bill 83
Pennell, Ken 232
Penny, J, & Sons 26
Peppin, John 200
Peppin, Pek 151, 196, 199-203
Perkins, Nick 111, 112
Perott, Winifred 163
Perrot, Wuggy 240
Perrott, Sam 163
Perry, Jim 149
Perry, Mr 149
Petheram, Bill 110, 111
Phelps House 165, 185
Phillips Grocery 137
Phillips, Fred 136, 155
Phillips, Miss 246
Pie Corner 273
Pierce, Mr 155
Pike, Jack 116, 117, 126
Pilton, 130, 131
Pindar, Stella 135
Pines, The 165
Pinkstones of Bristol 144
Pitching, The 15, 275
Pither, Charles, & Son 26, 28, 32, 228
Pither, John 253
Pither's Yard 295
Pitman, Harry James 116
Pitman, Mary 116
Pitman's Orchard, Woolston 231
Player, Thomas 15
Pond, Hannah 206
Pond, John 206
Poole 81

Pope, Lorraine 168
Porter, Mr & Mrs 163, 165
Porter's Nursery 131
Post Office 29
Pounds, Mr & Mrs 165
Powell 26
Powell, Les 231
Powell, Mr 154
Price Dr. & Mrs 163
Price, Tony 231-233
Prideaux's 81, 155, 162, 193
Priory Close 280
Priory Path 280
Priory View 302
Priory, The (Florida House) 30, 33, 122, 280, 281
Pullen, Judith 192
Pursey, Harry 145
Pylle 135
Quantock Poultry Packers 144
RAF badges 179
RAF Cardington 175
RAF Geilenkirchen 177
RAF Honington 176
RAF Weeton 175
RAF Wildenrath 179
Railway Hotel 29, 124
Rathbone, Mr & Mrs 56
Rathbone, Richard 162
Reed & Mallick 259
Reed, Mr 135
Remalard Court 146, 282
Ricardo, Miss 185
Ricardos 165
Ridout, Ann 212
Ridout, David 212
Ridout, Kathleen 212
Ridout, William 26
Rope Walk, Torbay Road 184
Rossi 132
Rossiter, Arthur 233
Rossiter, Ralph 233
Round House 268
Rowsell, Win 83
Royal Oak Farm, Clanville 111

Russ Bros. 29
Sage, Miss 209
St Anselms, 56
St Maur, Alice 14
St Maur, Nicholas 14
St Maur, Richard 14
Salisbury Terrace 103, 288
Sampson, Joan 186
Sandbanks 292
Sansom, Bob 230
Saunders, Mr & Mrs 248
Savage Cat 29
Scouts 173, 259, 263
Seaforth Highlanders 239
Sessions 40
Sessions, J B, 39
Sexton, Desmond 154
Shepton Mallet 23
Shepton Mallet Show, 137
Shepton Montacute 18
Sherborne, Jack 141
Sibley, Arthur 124
Silcocks 144
Silver Ash Farm 155
Simpson, Mrs Jane, née Boyd 165
Singer Junior car 55, 56
Small, John 206
Small, Stephen 206
Smallway Farm 149
Smith, Mr 209
Smith, Mr, of Pylle 135
Snook family 155
Snook, Samuel 26
Solomon's Lane 45, 302
Somerset Stay on a Farm Group 146
Somerset Young Farmers Club 136
Somerton 15, 119
South Bank 295
South Cary House 267
South Cary Lane 293
South Street 293
Sparkford 23, 53
Spearman's 219
Speed, Mervin 264
Spens, Mr 168

Sportsman's Lodge 149
Squatters Removal Band 259
Squibb, Jim 171
Squibb, Ruth 171
Squibb's Garage 172, 268, 283
Station Road 288
Steanbow Farm, Pilton 130, 131
Steer, Mr 209, 263
Steer, Sam 135, 255
Stickland, David 81-86
Stickland, Mr 135
Stickland, Veronica 163-166
Stickland, Winifred 165
Still, Mr, of Shaston 17
Stockley, George 147, 231
Stockman, Gordon 147, 228
Stockman, James 206
Stokes, Mrs 245
Stokes, Mrs 263
Stone, Norman 154
Street Names 271-309
Strickland, Mr & Mrs 168, 172
Strode Components Ltd 181
Stuckey's Bank 29, 295
Sullivan, Stella 83
Sunny Hill School, Bruton 209
Sutton, Anthony 17
Sweet, Ada 82
Sweet, Frank 81, 83
Sweet, George 279
Sweet, Joan 169
Tank Cottages 155
Targett family 153, 154
Targett, Colin 149
Targetts of Dimmer 144
Taylor, Dr. 29
Taylor, Godfrey 43
Taylor, Kenneth 43
Taylor, Leslie 56
Taylor, Mr & Mrs 29, 211
Tazewell, Richard 107, 109
Thomas, Mr 240
Thompkins, Rev. 23
Thorn 154, 155
Tidcombe, Mr 29

Tinknells of Wells 145
Titanic 279
Todd, Alastair 189
Tolley, Mr & Mrs 150
Toogood 26
Toop, Cyril 211
Toop, Mr 154
Tor View 207
Torbay 24, 59
Torbay House 155
Torbay Road 286
Totnes Costume Museum 50
Townsend 205, 295, 300
Triangle, The 276
Trickey, Miss 209
Trindall, Mr 135
Trott, Ruth 238
Trowbridge, Doris 213, 217, 219
Trowbridge, Tom 212, 213, 219
Trowbridge's Drapery 212, 216
Tucker Murder 303, 304-305
Tucker, Mr 258
Tuckers Lane 258, 303
Tullett, Joe 212
Tullett, William 218
Tulletts 116
Turtle, Mrs 211
Turtle, Roy 237
Upper High Street 295
Vaughan, Will 151, 196, 202, 271-309
Vaux's Bakery 211
Veryard, Stan 248
Vicarage 37
Victoria Court 283
Victoria Park 193, 280, 282, 288
Victoria Road 282
Villa, The (Beechfield House) 34, 37, 116, 297
Wade, Arthur 83
Wade, Mr & Mrs 244
Wadman, Claude 136
Waggon & Horses 29, 251, 260, 265
Waites of London 259
Waldegrave, Lord 264
Waldens at Trowbridge 144

Waller, Doris 237
Walsby, Jack 110
Ward, Sammy 29
Wareham 81
Warings of Portsmouth 259
Warren, Miss 173, 263
Watlington, Oxon 17
Webb, Leslie 236
Webber, Arthur 85
Webber, Walter 83
Weech, Mr 207
Weeks, Jack 115
Weeks, Ken 124
Well Farm, Alford 189
Wellard, Arthur 256
Wesleyan Chapel, Pithers Yard 105
West Lydford 13, 14
West Park 288
Wheaden, Mrs 164, 165, 247
Wheadon, Mr 165
Wheadon, Roy 165
Wheelan, Graham 185-188
White Hart 265
White, Alan 155
White, George 149
White, James 24, 25, 206
White, Norman 149
White, T and Sons 145
White, Thomas 29, 57, 149
White, William 17
Whitelock 26
Whittle, Tom 124
Williams 56
Williams brothers 155
Williams, Mrs R 53
Wilson, Harry 145
Wines, Enos 26, 27
Wingrove, Chris 144
Woman's Land Army 129-134
Woodcock Street 108, 275
Woodforde & Drewett solicitors 168
Woodforde Cottage 45
Woodforde, Alice 56
Woodforde, George 29
Woodforde, Helen 56

Woodforde, Rev James 18, 56, 258, 304-5,
Woodforde, Mabel 56
Woodforde, Randolph 29
Woodforde, Rev.Samuel 18, 258
Woodrow, Georgie 38
Woods, George 141
Woodville House 49, 275
Woolway, Brian 233
Wride, F C 45
Wyatt, Peter 155
Wyatt, Willoughby 41
Wyke Champflower 45, 263
Wyvern Waste 189
Yarlington Mill 249
Yeabsley, Mr 155
Yeabsley's Way 302
Yeovil Show 143, 145
Yockney, Jack 171-174
Youings, Ken 110
Zetor 145
Zion Chapel 23, 34, 293
Zouche, Sir William le 14, 200